UNDERSTANDING
ROBERT STONE

Understanding Contemporary American Literature
Matthew J. Bruccoli, Series Editor

Volumes on

Edward Albee • Nicholson Baker • John Barth • Donald Barthelme
The Beats • The Black Mountain Poets • Robert Bly
Raymond Carver • Fred Chappell • Chicano Literature
Contemporary American Drama
Contemporary American Horror Fiction
Contemporary American Literary Theory
Contemporary American Science Fiction
Contemporary Chicana Literature
James Dickey • E. L. Doctorow • John Gardner • George Garrett
William H. Gass • John Hawkes • Joseph Heller • Lillian Hellman
John Irving • Randall Jarrell • William Kennedy • Jack Kerouac
Ursula K. Le Guin • Denise Levertov • Bernard Malamud
Bobbie Ann Mason • Jill McCorkle • Carson McCullers
W. S. Merwin • Arthur Miller • Toni Morrison's Fiction
Vladimir Nabokov • Gloria Naylor • Joyce Carol Oates
Tim O'Brien • Flannery O'Connor • Cynthia Ozick • Tim Parks
Walker Percy • Katherine Anne Porter • Richard Powers
Reynolds Price • Annie Proulx • Thomas Pynchon
Theodore Roethke • Philip Roth • May Sarton • Hubert Selby, Jr.
Mary Lee Settle • Neil Simon • Isaac Bashevis Singer
Jane Smiley • Gary Snyder • William Stafford • Robert Stone
Anne Tyler • Kurt Vonnegut • Robert Penn Warren • James Welch
Eudora Welty • Tennessee Williams • August Wilson

UNDERSTANDING
ROBERT STONE

Gregory Stephenson

University of South Carolina Press

Published in Columbia, South Carolina, by the
University of South Carolina Press

Manufactured in the United States of America

06 05 04 03 02   5 4 3 2 1

Library of Congress Cataloging-in-Publication Data

Stephenson, Gregory, 1947–
   Understanding Robert Stone / Gregory Stephenson.
    p. cm. — (Understanding contemporary american literature)
   Includes bibliographical references and index.
   ISBN 1-57003-462-1 (cloth : alk. paper)
   1. Stone, Robert, 1937?– —Criticism and interpretation.
 I. Title. II. Series.
 PS3569.T6418 Z87 2002
 813'.54—dc21

                                   2002003107

For Birgit,
my link to realities,
virtual and other.

"Our interest's on the dangerous edge of things."
Robert Browning
"Bishop Bloughram's Apology"

CONTENTS

EDITOR'S PREFACE

The volumes of *Understanding Contemporary American Literature* have been planned as guides or companions for students as well as good nonacademic readers. The editor and publisher perceive a need for these volumes because much of the influential contemporary literature makes special demands. Uninitiated readers encounter difficulty in approaching works that depart from the traditional forms and techniques of prose and poetry. Literature relies on conventions, but the conventions keep evolving; new writers form their own conventions—which in time may become familiar. Put simply, *UCAL* provides instruction in how to read certain contemporary writers—identifying and explicating their material, themes, use of language, point of view, structures, symbolism, and responses to experience.

The word *understanding* in the titles was deliberately chosen. Many willing readers lack an adequate understanding of how contemporary literature works; that is, what the author is attempting to express and the means by which it is conveyed. Although the criticism and analysis in the series have been aimed at a level of general accessibility, these introductory volumes are meant to be applied in conjunction with the works they cover. They do not provide a substitute for the works and authors they introduce, but rather prepare the reader for more profitable literary experiences.

M. J. B.

CHRONOLOGY

1937	Born 21 August, in New York City, son of C. Homer and Gladys Catherine Stone. Father subsequently abandons family.
1943	Placed in an orphanage run by Marist Brothers. Attends parochial grade school.
1952–55	Attends Archbishop Malloy High School, NYC. Drops out to enlist in U.S. Navy.
1955–58	Voyage with Atlantic Fleet to Middle East. Voyage to Antarctica.
1958–60	Works as copyboy and caption writer for *New York Daily News*. Attends New York University. Meets and marries Janice G. Burr.
1960–62	Lives in New Orleans. Works at various jobs.
1962–64	Attends Stanford University on Wallace Stegner Fellowship.
1967	Publishes *A Hall of Mirrors*.
1968	Wins William Faulkner Foundation Award for notable first novel.
1967–71	Lives as freelance writer in London and Saigon.
1970	WUSA feature film based on *A Hall of Mirrors*.
1971–72	Works as writer-in-residence, Princeton University.
1972–75	Works as Associate professor of English, Amherst College.
1974	Publishes *Dog Soldiers*.
1975	Wins National Book Award for *Dog Soldiers*.
1977–78	Works as writer-in-residence, Stanford University.

CHRONOLOGY

1978	*Who'll Stop the Rain* feature film based on *Dog Soldiers*.
1979–80	Works as writer-in-residence, Harvard University.
1981	Employed as faculty member, University of California at Irvine. Publishes *A Flag for Sunrise*.
1982	Wins John Dos Passos Prize in literature, and *Los Angeles Times* Book Prize for *A Flag for Sunrise*.
1986	Publishes *Children of Light*.
1992	Publishes *Outerbridge Reach*.
1997	Publishes *Bear and His Daughter*.
1998	Publishes *Damascus Gate*.

UNDERSTANDING
ROBERT STONE

CHAPTER ONE

Understanding Robert Stone

Among contemporary American authors, Robert Stone is something of an anomaly. Independent of changing literary fashions and trends, unaffiliated with groups or movements, and undisposed to self-promotion, Stone has for more than thirty years quietly cultivated his craft, refined his imaginative vision, and produced a series of remarkable novels and short stories.

While Stone's work has generally been well received by reviewers, been honored by literary awards, and been adapted for two feature-length films, it has not yet achieved the critical recognition it merits and has remained less widely known than it deserves to be.

Aside from reviews, the fiction of Robert Stone has received relatively little critical attention. One book-length study of his writing has been published, a handful of scholarly articles has appeared, and certain of Stone's novels have been treated in studies of the literature of the Vietnam War. Yet in view of the praise accorded the author's fiction and the wide recognition of at least one of his works as a masterpiece of postwar American literature, the critical response has been rather sparse. Moreover, all of it has appeared before the publication of *Bear and His Daughter* (1997) and *Damascus Gate* (1998).

The distinctive manner of Robert Stone's fiction, its combination of a stark, hard-boiled realism with the hallucinated and the mystical, has its origin in the experience of the author—in his personal encounter with the terrors and mysteries of the worlds of inner and outer reality. For though Stone's novels and stories are not overtly autobiographical, they clearly draw on circumstances and events of his life and derive from his acquaintance with particular institutions and milieus, with certain modes of behavior and their motivations, and with specific conditions of mind and states of the spirit.

Born in the borough of Brooklyn, in New York City, on 21 August 1937, Robert Anthony Stone spent his childhood on the West Side of Manhattan either in the company of his schizophrenic mother or in a Catholic orphanage, Stone's father having abandoned his wife and child during the author's infancy.

After Stone's mother lost her job as a schoolteacher in New York for medical reasons, she and her son subsisted on her very small pension. Because of her unstable psychological state, she was in and out of hospitals. At the age of six the boy was placed in an orphanage run by Marist Brothers, where he remained until he was ten years old.

An early influence on Stone's imagination was radio, particularly radio dramas such as the mystery program *Sam Spade*, based on the figure Dashiell Hammett created:

> When I was seven or eight, I'd walk through Central Park like Sam Spade, describing aloud what I was doing, becoming both the actor and the writer setting him into the scene.[1]

Another radio program, *Tell Me a Story,* helped fashion the boy's narrative imagination. The technique of presenting competing panel members with three different elements that were to be woven together into a story has affinities with the general structure of Stone's novels, in which multiple characters starting at different points gradually converge.

Between the ages of ten and seventeen, while Stone finished parochial grade school and attended Archbishop Malloy High School, he lived again with his mother, in rooming houses and cheap hotels. Occasionally, his mother would embark with him on long, futile journeys, to Chicago once and another time to New Mexico. Traveling together by bus, they lived on welfare and in Salvation Army shelters at their destinations, before returning to New York.

In 1955, at seventeen and without completing high school, Stone enlisted in the United States Navy. The following year, as a radioman with an amphibious force of the Atlantic Fleet, he witnessed from the ship the aerial bombardment of Port Said by the French, a fearsome, piteous spectacle that made a profound impression on him:

> It was quite horrible. You could look through the
> glasses and see donkeys and people flying through the
> air, chewed up by 7.62s and rockets. It was a slaughter
> of civilians. But it always is.[2]

Much later, especially in *Dog Soldiers* and *A Flag for Sunrise*, there are echoes of this event and the insight that it provoked in the youthful sailor and budding writer "that the innocent suffer at the hands of people or forces driven by ignorance and greed."[3]

Stone's memories from service as senior enlisted journalist on Operation Deep Freeze Three, during a voyage to Antarctica, kept vivid the extraordinary landscapes and that he later summoned in writing *Outerbridge Reach*.

During his teenage years and early twenties, Stone read widely and deeply American, English, and world literature, encountering authors whose work was to influence his own development as a writer, most notably Herman Melville, Joseph Conrad, John Dos Passos, and Ernest Hemingway.

After his time in the navy, Stone returned to New York City, studying at New York University and working as a copyboy and caption writer for the *New York Daily News*. At NYU, Stone met and married Janice Burr, a fellow student, and also began an affiliation with the counterculture in its Beat Generation phase, becoming a habitué of Beat cafés and experimenting with marijuana and peyote.

In 1960, Robert and Janice Stone traveled to New Orleans, where they remained for nearly two years. While he was there, Stone wrote poetry, read it aloud in cafés to jazz accompaniment in the best Beat tradition, and eked out a living from temporary employment as a census taker (visiting households in every quarter of the municipality), and by working in a coffee factory and unloading ships at the pier, as well as by occasionally acting. Both his acquaintance with the city of New Orleans and his experiences of working in the factory and as a census taker were later to provide grist for his first novel, *A Hall of Mirrors*.

Only upon returning to New York City did Stone—inspired suddenly by a rereading of F. Scott Fitzgerald's *The Great Gatsby*—begin writing *A Hall of Mirrors*. On the strength of the early chapters, he received a Wallace Stegner Fellowship to Stanford University, where he encountered Ken Kesey among the writing students and through him became involved in the nascent West Coast psychedelic scene, behind which Kesey was the primary driving force.

The result was that he altered his novel, which he had begun as realistic, somewhat naturalistic fiction in the tradition of Dos Passos and John Steinbeck, to accommodate other modes of perception, other levels of reality, as drugs transformed his concept of reality.

UNDERSTANDING ROBERT STONE

Stone's acquaintance with Ken Kesey and his stoned cohorts, the Merry Pranksters—among them the legendary Neal Cassady—led to fictionalized versions of the company and its members. Kesey and Cassady are partial sources for the characters of Dieter and Hicks in the novel *Dog Soldiers*, and for Fletcher and Willie Wings in the short story "Porque No Tiene, Porque La Falta." The Merry Pranksters and their psychedelic citadel at Kesey's ranch at La Honda, California, become in *Dog Soldiers* the mystical band known as Those Who Are, whose spiritual headquarters is the former monastery El Incarnacion del Verbo.

Despite distractions and interruptions, and despite having to earn a living after the expiration of his fellowship, Stone completed *A Hall of Mirrors* in 1966. The novel appeared the following year, receiving considerable critical praise and winning the William Faulkner Foundation Award for notable first novel. Paramount Studio purchased movie rights to the book and placed Stone under contract to convert the novel into a screenplay.

In the late 1960s, Stone and his wife moved to England, where he worked intermittently on the screenplay and made a beginning on a second novel, which was to become *Dog Soldiers*. He felt that the characters in it "must have been in Vietnam, even though I didn't quite know who they were. I thought, 'what is their relationship to this Vietnam situation?'"[4] Seeking to answer the question, Stone traveled to South Vietnam in mid-1971 accredited as a correspondent to a fledgling English countercultural weekly, *Ink*.

Stone spent approximately two months there investigating the drug trade and black market in Saigon and visiting forward areas around Bien Ho where ARVN troops were engaged in operations against Vietcong guerrillas and units of the North Vietnamese army.

Witnessing widespread and unbridled corruption against the back-drop of a brutal, futile war clarified in the author's mind the novel he was starting to write: "I began to see what this book was going to be and who these people were going to be."[5]

Returning to live in the United States later in 1971, Stone encountered the rapid and dramatic changes wrought by the explosion of racial tensions, by the bitter political controversy over the Vietnam War, and by the spectacular expansion of the drug culture. Stone's dismay and disorientation at the spectacle of a nation seemingly on the verge of dissolution lent *Dog Soldiers* its apocalyptic undertones.

Stone completed the novel in two and a half years, while he was writer-in-residence at Princeton University and, then, a member of the English department at Amherst College. Published in 1974, *Dog Soldiers* won the National Book Award. The novel later provided the basis for a motion picture, for which Stone was coauthor of the screenplay, entitled *Who'll Stop the Rain*, released by United Artists in 1978.

Neither of the films based on Stone's novels has been particularly successful either critically or at the box office. The author maintains that the finished films bear only the most casual and incidental resemblance to his screen treatments.

During the mid-1970s, Stone traveled to Honduras and from there by bus to Costa Rica, in the first of several journeys he was to make in Latin America. His observations and experiences formed the basis for his third novel, *A Flag for Sunrise*, published in 1981. The book is set in an imaginary country named Tecan that combines essential elements from several Latin American nations.

Despite wildly misconceived, ideologically motivated carping from critics on both the right and the left over what they take to be the political implications of the novel, *A Flag for Sunrise* was generally well received by reviewers, winning the *Los Angeles Times* Book Prize, receiving nominations for the American Book Award, the National Book Critics Circle Award, and the PEN/Faulkner Award, and placing as runner-up for the Pulitzer Prize in fiction.[6]

Stone's fourth novel, *Children of Light*, appears to have had a long gestation. Obliquely, the book draws on Stone's experiences as a child and adolescent living with his schizophrenic mother. Stone's insights into his mother's condition contribute to his portrayal of a central figure in the novel, Lu Anne, a dedicated and accomplished actress beset by recurrent seizures of delusion. The plight of a mind tormented by conflicting experiences of reality and causality receives sensitive rendering in Stone's hands.

Published in 1986, *Children of Light* evoked a mixed and guarded response from reviewers. The novel was seen as Stone's least characteristic work, and though widely praised for its rigorous craftsmanship and the power and grace of its prose, it was viewed as somewhat slight, and rather disappointing in the light of the author's earlier achievements.[7] It is worth seeing how the book is more complex and more acute than the early critical estimates recognized. The novel represents, moreover, an important extension of Stone's central thematic concerns.

Stone's fifth novel, *Outerbridge Reach*, draws in part on the author's love of sailing and the sea, in part on his vivid memories of voyaging to Antarctica with the United States Navy in 1958, and in part on a bizarre incident the author read about in the *Sunday Times* in 1968, while living in London. The newspaper story that struck a resonant chord in Stone's imagination and that remained in his mind for many years was written by Nicholas Tomalin and Ron Hall and concerned an English sailor, Donald Crowhurst, who entered a solo around-the-world boat race but contrived to deceive the sponsors of the race by radioing false positions. Instead of circumnavigating the globe, Crowhurst sailed in circles off the coast of Patagonia, feigning a winning lead with the intention of claiming the prize. Instead, Crowhurst went insane and was lost overboard. A passing ship recovered the boat containing his encoded journals.

Employing the general outlines of this event—together with a few of its particulars—for an episode in his novel, Stone transformed the story into powerful and affecting literary art.

Curiously, after the novel's publication in England, certain voices raised objections to Stone's fictional use of the story as constituting unfair appropriation of the work of the reporters, who had developed their *Sunday Times* account into a book-length chronicle.[8]

In a prefatory note to *Outerbridge Reach*, the author acknowledges that passages of his novel were "suggested by an incident that actually occurred during a circumnavigation race in the mid-1960s." Not wishing readers to believe that he is merely retelling in fictional guise the story of the Crowhurst tragedy, nor wishing to cause Crowhurst's family any further distress or embarrassment, Stone refrains from mentioning Crowhurst by name. But this was interpreted as subtle and cunning plagiarism in a newspaper story in the *Sunday Telegraph*, in a review of the novel in the *London Review of Books*, and in the Letters to the Editor column of the *Times Literary Supplement*.

Stone felt compelled at last to defend his imaginative use of the Crowhurst story in a short article entitled "The Genesis of *Outer-bridge Reach*."[9] He takes strong exception to the notions that the episode in the novel is scarcely more than a replication of the story by Tomalin and Hall and that the story was not in the public domain. He insists on the right of novelists to use press accounts "if they create and dramatize characters of their own devising."[10] Later in the Letters to the Editor column of *TLS*, Stone reaffirmed his position that the public record constitutes "a traditional and proper source for fiction."[11]

Apart from this, *Outerbridge Reach* has received high praise from critics in both the United States and the United Kingdom. A work of complexity and depth, of humanity and intelligence, rendered with skill and informed by a distinctive and compelling vision, *Outerbridge Reach* is arguably one of the finest American novels of its era.

Two extended journeys to the Middle East by the author and his wife during the eighties and the nineties inspired his latest novel, *Damascus Gate*, set in the conflict-ridden city of Jerusalem. Epic in scale and in the resonance of its action, the novel may mark the culmination of the author's moral and psychological, political and metaphysical concerns. It also confirms Stone as a writer whose work advances steadily in the range of experience it concentrates and in the power of its technical means.

If Stone's work remains to a marked degree isolated from changing literary fashion, that is true, I think, for two mutually reflective reasons: because Stone's writing is the expression of an achieved individual vision, the product of a direct and energetic engagement with the essential questions of human existence, and because his fiction is rooted in a central tradition of the American novel, a romantic-realist strain running from Herman Melville to Norman Mailer. This tradition is urgently concerned with understanding the nature and meaning of the human condition, by penetrating the surfaces of the social and the natural worlds, by exploring extremes of human experience, by confronting violence, chaos, and terror, and in the end wresting from the encounter some ethic or redemptive insight, some manner of metaphysical vision, or some hint at least pertaining to the mystery of our lives.

Robert Stone's oeuvre is not large, but it is strong and individual. And he does not give the impression that his best work is behind him.

CHAPTER TWO

A Hall of Mirrors

The title of Robert Stone's first novel, *A Hall of Mirrors* (1963),[1] evokes an image of illusion and confusion, some corridor lined with mirrors in which myriad reflections afflict the beholder with bewilderment and helplessness. As the phrase occurs in Robert Lowell's poem "Children of Light," from which the epigraph of Stone's novel is taken, "a hall of mirrors" serves as a metaphor for America, for a society the poet views as inheriting from the pilgrim fathers dangerous delusions—beliefs and attitudes that lead inevitably to racial conflict, violence, and a betrayal of Christian sacramental vision. The title, with its own potent poetic resonance and fortified by the additional connotations arising from Lowell's poem, serves to suggest certain of the novel's major preoccupations: America, the life of the spirit, and the theme of illusion.

The America of *A Hall of Mirrors* belongs to the early 1960s, an era usually remembered as prosperous and confident but here depicted in imagery of desolation and decay, rankness and desiccation: bleak oil barrens and heaps of ash and gravel, grimy industrial landscapes and sterile, prisonlike factories, concrete freeways and squalid cityscapes, streets of chrome-plastic stores and stiff, gray-faced city dwellers, frost-blighted rosebuds in the spring, and dry stalks and dead trees in the summer. Stone's America is a wasteland whose New World equivalent to T. S. Eliot's "unreal city" is New Orleans, "Land of Dreams" (28). There seems even to be an echo of Eliot's London with its rats and its brown fog in Stone's descriptions of New Orleans: "a large and unafraid rat wheeled and darted . . . the mist . . . brown, foul, smelling of river water and things rotting" (28).

If New Orleans represents the essential characteristics of America, then the epitome of American manners, values, and aspirations lies in the brightly lit window display of a nameless shop on the corner of Rampart and Canal Streets:

> In one of the case windows, neat rows of steel telescopes sparkled under white light; there were binoculars, tiny radios, cocktail shakers and medals of the saints. In the second, spread across a background of rich dark cloth like velvet, there were revolvers, switchblade knives and razors. (40)

The alternatives embodied in the objects in the windows are clear: we may seek to extend our vision, be heartened and uplifted by music, value an even temporary abatement of our cares, cultivate spiritual comforts and ideals, or we can hurt and murder one another.

The citizens of Stone's American wasteland consist of essentially two kinds: liars and believers, predators and their prey, the powerful and the powerless. These two groups are not, however, entirely distinct but are sometimes manifest as different tendencies within the same individuals, who behave like organisms in a food chain, feeding even as they are fed upon.

Consider the young Bible salesman present at the very beginning of the novel. An eighteen-year-old country boy, he has been recruited through an advertisement placed in a local church magazine by a company whose interest is solely in selling Bibles—in the associated profits, though, rather than in prophets and souls. In sober ministerial attire, including an old-fashioned fedora and a pair of pane-glass spectacles—all of which he has purchased from the company—he is taken from city to city and from town to town "in the company's relentless transport" (3) to sell Bibles door to door. When he misses the rendezvous with the company car, he is left behind either to catch up on his own or to return home alone. Although frightened, lonely, even a little dazed, the boy accepts the pitiless, do-or-die principles of the company's operations, convincing himself, "That's the way it's got to be" (5).

Not only is the boy a victim of a ruthless survival-of-the-fittest business ethic, he is also the agent of an organization exploiting the hopes and goodwill of others. He deceives simple and gullible customers with his memorized sales pitch and his false ministerial appearance, ascetic behind the false eyeglasses. Seduced by the guile and greed of the company, he can survive only by seducing others.

Or consider Jack Noonan, a high-ranking executive in the Bingamon Corporation, casually and confidently wielding power over his subordinates but himself constantly insulted and humiliated by his superiors. Or, at the other end of the social scale, Dornberry, the former convict who labors for a pittance in one of Bingamon's factories, believing that Mr. Bingamon "don't even keep this place goin' but to help us boys out" (91) and reserving his aggression for those of his own class. Or the unfortunate Aloysha, the attendant of the Living Grace Mission. Among the lowest of the low, his faith and labor exploited by his con-man employer, he seizes every opportunity to intimidate and humiliate the hopeless alcoholic stumblebums who seek his help.

A Hall of Mirrors is informed by an aggrieved sense of the broken promise of America, a tragic vision of the betrayal of American ideals. "What's going on . . . Who are you and what the hell do you think you're doing?" (290), the novel asks of America as a nation. How is it, the book inquires, in the land of the free and the home of the brave, whose alabaster cities gleam undimmed by human tears, that so many citizens live in such wretchedness, degradation and fear? How is it that men such as Claude Torneille, who grow "rich and respectable" (112) by shabby scams and fixes, are exalted even as a kind of heroic ideal, while unfortunates such as the crippled Philomene and the maimed Lucky Hoskins live in desperate squalor, and pitiful innocent figures such as the gay Mardi Gras reveler are ruthlessly persecuted? How do corrupt public servants, bullying, brutal cops, cynical demagogues and paranoid superpatriots so proliferate and thrive? Why has a nation raised from the wilderness reverted to a wilderness of self-interest?

The central characters of *A Hall of Mirrors*—Rheinhardt, Geraldine, and Morgan Rainey—all stand apart from or in opposition to "the fabric of predatory power" (268) that makes up modern America. The response of each character to the knowledge of life's underlying brutal structure reveals the most distinctive qualities of his or her identity. In order to represent vividly the nature of their separate responses, the author employs a triple character focus, presenting the inner life, thoughts, and feelings of each of those characters. In both extent and importance, however, Rheinhardt's point of view dominates the narrative, and he must be considered the chief character of the novel—though, deeply flawed as he is, he can scarcely be named the hero, however keenly he engages our interest.

Rheinhardt is a self-divided figure, locked in struggle with himself. He is a man who deliberately has rejected the best within him and assiduously cultivates the worst. Once an exceptional classical clarinetist with much promise, he cast aside his gift out of a sort of moral cowardice, lacking "the energy and manhood" (48) necessary to develop his talent. He now works as an itinerant disc jockey, but his true vocation is drinking: he is a confirmed and dedicated drunk. Rheinhardt aspires to the condition of insensate matter, but he is too ignoble to accept the full consequences of his desire—and so he drinks. The liquor provides temporary oblivion, but at the cost of increasing terror and psychological dissociation as his bouts of delirium tremens escalate in intensity and frequency. Although he seems bent on extinguishing within himself all feeling, all compassion and concern, because they are painful to him, he has not yet altogether succeeded in doing so. Within him still lives a man of conscience and fine sensibility, a man acutely conscious of the distress of others, and who wants to alleviate their pain and plight.

The opening passages of the novel establish Rheinhardt as a man contending with himself. He sympathizes with the predicament of the frightened young Bible salesman, and offers him comfort and advice. Moreover, he understands the social and psychological components—ambition and greed—that shape the boy's situation. Rheinhardt further comprehends how the old-fashioned, simplistic pieties of McGuffey's *Eclectic Reader* (according to which the boy was educated), are hopelessly inadequate to prepare anyone to cope with the varieties of human weakness and the world's temptation. We see Rheinhardt's familiarity with and love of music—he is momentarily inspired to hum an aria from Puccini's opera, *Manon Lescaux*—and his immediate and emphatic repression of this aspect of himself. We also see his attraction to the dark and negative aspects of life: to oblivion—his prodigious drinking—and to death—his envy of the dead in their graveyards.

Rheinhardt's conversation with the Bible salesman and his attempts to help the boy by making him recognize the humiliating truth of his situation are later paralleled by a conversation that Rheinhardt has with Jack Noonan in which Rheinhardt attempts to save Noonan from his own greed and ambition. Rheinhardt urges Noonan to quit the employ of M. T. Bingamon who deliberately demeans Noonan and treats him with indignity and contempt. In both instances Rheinhardt's efforts are in vain. On another occasion, occurring between these two expressions of Rheinhardt's vestigial altruism, he engages in a dialogue with himself in which his conscience tries to persuade him to acknowledge the guilty fact of his complicity in the propagation of untruth for wicked purposes— namely the highly slanted newscast he has prepared for Bingamon's right-wing radio station, WUSA. When Rheinhardt's conscience admonishes him in the name of moral responsibility and personal integrity, he stifles its allegations of wrongdoing as quickly and resolutely as he earlier repressed his musical inclinations. He silences it by drowning it in alcohol, embarking on a prolonged binge. Yet a significant factor in each of these instances is the persistence of moral awareness in Rheinhardt. Try as he might to abolish his conscience, it still survives to perturb him and to disturb the false repose he cultivates through his studied indifference.

Rheinhardt's two dreams also show the power of his moral awareness. The first occurs at the outset of the narrative (3–4), the other in Book Two (177–78). Both are self-state dreams, or symbolic expressions of the mind's condition by the unconscious. In the first dream, the snowy winter streets represent the aloofness to which Rheinhardt aspires. The house he enters represents the citadel of apathy, the inner stronghold he has constructed in his mind as safety from the pain of knowing and feeling. But instead of feeling secure and triumphant upon passing through the glass doors and entering the building, he feels a sense of loss. This mood is succeeded by a sequence of infernal imagery—the white glass towers, the bright green boiling vegetation. The dream diagnoses Rheinhardt's condition and warns him of what the consequences of his attitudes and actions will be: madness and damnation. Similarly, in the second dream, the loft-like setting of the dream represents Rheinhardt's mind, while the coffin-like booth which confines him represents his willed unfeeling, uncaring state, an insulated, restrictive condition of death-in-life. The dust, the darkness, the mold, and the rodents represent his moral squalor, while the sudden intrusion of the ghastly light and terrible boiling vegetation again suggest the consequences of his chosen conscious existence: infernal terror and madness.

These appalling visions affirm that, at a deeper level of being than his conscious will and awareness, Rheinhardt's psyche is attempting to warn his ego-consciousness of the inevitable, dire effects of his perverse mode of life, and thus to defer him from such a course.

Rheinhardt's inner desire for lucidness rather than oblivion, for beauty rather than sordidness, is revealed also through his recurrent drunken or dissociated fantasies that he has only just lost his clarinet. At such moments it is as if he suddenly comprehends the enormity of his having forsaken his musical vocation, having betrayed the part of himself that might have, in the words of Oscar Wilde, "struck one clear chord to reach the ears of God" ("Hélas").[2] Significantly, the clarinet derives its name from the Latin word *clarus*, meaning clear. In having willfully ceased to maintain his gift, to practice and play his clarinet, Rheinhardt has renounced clarity of mind and spirit. Yet

the appetite of the mind and the spirit for clarity is implacable, ultimately uneradicable, and though Rheinhardt can deny and suppress
that appetite, he cannot free himself from it.

Repeated allusions to Shakespeare's *Hamlet* suggest another
perspective on Rheinhardt's self-dividedness. With his skeptical,
self-lacerating intelligence, his keen wit and acute awareness of the
hypocritical, corrupt nature of the world, Rheinhardt would make
a modern Hamlet figure, but he has chosen instead the part of
Claudius, the poisoner, the usurper. Rheinhardt's most frequent and
telling citation from the play is Claudius's cowardly ejaculation
"Defend me friends, I am but hurt" (21, 24, 181, 398). Through the
quotation, Rheinhardt denies that he is mortally wounded by the
terror and tragedy he experiences, and suggests an affinity between
him and Claudius. In a sense, Rheinhardt is both Hamlet and
Claudius: a heroic, noble self plotted against by a cowardly, treacherous, usurping self. Just as Claudius deliberately poisons his brother
and his nephew, and inadvertently poisons his own wife, Gertrude,
Rheinhardt's usurping self poisons his better self with alcohol, cynicism, and apathy, and inadvertently also poisons Geraldine, the
woman who loves him.

Geraldine remarks to Rheinhardt, "You're your own worst
enemy, ain't you?" (100). Later, she recognizes that Rheinhardt's
cruelty, destructiveness, and indifference have also poisoned her
spirit:

> She had gotten all his dreams and shakings; she had
> caught them. It got at her now his way and that was
> too much. (328)
>
> He'd hollowed it all out beneath her. . . . Now it
> would cave. Now it would all go the long way down,

everything in the big hole, everything under. He
undermined her. (332)

Finally, like Claudius, the usurper within Rheinhardt is caught in his
own trap. Having destroyed those who stood between himself and
the possession of the crown and kingdom, Claudius perishes from
his own poison. Similarly, at the end of the novel when the affectless Rheinhardt is in full possession of the mind and fate of the man
he inhabits, he forfeits all triumph or satisfaction in having survived
and prevailed, because now all life within is poisoned and sickened
by irredeemable loss.

Another aspect of Rheinhardt's character is suggested by the
allusions he makes in conversation to the Book of Job. At one point,
when asked by Geraldine where he's "coming from," Rheinhardt
replies by quoting Satan: "From going to and fro in the earth, and
from walking up and down on it" (133). Subsequently, in a confrontation with the idealistic Morgan Rainey, Rheinhardt exhorts
him to "Despair and die" (256), echoing the advice of Job's wife
to her husband in the face of their overwhelming personal disasters. These quotations illuminate his central, fatal flaw. Like Satan,
Rheinhardt has turned his back on the good: he declines to serve the
divine power within him—his capacity to create beauty—and turning from the joy and beauty of music, he cultivates instead baseness
and ruin. And like Job's wife, Rheinhardt responds to the pain of life
not with patience or with faith but with defiance and despair.

Rheinhardt's plight as an individual American may be seen to
epitomize that of the larger community, and even of the nation as a
whole. In the novel, Rheinhardt is by no means unique in his self-
betrayal and his unprincipled pursuit of a dollar. Other characters,
most notably Noonan and Irving, the WUSA engineer, sell their

integrity for money and prestige, while still others, including Bingamon, Mr. Cefalu, Lester Clotho, Calvin Minnow, Claude Bourgois,
Senator Pickens, and Jimmy Snipe, would seem never to have possessed the least jot of conscience, but instead only a ferocious, voracious appetite for power. The cumulative effect of such individual
acts of perfidy and relentless egocentrism performed at all levels of
society has been the transmogrification of "the land of dreams" into
a wasteland. Just as Rheinhardt turns away from the best within himself, so the nation, as depicted by Stone in *A Hall of Mirrors*, has
proved false to its ideals, betrayed its promises and dreams, and poisoned itself with materialism, selfishness, and self-gratification, with
intolerance, violence, and the politics of paranoia.

There is one fleeting moment, when stunned by the explosion
at the Restoration Rally, Rheinhardt almost realizes and regrets
his much-reduced and wrong-headed state. He wonders suddenly
whether "there was something some vital piece of equipage without
which . . . what? Without which all was lost?" (372) The lost, vital
piece of equipment, the lack of which Rheinhardt so briefly, so
keenly feels, is, as his name suggests, the very apparatus he has
spurned: the heart. More fortunate than he deserves to be, Rheinhardt has been given a second chance, an opportunity to recover his
missing part through Geraldine.

Geraldine possesses all those qualities—humility, compassion,
tolerance, love—that could redeem Rheinhardt, could revive and
renew him. She possesses those qualities that could, if fostered and
embraced, redeem and renew the nation.

Geraldine is a hard-luck hick: uneducated, unsophisticated,
unfortunate. Almost since her birth, she has been a handy victim for
a series of broody, brutal men, and a victim of economic exploitation

and social exclusion. She has literally, as well as figuratively, been scarred by life: her last boyfriend cut lines in her face with an oyster knife. Yet she endures and remains intact and only a little worse for wear. Through her sorrows and misfortunes she retains a fatalistic dignity, belief in life and hope of heaven.

In contrast to Rheinhardt, who lives in a hell of his own creation and who feels the magnetic pull of graveyards on his mind, Geraldine, despite her griefs and afflictions, cherishes visions and ideals. Her essential, irrepressible innocence is shown when she rides in a stranger's car at sunset in the rain across the oil barrens, and she is heartened to see among the clouds "a little patch of blue open sky . . . looking very far off, clean, remote, inviolate" (16). Although she is feeling sad and vulnerable—"small and cold" and "twice lost" (17) among the endless oil towers and giant pumps that symbolize the power and avarice that have excluded and exploited her in her life— the patch of clear sky inspires her to dream of human charity and divine mercy. She imagines a kind and caring place, the sort of loving community that was among the earliest American ideals. She envisions a place she associates with her childhood memory of President Roosevelt, and she yearns for "Heaven and rest and God" (19). Similarly, later in the novel, a quotation from the marginal gloss of Samuel Taylor Coleridge's *The Rime of the Ancient Mariner*—when the mariner "In his loneliness and fixedness yearneth toward the journeying moon and the stars"—excites her admiration and expresses the profound longing of her spirit for belonging, joy, and rest (170).

Not only is there no place in the world for Geraldine's rare and precious spirit, but it is as if by radar the agents of negativity— the pimps, cops, thugs, crazies and haters—single her out for special destruction. Perhaps in some primitive fashion they sense the subversive potential of her tolerance, tenderness, and generosity, her capacity for love and hope. In the end, of course, she is successfully destroyed by them, driven to die by her own hand in a narrow jail cell, using cold, hard metal as the instrument of death—the same metal of which the oil towers and the giant pumps are made. Geraldine dies a victim of and martyr to the mentality of metal, the greed of machinery and the pitiless prisons and factories, the rigid, relentless selfishness and the demented, obsessive desire for power that blight the mind of America.

Morgan Rainey represents another mode of opposition to the networks and agencies of "predatory power." Like Geraldine, Rainey is well acquainted with the cruelty of the world. He once worked as an investigator for the Massachusetts Children's Bureau, encountering instances of unbelievable, savage violence against helpless children. He subsequently worked with the American Friends Service Committee in rural Venezuela, helping barrio children, attempting to mitigate in some measure the wretchedness and privations of their lives and instill in them some hope and dignity. When he first appears in the novel, he is a temporary interviewer in a survey of welfare clients commissioned by the State Attorney's Office. Rainey's job interviewing welfare clients in their homes in the black ghetto of New Orleans brings him into daily contact with human suffering, degradation, and injustice.

Rainey's social conscience is a direct extension of his religious sense of life, his belief in a covenant between God and humanity. Yet his faith in God has not come easily, nor has it always been easy to maintain. Rainey's childhood faith was shaken and shattered by a convergence of events over a period of about ten days when he was a teenager. The first of these events was the sudden death of his father. Then, only a week after his father's death, Rainey witnessed the brutal murder of a Negro man. The very next day, Rainey began to fall ill with rheumatic fever, and that night, a violent hurricane struck, ravaging the area for days and nights on end:

> —voices roared from that wind, and the quiet joyous voice that for him was the voice of God, had broken, grown distant and fallen away before a terrible maimed chorus, the million-throated howl of a Godless earth, transfixed with hate, with death, with darkness. (219)

Later in life, just prior to the events of the novel, Rainey had what he subsequently refers to as a "breakdown," a combination of nervous collapse and existential crisis. He credits the grace of God for his eventual recovery from this condition and resumes his belief in a covenant. Later still, Rainey faces a final temptation, an enticement to succumb to despair and madness, when Lester Clotho induces in him a trance state, provoking in Rainey's mind a waking nightmare wherein he is again confronted with the vision of a world devoid of mercy and meaning, a world of darkness, depravity, and brutality. Rainey withstands this assault on his faith as well and emerges strengthened in his sense of mission. The experience reaffirms his determination to challenge those in control, the unscrupulous powerful, and to denounce their falsehoods and intrigues.

Yet for all his noble qualities and worthy ideals, Rainey is an ambiguous figure. His character holds an element of the grotesque, as reflected in his repugnant physical appearance and manner, but more especially in his inclination toward morbid self-indulgence, which can be seen when he and Geraldine become amorously attracted to each other. Rainey destroys the mood between them by devoting his kisses exclusively to the knife scars on Geraldine's face, as if attracted only by pain and suffering, or as if pursuing some perversely gratifying form of self-immolation. Perhaps, as his surname suggests, there is in Rainey something of a lugubrious quality, an exaggerated, excessive pity. The tears he sheds for the world are immoderate, dropping like rain.

Rainey embraces in more abstract form, as theology or ideology, those impulses which Geraldine embodies in a more natural, purer form, as spontaneous compassion, as childlike trust, innocent hope. In this way, there may be a sort of allegorical level to each of the three principal characters: Rheinhardt, Geraldine, and Rainey representing, respectively, the mind, the heart, and the spirit. In isolation from the others, each is partial, inadequate, and ineffective.

Among the secondary characters of the novel, a similar range of deficient responses to life in America and to the human condition exists. For example, the two hipsters, Marvin and Bogdanovich, cultivate a detached appreciation of the phenomenon of existence, an acceptance of things as they are. Assisted by abundant quantities of marijuana, they seek a state of nondiscriminatory, nonjudgmental awareness, passively being absorbed into the varieties of experience. As Bogdanovich remarks, "I'm always going to places. Riots, the dog races, the hockey. Anything like that" (393). Their pothead code of cool constitutes a neutrality of mind that precludes any genuine interest or feeling, any passion or compassion, and represents ultimately a flight from humanness.

S. B. Prothwaite responds altogether differently to life in America. He, for reasons of ideological conviction and personal grievance, drives a truck loaded with dynamite into the Restoration Rally, killing at least nineteen people in the ensuing explosion. Prothwaite is at least seventy-five, a relic of early twentieth-century labor radicalism, still inveighing against "the banks and railroads" (352) and the "malefactors of great wealth" (354). Yet despite his impassioned, antiquated IWW (Industrial Workers of the World) rhetoric, his act of terrorist violence is clearly motivated more by a sense of personal insult than by political ends. Prothwaite embodies the most pernicious features of the ideological mentality: the capacity for determined action without the power to grasp moral issues, and the self-deceiving belief that violent and inhuman acts of personal vindictiveness are nobly undertaken to serve history and human progress.

Farley, also known as Farley the Sailor, shows quite another response to life and the human condition. Farley is a man dedicated exclusively to his own survival, to his own prosperity and well-being. Neither scruple nor restraint impede him in his enterprise. Principally a confidence trickster by profession, he does not balk at theft or even murder. Farley's most successful con is his impersonation of a clergyman, and in this capacity he eagerly lends his rhetorical talents to the right wing, racist machinations of M. T. Bingamon.

Yet Farley has a peculiar touchiness, even among fellow hustlers, regarding his imposture. In his conversations with Rheinhardt, Farley repeatedly declares the sincerity of his religious outlook, mouthing pieties such as "we're all to blame for each other's sins" (78) and "I always try to think like St. Francis. Everyday each man must hoe his own small garden" (82). These are incongruous sentiments in so ruthless a man. Although it is possible that his pose is maintained even among friends out of a sense of caution or irony (which clearly he possesses), it seems more credible that he is, convinced of his own devoutness and of God's special favor. Farley appears to be in earnest when he makes remarks such as "saved again and His hand was in it" (81), or when after having murdered and plundered his way out of the disaster at the Restoration Rally, he observes, "Life, however bizarre it may appear, is ordered to an end" (383).

Through his many metamorphoses—from simple sailor to RCN Lieutenant to hairdresser and dietitian to "cosmic philosopher" to man of the cloth—Farley is another example of that common phenomenon, the con man who ends by conning himself, losing all sense of his original identity and becoming the dupe of his own poses and pretenses.

Self-deception is the common denominator of the varied approaches and responses to life as embodied in the secondary characters of the novel. This is most apparent in the cases of Prothwaite and Farley. Both figures profess allegiance to an ideal, political or spiritual, but in actuality both practice only the ethic of self-love, asserting their desires and imposing their wills without regard for others. Marvin and Bogdanovich deceive themselves in more subtle but no less fundamental ways, mistaking a mindless euphoric aloofness for serene detachment and confusing atavism with evolution. All of these figures isolate themselves from the human community, imprison themselves in their disguises and obsessions, in greed and anger, in glibness and flippancy, and ultimately in illusion.

Illusion and deception in their many forms are fundamental ingredients of human society as it is depicted in *A Hall of Mirrors*. The kind of imposture perpetrated by Farley represents only the least degree of the scope of fraud as practiced in the larger community. A far more extensive, more pernicious misrepresentation of reality is the kind undertaken for profit by Lester Clotho, who creates, as it were, frauds-to-order at the behest of political figures aiming to further their careers. Clotho specializes in the kind of elaborate, grand scale fakery known among professional confidence men as "the Big Store." Clotho can serve up any number of deserving, undeserving, or even completely fictitious welfare recipients as the occasion may require, organize bogus civil rights protests or even help stage a race riot upon request, when such events are needed to fulfill a client's political ambitions. So masterful is Clotho in the arts of deception that he is even able to turn black into white, night into day, as when he practices some of his most diabolical illusions on the gullible Morgan Rainey.

State's Attorney Calvin Minnow and wealthy demagogue M. T. Bingamon are further up the pyramid of illusion. Minnow is the evil intelligence behind a fraudulent welfare survey, of which the falsified data will enhance his political image—though it will also inflict misery on helpless, hopeless people. But as his name suggests, Minnow is a small fish in comparison to those more powerful. Among these bigger fish is M. T. Bingamon, whose "patriotic" crusade represents in reality a betrayal of every American ideal, and whose "vision" of a revitalized America is no more than a blind for his delusions of grandeur, his raw and ruthless will to power.

Those who perpetrate illusions on others are themselves victims of illusion—they fail to comprehend the illusory nature of desires and ambitions, worldly possessions and temporal power. Consider Bingamon's ultimate fate. At the very moment when he might at last be on the verge of attaining to the power he has so avidly pursued, he becomes utterly helpless. Despite his continued possession of the instruments of power—his pistol and his telephone—he is rendered completely devoid of strength and resources, control or influence. For all his vast wealth, his cunning and craft, his unquestioning confidence in his own destiny, Bingamon is overthrown and undone in an instant by an unforeseen event, an accident, a trick of fate, forfeiting not only his illusory power but his life as well.

Men like Clotho, Minnow, and Bingamon who perpetuate illusion may be understood best in metaphysical terms. Consider Morgan Rainey's moments of visionary insight in his encounters with these men. After confronting and challenging Minnow, Rainey recounts to Geraldine his preternatural understanding of the man: "It was given to me to see that man in a more than ordinary way. I knew him and I recognized him in a more than ordinary way" (272). Later, both when he is perturbed by the nightmare visions inflicted upon him by Clotho and when he is striving to foil Bingamon's plot to provoke a race riot, Rainey recalls the counsel of Saint Paul in his *Epistle to the Ephesians*:

> For we wrestle not against flesh and blood but against
> principalities, against powers, against the rulers of the
> darkness of this world . . . (349)

According to this mystical mode of perception, Bingamon, Clotho, Minnow and their counterparts are seen not merely as men but as agents of a negative principle, servants of a cosmic falsehood.

Rainey's vision of individuals in the visible, material world as manifestations of a supernatural order leads us closer to the deep structure of *A Hall of Mirrors*, to those images which establish the basic tonality of the text and through which the informing ideas of the novel are conveyed. The recurring salient images of the text form two essential opposing groups, each of which in turn consists of two allied sets. The two conflicting groups of images express two antagonistic views of human nature: humans as creatures of base instinct, represented by motifs of animalism and cold, and humans as spiritual beings, represented by the spiritual and music motifs.

Throughout *A Hall of Mirrors* there are comparisons of human beings with creatures. Relatively early in the novel, for example, the identification number tattooed on the arm of a former concentration camp inmate is referred to as "the beast mark" (48). Later, a sullen, menacing motorcycle policeman is likened both to an "insect" and an "animal" (124). Philomene compares humans to cats in terms of their sexuality (128), while Marvin compares humans to fish in terms of their predatory behavior (252). Similarly, Rheinhardt experiences a vision of the crowd attending the Restoration Rally as an assembly of raptors:

> Rheinhardt looked into the lights and saw dead whitened eyes, the twitching of stalk necks, bloodied bone, pecking—a huge groaning aviary, beak and claw. (328)

The "reptilian speed" of Farley in pursuit of loot (377), the "antlike" (380) appearance of running figures in the riot, together with their resemblance to "panicking night feeders" (380), also imply that humans are no more than creatures preoccupied with their own survival and with the satisfaction of their physical appetites.

The motif of animalism in the novel culminates in the image of the vampire, the ultimate human beast. Introduced through allusions to the film *Dracula* (133, 135), the vampire is a metaphor for the universality of human predation: "it's the dracula syndrome. It's the drink blood or die bag" (257). Even Rainey accepts the vampire metaphor as descriptive of the nature of certain humans, but not of human nature in general:

> I believe that there's a kind of man among us who
> feeds on pain to keep himself alive. I believe it because
> I saw one man in one office who lives on blood and it
> came to me that he wasn't the only one, you under-
> stand. He couldn't be the only one. (273)

The motif of animalism is closely allied with recurrent imagery of cold. Cold weather figures prominently in the book, and the tempo- ral movement of the story is from a chill spring to a cool fall and the approach of winter. The atmosphere of cold is metaphorical, sug- gesting lack of emotion, selfish calculation, and the absence of con- science or compassion. According to the terms of the novel, we are entering a sort of ethical ice age, a new epoch of insensitivity, avarice, and unrestrained egotism:

> "What in fact is happening," Rheinhardt said, "is that
> things are taking a cold turn. . . . One by one the warm
> weather creatures will topple dead with frosted eye-
> lids. . . . The creatures of cold will proliferate. The
> air will become thin and difficult to breathe. . . . Very
> shortly it will start to snow. It will be Cold City."
> (252–53)

Or as the cold-blooded Farley, the very man for cold weather, later remarks:

It'll get colder than this, Rheinhardt. This is nothing.
When it gets right frosty, I'll be back. That's the way
I like it. (383)

If some characters, such as Farley, or Bingamon with his "singular and formidable cool" (114), successfully adapt, others accommodate themselves more slowly to the cold, while still others—the warm-blooded, warm-hearted creatures—are not disposed to adjust to the changing environment and consequently are threatened with extinction. Rheinhardt is of the second category, habituating himself to the low moral temperature, bringing himself by degrees into concord with the cold. An early sign of Rheinhardt's gradual adaptation occurs on the morning after one of his binges, when he notes that his body "was cold and numb somewhere inside" (20). He attains a more advanced stage of adaptability just after he has prepared his first slanted WUSA news broadcast, and he feels "a curious chill about the edges of his spinal column" (109). Collaborating more closely now with the powers of cold, the signs of his adaptation become more manifest. At the end of the novel, Rheinhardt has by virtue of his successful adjustment to the cold earned the status of "a survivor" (397, 406)—though as Bogdanovich remarks, "That's not a compliment" (397).

The warm-blooded victims of the new epoch of cold are Geraldine and Rainey. Both of them are particularly susceptible to catching colds (14, 15, 231), and neither can sustain life in the absence of the heat and light of love. Geraldine perishes as a result of cold, undermined by Rheinhardt's coldness and destroyed by the emblematically cold metal of her jail cell. Rainey also ends in the grip of the powers of cold, incarcerated, accused, though his ultimate fate is not related. Since Rainey carries within himself a kind of self-generating heat in the form of his love of God and humanity, he may be able to endure the cold and perhaps even ultimately flourish in his own season. Or he may heed the advice Rheinhardt gives to him: "Despair and die."

The interrelated clusters of spiritual and musical images oppose the animal and cold motifs. The spiritual motif is introduced at the very beginning of the novel through the Bible salesman, who shows how religious ideals may become corrupted by mercenary considerations. Spirituality is then no longer a potent force in the life of humankind, but is reduced to being misrepresented by intolerant fanatics like Aloysha and the Reverend Orion Burn of the Four Square Christianity Church, impostors such as Farley, and commercial interests such as the Bible company. What survives of traditional religion is largely ignored by the populace. For example, although it is Ash Wednesday at the beginning of the novel, there is no indication that anyone in the offices or shops, the restaurants and bars, or on the streets of the city pays the least heed to the meaning of the Lenten season. And though throughout the novel the church bells of the city chime various hymns—"Abide with Me," "A Mighty Fortress Is Our God," "Rock of Ages," and others—the exhortations in these songs have no apparent effect on the citizen's venal, sensual lives.

Yet the hope of a higher, truer life, of some transcendental state of being persists, resisting all destructive forces and agencies, surviving even gross exploitation and grotesque misrepresentation. Such hope endures in the Geraldine's longing for "some place at the end of it," a place where there is "no pain, no toil, no danger" (18). It manifests itself in Rainey's prayers and acts of witness, and even in the marijuana reveries of the hipsters who envision a paradisiacal "California of the mind" that exists "At the end of that dry hairiness, on the other side of the skeletons and the windies and the terrible salt flats, at the further edge of the bad trips" (183). Such hopes of paradise, such beliefs in redemption and divinity, represent an essential antidote to animality. "Otherwise," as Rainey remarks, "we keep finding out the insect in each other. We tear like insects. Without God." (214)

Thus, though betrayed and rejected, the spiritual impulse still shows itself to be resiliently protean and perhaps ultimately irrepressible.

Like the spiritual impulse with which it is closely associated in the novel, music assumes different forms, manifesting itself through different modes: radios and jukeboxes play rock 'n' roll and country-and-western tunes, the church bells carol hymns, Beethoven's *Pastoral Symphony* and Berlioz's *Requiem* drift out of open apartment windows; Philomene sings a folk song; Geraldine and Rheinhardt sing drunken duets; an anonymous, hopeless voice in the room of a cheap hotel sings "Onward Christian Soldiers." These are sounds of lamentation, celebration, aspiration—the flawed, faltering, determined spirit of humankind expressed in music.

Music, like religion, can become distorted and perverted, as is the muzak that permeates the offices, corridors, and elevators of City Hall, or the insipid "pastel sound" (324) of the band at the Restoration Rally. But, like spirituality, music is ultimately irrepressible, arising spontaneously from even the most daunting circumstances, as, for example, when the barrio children sing the "Los Chimichimitos," the Venezuelan children's song, and the black children in the ghetto sing about the goose and the monkey.

Music's highest function in *A Hall of Mirrors* is to exalt and elevate the mind and spirit, to liberate the isolated ego from its narrow bounds, uniting with other human spirits. This sovereign power of music is recalled by Rheinhardt, who once experienced such a moment of transcendence while playing a Mozart quintet:

> just above the barrier of form was a world of sunlight in which he could soar and caper with an eagle's freedom . . . there was perfection in this music, something of God in this music, a divine thing in it—. (46)

Rheinhardt also recalls how he observed the transfiguring effect of music on an elderly cellist who was a former concentration camp inmate, a man who had experienced unspeakable suffering and degradation and who knew firsthand and in full measure the human capacity for evil:

> He opened his eyes to see the cellist bent low over his strings; the man's eyes were bright with love, and as his fingers moved tenderly across the board his upturned wrist displayed the five blue characters where they had taken that caressing arm and tattooed upon it DK 412. Just before Rheinhardt picked up on his next note the old man had turned expectantly towards him with the rapture and tenderness still shining in his face. (47)

The power of music also reveals itself in Rheinhardt's later life. For although he attempts to reject music, he cannot altogether resist the pull it still exerts upon him. He is drawn irresistibly into the music room at the library, for example, and compelled to read the music for the Mozart Quintet, testifying to the latent power that music still retains in his psyche. Later, at the Restoration Rally, as he mounts the stage before the howling crowd, called upon to deliver a "God and country" (366) harangue, Rheinhardt, in fact, believes that he is about to conduct Mozart's *Symphony in G Minor*. And, as previously mentioned, Rheinhardt is often subject to the misapprehension that he has only just lost his clarinet, searching for it and inquiring after it.

The image patterns of *A Hall of Mirrors* represent a contest between redemptive energies and forces of negation, and every choice made, every action undertaken by every individual human being bears on the ultimate issue of the conflict. In the novel, the forces of negation would seem to be carrying the field, the redemptive forces in disarray and full retreat.

A Hall of Mirrors does seem distinctly gloomy in this regard. Geraldine is destroyed. Rainey's ineffectual protest leads only to his incarceration. Rheinhardt ends as irredeemably damned. Only the persistence and resilience of conscience, spirituality and music seem to suggest the smallest grounds for hope. Yet, clearly, *A Hall of Mirrors* is an admonitory work that aims to disturb and provoke the reader, and there is an implicit sense that the malady has a remedy. Finally, the novel's diagnosis of the spiritual crisis, the decay, discontent, and corruption of contemporary society represents the essential vision which the author intensifies, extends, and refines in his subsequent works.

Though it is Robert Stone's first novel, *A Hall of Mirrors* displays virtually none of the flaws of an apprentice work of fiction. The novel is vigorous and subtle, deft in its evocations of character and atmosphere, and skillful in its building and sustaining of narrative momentum. Its multifaceted style accommodates realism, delirium, wit, and a richly suggestive texture of image and allusion. With this debut, the author lays claim to an area of experience that is his special domain as a writer: the region that, quoting Robert Browning, we may name "the dangerous edge of things"[3]—the frontier that lies at the farthest end of alienation and psychic fragmentation, that baleful place where, in the face of terror, despair, and the demonic, there may be a moment of ultimate choice and grace and redemption may at last become possible.

CHAPTER THREE

Dog Soldiers

The opening pages of *Dog Soldiers*[1] present an ontological and spiritual understanding of the characters and events of the novel. This perspective is developed in the course of the novel, primarily through Christian and Buddhist theology. These two widely divergent religions are used as metaphorical descriptions of the core truth and insight which informs them, and of the ultimate end—human liberation—that they both serve but which they conceptualize differently and express according to their separate tenets.

The novel's interpretation of the human predicament, expressed through Christian imagery, is that we inhabit a Fallen World, one stricken and afflicted to the very core of its being, and that we are ourselves corrupted and depraved, though we retain at the deepest level an essential, latent innocence. Our world is one in which religious teachings are ignored or disbelieved and disdained, and in which the only universal creed is the pursuit of power and pleasure. Our contemporary Fallen World is full of confusion, disorder, and senseless, ruthless violence; it is a world in which the power of evil continually augments its potency from ever-increasing human weakness. And yet even amid the darkness of human life's mutual devouring in such a fallen state, there is the constant presence of the numinous, and the constant opportunity for salvation.

Such a perspective is suggested already in the opening scene of the novel in which the main character, Converse, sitting in a park in Saigon just prior to an appointment at which he intends to obtain a large quantity of heroin, engages in conversation with an American missionary woman. The contrast between the two figures, as revealed in their exchange, is striking: Converse, amiable, sophisticated, but lacking in conviction, conscience, and courage; the missionary lady, "clear-voiced and clear-eyed," a woman of "formidable strength" and of deep belief and commitment. In the course of their conversation, they discuss the acceptance of God's will, eschatology, evil, Satan, and salvation.

Even while Converse and the missionary woman sit talking in the park, prostitutes, moneychangers, and hustlers of all sorts are pursuing their predatory trades in the arcade of the nearby "Eden Passage" (1, 3, 9). Repeated references to this location and the business conducted there imply how far we have fallen since we dwelt in Eden. Further contrast to prelapsarian innocence and to the religious beliefs of the missionary woman is provided by Converse's reading of a letter from his wife, Marge, in which she expresses her moral relativism and general lack of restraint. Charmian, Converse's partner in the heroin transaction, provides an even stronger contrast. An utterly unscrupulous and selfish woman, she is the diametric opposite of the missionary lady.

Recurrent allusions to Buddhism and its tenets and practices provide a supplementary view of the state of humankind. According to the Buddhist perspective implied in the novel, consciousness and the phenomenal world are illusions, and all the suffering and death that is endured by humanity is an inevitable consequence of this fallen state of being, the condition of illusion. Liberation from illusion is possible through right thought and right action, through which desire and self-consciousness are overcome, and transcendent being or selflessness is attained.

This perspective is introduced obliquely in the first chapter of the novel in the description of Charmian's bedroom, "filled with

Buddhas and temple hangings" (10). It is subsequently developed through the characters of Ray Hicks and Dieter Bechstein, both of whom embrace versions of Buddhism and who think and act in accordance with Buddhist principles. This Buddhist view of humanity and reality can also be seen in the recounting of the oriental fable concerning desire (183) and in various incidents, which by virtue of their obsessive, compulsive, false, and illusive character invite a Buddhist interpretation.

The Christian and Buddhist perspectives in the novel share a sense that the human plight is our exile from true being, and that by turning away from the illusions of the material world and the false identity of subjective consciousness, we can discover our true identity in union with the Absolute. Human endeavors that do not in some manner address this form of redemption partake of illusion and are by their very nature spurious and futile. Thus by the end of the opening scenes of *Dog Soldiers*, the social and personal consequences of lack of belief have been set forth and the ultimate alternatives of the novel have been proposed.

As the very embodiment of desire and illusion, the three kilogram package of heroin that passes from hand to hand in the course of *Dog Soldiers* constitutes the axis of all relationships in the novel. It is in relation to this substance that the various characters of the novel discover or disclose their inherent nature.

Dog Soldiers employs an anonymous third person narration that follows the point of view of three main characters: Converse, Hicks, and Marge. Converse and Hicks are given about equal attention as narrative foci, while much less space is devoted to a rendering of Marge.

Converse is as his surname suggests, a man reversed in every sense: in thought, word, and deed. By slow degrees and by sudden transformations he has become quite the opposite person from the one he wishes to be. As we learn in the course of the novel from various scattered remarks, references, and recollections, Converse was once a promising young man, talented and idealistic. He served in the United States Marine Corps, wrote a successful play, and was— or so he and others thought of him—"a moralist," even a "world-saver" (54). But when we first encounter him at the beginning of the novel, he has wasted and betrayed his talent, and forsaken all notions of saving the world, or, indeed, of saving anyone except himself.

Converse abuses and dissipates his gifts as a writer through his work on the staff of a sordid and sensationalistic tabloid newspaper, where he writes lies for a living, inventing grotesque stories to satisfy the perverted appetites of the paper's prurient readership. Hoping somehow to salvage what remains of his integrity as a writer, and with the intention of gathering material for a possible novel, Converse spends eighteen months in Vietnam and Cambodia covering the war as a freelance journalist. There, however, he begins to discover that he is hollow, without any real ideals or any deeply felt, deeply held moral apprehensions. Converse continues, though, to pretend in his social intercourse and in his capacity as a journalist to possess such moral perspectives, but he recognizes that his stories are "false, facile" (261), travesties of the real and the true. In this sense his work as a war correspondent is merely a continuation of his tabloid journalism—he is still writing lies for a living.

The final stage of Converse's recognition of himself as a man without substance occurs on the battlefield in Cambodia, when under accidental aerial bombardment by friendly forces, he is reduced to quivering terror and the desperate desire to live. Surely this is not an uncommon reaction to such an experience, but for Converse the profoundly dismaying revelation of the event is that "That was all there was of him, all there had ever been" (186). From this point forward, Converse is a man utterly without metaphysical orientation or moral direction, without code or values. He has become what he calls a "dog soldier," that is "the celebrated living dog, preferred over dead lions" (186) who blindly soldiers on in life, submitting to it without dignity, suffering without hope, enduring existence merely out of fear of death.

Significantly, it is after this confrontation with raw terror and the consequent collapse of his sense of identity that Converse meets Charmian, who proposes that they form a partnership to smuggle a quantity of heroin from Vietnam to the United States. Converse's motives for accepting her proposal are various, but chiefly it is the fatal combination of "his own desperate emptiness and her fascination for him" (24–25) that persuades him to consent to her plan. By this point, Converse has developed a passive, fatalistic condition of mind. The conjunction of Converse's anomie and the enticements of Charmian suggests that seduction by evil is facilitated by the presence of a moral and spiritual vacuum and may suggest that such a void serves to attract evil.

The progress of the persistent fever that Converse follows with such concern at intervals through the opening chapters of the novel is a metaphor for his infection by evil. The trope of infection is specifically associated with the briefcase full of heroin that he carries: "he bore it through the heat like a festering limb, expecting at any moment some passerby might protest at the smell of it or its unsightliness" (49–50). A more subtle and debilitating symptom of his disease is the scrupulously reasoned but thoroughly specious formal argument he rehearses to himself in favor of smuggling the heroin;

he convinces himself that moral objections against such an under-taking are invalid, since in an absurd world "people are just naturally going to want to get high" (42).

Having once yielded to what is weakest and most vitiated in himself, Converse's descent is relentless. He is double-crossed, pur-sued, beaten and tortured, threatened, dragooned, humiliated, badly frightened, and nearly murdered. Yet other than the keen regret that he quite naturally feels at having involved himself and his wife in such danger and disorder, there is very little indication that Converse changes in any way as a result of his ordeals. He seems not to feel any real contrition, recovers neither his courage nor his conscience, and apparently achieves no noteworthy insights into human life and fate.

There are, however, occasions on which Converse nearly begins to grasp the deeper significance of his act, and seems almost to catch some glimpse of an ethical mechanism that governs exis-tence and destiny. While in the custody of the two vicious criminal-drug agents, Smitty and Danskin, Converse is on more than one occasion made uncomfortably aware that through his transgression he has forfeited all moral credibility, all grounds for drawing moral distinctions or making pronouncements. Once, for example, in the course of a discussion with Danskin, Converse attempts to invoke moral principles of a sort and is contemptuously rebuked:

> "Don't you think sometimes," Converse ventured . . . "don't you think there ought to be more to life than that?"
>
> "You should talk," Danskin said. "What have I got to learn from you about what there should be?"
>
> Converse was silent. (252)

Later, when facing the likelihood of his imminent death, Converse recalls the way in which he once betrayed one of his purest impulses by writing a newspaper story that cheapened and sullied his inmost feelings:

> The notion struck him that it was the writing of that story he was paying for. The idea of such justice both comforted him and terrified him. (262)

In the end, though, such moments of potential insight are without meliorative effect upon him. Fear remains the defining factor of his existence, when we last see Converse in the novel, he is fleeing for his life.

Diametrically different in character to Converse is his old friend from Marine Corps days, Ray Hicks. While Converse is dominated by intellect and fear, Hicks lives by intuition, readiness, and grace in physical activity. And while Converse is without religious belief and moral or personal integrity, Hicks is a devotee of Zen Buddhism and a man who adheres to a clear and rigorous personal code. In metaphoric terms, the difference between the two men lies in the head and in the heart. Yet while Hicks admires and even loves Converse as a friend, Converse for his part largely avoids Hicks and regards him as a psychopath.

There are, certainly, aspects of Hicks's character that might lead to such a pronouncement. He is given to rage and violence and to irrational acts, and he is jealously, vindictively, protective of his very personal and, at times, peculiar sense of honor. It is this facet of his personality that impresses Marge when she first encounters with Hicks:

> He had a hungry face . . . Deprivation—of love, of
> mother's milk, of calcium, of God knows what . . . His
> eyes seemed as flat as a snake's. There was such cold-
> ness, such cruelty in his face that she could not think
> of him as a man at all. (95)

But as both Marge and Converse ultimately discover, Hicks is a far
more complex and ambiguous person than his fierce mien and his
occasional erratic behavior might immediately suggest. He is a man
at odds with himself—one part of him resentful and wary, capable
of impetuous folly, while other aspects of his character include his
sincerity and strength of spirit, and his capacity for love and for self-
sacrifice. Hicks is certainly no paragon, but is nevertheless an inherently virtuous, even heroic man. Like a hero of Sophoclean tragedy,
he is self-willed, almost obsessed, but grandly persevering in his
contest with fate and death.

Hicks's contradictory nature is suggested when we first
encounter him as he sits drinking beer and re-reading Nietzsche in
a merchant seaman's canteen in Vietnam. At the outset of his conversation with Converse, Hicks declines the heroin that has been
brought for him to smuggle into the United States, citing spiritual,
moral, and practical objections. The prospect of easy money holds
no apparent appeal for Hicks, nor does he respond to the pressure
that Converse exerts on him with threats of certain retribution at the
hands of the CIA. Hicks's eventual decision to move the heroin for
Converse is motivated solely by his desire for some form of challenge and stimulation: "He felt the necessity of changing levels, a little adrenalin to clean the blood. It was interesting and kind of scary"
(55). This incongruous combination of action and motivation manifests again later in the novel when we are told that "Even dealing, he

endeavored to maintain a spiritual life" (75). Again, like a Greek hero, Hicks's defects seem to be inseparable from his merits and his virtues inextricable from his vices.

Hicks's interest in Nietzsche is a clue to the serious temper of his mind and to his urge to create himself anew through will and discipline, like a Nietzschean superman, to grow beyond himself. But, in a sense, Hicks has grown beyond Nietzsche, finding that he can no longer read him with any interest or appreciation. The Nietzschean ideal has been supplanted in his spirit by the philosophy of Zen and by the samurai ideal.

Hicks's involvement in Zen derives from his exposure to Japanese culture while stationed in Japan with the Marine Corps. He has also studied under a western roshi, or Zen master, Dieter Bechstein, who describes Hicks as being "a natural man of Zen":

> He was incredible. He acted everything out. There was absolutely no difference between thought and action for him . . . It was exactly the same. An enormous self-respect. Whatever he believed in he had to embody absolutely. (271)

Hicks's affinity for Zen correlates with his view of himself as "a kind of samurai" (75), a warrior adhering to a chivalric code and fighting only in defense of honorable goals. In accordance with this code, Hicks renounces his career in the Marine Corps after serving in Vietnam because "it was not a war for a man who maintained a spiritual life" (75).

His lapses and his errors notwithstanding, Hicks lives the ideal of the Zen warrior as truly as he is able, striving for self-clarification, refining his desires:

> In the end there were not many things worth wanting
> —for the serious man, the samurai. But there were
> some. In the end, if the serious man is still bound to
> illusion, he selects the worthiest illusion and takes a
> stand. (168)

In the end, the worthiest illusion for Hicks is love—love for Marge
and love for his friend Converse. There are crucial occasions in the
course of the novel when Hicks might easily have avoided further
dangers and difficulties and even have saved his own life by abandoning Marge or Converse, but he declines to do so, instead embracing his fate, affirming his code. Hicks's last and most decisive act
of samurai valor toward Marge and Converse is when he single-
handedly takes on the four armed malefactors who have pursued and
assaulted them.

Among all the confusion and cowardice that afflict the various
characters of *Dog Soldiers*, all the weakness and waste, the ignominy
and the corruption of will, Hicks performs a noble, selfless act, an
act of love. Already, however, only minutes after the deed of valor,
Hicks invalidates it by killing Dieter, whom he mistakenly believes
is stealing from him.

Yet, in the hours that follow, Hicks again redeems himself,
expiating his guilt through an extraordinary penitential ordeal.
Gravely wounded and bleeding steadily, Hicks walks for miles and
miles in the heat of day across a harsh desert landscape, bearing his
pack (containing the three kilograms of heroin) and his rifle. With
exemplary discipline and fortitude, Hicks resists self-pity, despair,
and terror, maintains his dignity, and perseveres in his chosen mission to the very limit of his strength. In the process, he also confronts

and triumphs over the negative apprehensions that have hindered and misled him in his life, attaining a new clarity and discovering a new identity as "the pain carrier" (330).

Hicks's role as "the pain carrier" represents the highest refinement of his vocation as a samurai. In the extremity of his own suffering and weakness, he willingly assumes the function of a scapegoat or a sacrificial figure, taking upon himself the humiliation and the pain of others:

> "All you people," Hicks shouted, "let it go! Let it go, you hear! I'm out here now. I got it! . . . Everybody! Everywhere! Close your eyes and let it go. You can't take it—you don't have to take it any more. I'll do it all." (328)

Hicks's earlier ambivalence is resolved in his end. Whatever his imperfections, he is moving and impressive in his final magnanimous ordeal. Alone among the principal characters of the novel, Hicks embodies something noble and heroic.

Marge comes closest to Hicks in terms of a spiritual and mental refinement. Marge is similar in character to both Converse and to Hicks, who externalize the poles or potentials of her psyche. Accordingly, Marge's inner development in the course of the novel may be seen as a movement away from the values and attitudes represented by Converse and toward those represented by Hicks.

Like Converse, Marge is, at the beginning of the novel, betraying her gifts, turning her back on the best in herself. Formerly a student of anthropology and drama, she now sells tickets at a pornographic cinema (like Converse, in this regard, serving the perverted appetites of the public). Formerly an idealist and political activist, she has become cynical and is becoming addicted to dilaudid, an opium derivative. Also, like Converse, she is a moral relativist and is adept at rationalization. In a letter replying to Converse's proposal concerning her role in the the heroin smuggling, Marge insouciantly writes:

> Why the hell not? I'm prepared to take chances at this point and I don't respond to the moral objections. The way things are set up the people concerned have nothing coming to them and we'll just be occupying a place that someone else will fill fast enough if they get the chance. (39)

The sort of engagement that Marge previously had with intellectual, artistic, or political issues has now been replaced by a devotion to dope and its dark glamour:

> Not since she was much younger had she felt so satisfying a commitment as she felt to the caper and to the dope that would be on the water. (71)

Yet, in spite of Marge's attraction to the escape and oblivion afforded by opiates—an attraction that intensifies as the novel proceeds— she still retains a contrary desire to confront reality, to partake of it fully, and even to challenge it. Marge expresses this latter desire, in inverted form, through her dismay at the blank trance state into which her daughter Janey habitually passes while riding her plastic rocking horse in the backyard. (Clearly, there is a parallel here between Janey's addiction to her horse and Marge's addiction to her "horse," as heroin is sometimes known.)

Marge's residual, latent desire for action and experience, in preference to inertia and stupor, also manifests in her response to Hicks. Afraid of and repelled by him initially, she is astounded to discover the magnetic attraction he exerts on her: "When she felt his lips, his bitter greedy mouth against her face, it came to her clearly that it was what she wanted" (96).

Hicks represents for her the very embodiment of the raw, vigorous life she craves even as she flees from it into the indolence and dreamy contentment of her opiates. Hicks is for her "the fear, the danger, the death. The thing itself" (96). Marge's deep affinity with him is further underlined by the dream she has of him on the morning before their encounter and by the simultaneous shiver they experience on a later occasion.

Yet even as the weaker aspects of Marge's character gain influence over her psyche—as measured by her increasingly frequent recourse to the heroin—energies of another kind also become available to her, and she manifests courage and strength in the face of danger. She first displays these qualities when she and Hicks bluff a group of vicious white-trash freaks who have occupied Hicks's house. Marge carries off her part successfully, "looking cool and arrogant" (107), winning Hicks's unspoken approval.

This relatively minor event serves to prefigure Marge's later act of courage and atonement when she decides to surrender the heroin to the crooked narcotics agents. Acting on her own, knowing that she may be killed, Marge acknowledges that the responsibility for the entire misadventure rests on her and Converse alone. Arguing the issue with Hicks, Marge insists: "It was my goddamn thing. Mine and his. We ought to pay in our own way" (287). "We did this—John and I. I won't have anybody else fucked up over it" (289). Again, Hicks is filled with admiration for her bearing and her bravery: "You dig her walking to her fate thataway? Nothing but class" (291).

Marge shows a further and final act of courage when she insists on keeping the appointed rendezvous with Hicks, in the face of her husband's arguments that it may be fatally dangerous to do so. In contrast to Converse, Marge's personal loyalty takes precedence over personal safety.

In the end, though, there are no conclusive indications as to what will become of Marge. It is not clear what she has learned or gained, whether she will remain with Converse, what kind of life she will lead in the future, and whether or not she can redeem herself from her drug habit. Somehow, though, the sheer defiant fact that Marge has survived the long nightmare of violence and ruthless pursuit seems grounds enough for hope.

As for the pursuers themselves, in the figures of the three corrupt narcotics agents the author has created vivid and chilling portraits of human depravity. By virtue of his ability to inspire cold terror, Danskin rises preeminent among the three. Though intelligent, tasteful, and affable, Danskin is a man with destructive impulses, whose motive power is his blind, violent assertion of himself. Calculating, intimidating, driven by rage, pride, and the desire for power, unrestrained by morality or compassion, Danskin probably could be categorized by a psychologist as a sociopath. But he represents a devil incarnate, a man who has surrendered his humanity to the demonic within himself.

Danskin's companion, Smitty, seems at first to be the more malevolent of the two, and certainly he shows himself capable of every base and cruel act. Yet, he is at times incongruously vulnerable and ingenuous. Naïveté and a kind of random compassion alternate in Smitty's behavior with mindless violence. And his dream (which later will be considered further) suggests that there is a level at which he still retains some form of moral awareness. He is a strangely vile and pitiful, vicious and pathetic figure.

The sinister eminence behind the entire heroin operation is Antheil, who uses his position as head of a federal regulatory agency to engage in profitable criminal activities, including the sale of narcotics. Antheil constitutes a link between the upper reaches of political and financial power, where he is well connected, and the lower depths of the criminal underworld—between two unprincipled, predatory realms. Thoroughly ruthless, Antheil is at home in both domains and able to turn his suave ferocity and consummate deceitfulness to good economic account. Appropriately, his name suggests the insect world, and ironically, he has a degree in law.

Danskin, Smitty, and Antheil, together with the novel's other malefactors, such as Charmian, Antheil's cold-blooded coconspirator in the heroin transaction, and Eddie Peace, the maximum middleman for illicit kicks in Los Angeles, all embody the self-aggrandizing, self-indulgent, infantile, aggressive impulses of human consciousness. This unsavory lot share a common grasping, selfish preoccupation with power and possessions, a complete lack of moral code, and an utter indifference to the lives of others.

Additional secondary characters of *Dog Soldiers*, however, embody quite other desires and directions, and by their presence somewhat redress the pervasive wickedness in the novel.

Dieter Bechstein's enterprise, for example, is utterly dissimilar from that of Antheil and his associates. Dieter's goal is to elevate, enlighten, and liberate humanity, or at the very least, to create a spiritual counterforce to the "degeneracy and murder" (274) of the age. His one crucial error of judgment in the pursuit of this noble aim—the introduction of drugs as a mode of transcendence to those who join him in his quest—weighs heavily upon him, and when we first encounter him in the novel his project is in abeyance. Significantly, Dieter attempts to destroy the very object that Antheil and the others crave to possess, the heroin: the objectification of their ignorance and folly. Futile and fatal to him though this effort proves to be, it expiates his earlier embracing of drugs, and represents a reaffirmation of his spiritual ideals.

Ken Grimes is another figure who lives and dies according to an unselfish ideal. A combat medic who is killed in Vietnam at the age of twenty, Grimes initially fled to Canada to avoid the draft, but then, placing fidelity to his moral code above his personal safety, he returns to the United States to be inducted as a noncombatant. Grimes is the only figure in *Dog Soldiers* to employ drugs in a truly humane manner: for the relief of pain. He is also one of the few in the novel who accept the conditions of life and death and who attempt to act compassionately within those limitations. His motto, taken from Edgar's speech in the last act of Shakespeare's *King Lear*, is that "man must endure his going hence even as his coming hither" (261). More fully and more bravely than any other figure in the novel, Grimes embodies a view of life according to which "people acted on coherent ethical apprehensions that seemed real to them" (261). Such an attitude is, of course, utterly alien and incomprehensible to the likes of Antheil, Charmian, Danskin, and their ilk, and even to a man like Converse, though he admires and envies it. Indeed, Grime's death moves Converse to feel love and "even pride in humanity" (261), surely the noblest emotions that he experiences at any time in the entire narrative. It is as if persons such as Ken Grimes, in the poet Stephen Spender's phrase, "leave the air signed with their honor."[2]

Two other secondary characters, Jill and Ian Percy, also act in accordance with moral principles. The Australian couple has lived in Vietnam for many years. The Percys are profoundly attached to the country, and thoroughly familiar with its language, culture, and politics. A former agronomist for the United Nations Relief and Rehabilitation Agency, the World Health Organization, and other organizations, Ian now works as a journalist, as does Jill. In their reporting, both attempt to convey, "for the information of the civilized world" (28), something of the suffering and plight of the people of Vietnam —notwithstanding their persuasion that "the civilized world" is not particularly interested. In an effort to deflect from themselves some of the appalling human tragedy that has confronted them for so long in Vietnam, Ian affects a gruff, sardonic manner, while Jill adopts a bluff and hearty one. But their dissolute drinking and their unguarded moments betray the rage and despair that oppresses their spirits. When there is an explosion in front of the Saigon tax office, resulting in the death and injury of a number of bystanders, Ian and Jill are clearly overcome with emotion at the dreadful spectacle. Even after having witnessed so much death and suffering during their years in Vietnam, they remain uninured. Yet they intend to stay in Vietnam "forever," as Jill puts it, continuing to try against all odds to mitigate some of the pain of the Vietnamese people. "Engagé" is the Sartrean existentialist term that Converse applies to the Percys: committed. Like Ken Grimes, they adhere to a code in which personal welfare and safety are only of secondary importance.

In a sense, the various characters of *Dog Soldiers* occupy positions along a scale of vanity, in the sense of both its definitions: self-conceit and emptiness. These two definitions can be mutually reflective, that is we may be said to pursue vanities in direct proportion to the degree of our own vanity. Vanity in this double sense is the measure of man in *Dog Soldiers*. There are those, such as Antheil, Charmian, and Danskin, who know only vanity, and there are those like Dieter, Ken Grimes, and the Percys, who strive in their lives to liberate themselves from vanity. And finally, there are those, such as Hicks, Converse, and Marge, who oscillate, drift, and travel along the scale.

Deception, delusion, desire, ignorance, falsehood—all the corollaries and consequences of vanity—constitute a central theme in the novel, which we may call the theme of illusion. One main constituent of this theme is mendacity: Converse's newspaper stories for *Nightbeat* are all lies, and he lies to Hicks in an effort to persuade him to smuggle the heroin; the marines at My Lat lie to Converse about the sappers, and they perpetuate an elaborate hoax about them, perhaps for the benefit of those in command; Smitty lies repeatedly about having been in Vietnam, concocting atrocity stories to titillate and seduce his listeners; Danskin lies for a living, impersonating political radicals and drug users for the FBI and the Bureau of Narcotics; Charmian lies to Converse from the very outset concerning the heroin transaction; and Antheil lies and lives a lie, pretending that he is an enforcer of the law when he is, in fact, a criminal on a grand scale.

Similarly, numerous other characters, objects, or events in the novel hide themselves under false appearances: prostitutes simulate lust; silicone breasts pose as real breasts; criminals pose as law enforcement agents; sand passes for heroin; flashing lights and loud noises over speakers simulate battle; Charmian resembles "a figure of ceremony . . . to be sacrificed or baptized" (10) as she sets up

Converse; Antheil looks like "a sympathetic young dean at an eastern liberal arts college" (206); the ordinary physical world dissembles the fact that it is "a massive instrument of agonizing death" (185); existence itself deceives us with its assurances and promises, but ultimately reveals itself as "a trap" (185).

Desire is another trap, another illusion. The lonely "mooches" masturbating before insubstantial images projected upon a cinema screen are the very model of our universal condition: craving, grasping after shadows and phantasms. Another such intersection of desire and illusion in the novel is the use of opiates. Promising delight and surcease from the pain of life, these drugs exact strict servitude and confine the user within a dungeon of delusion ever narrower and ever more tightly shut.

Enduring somehow amid all the blindness and deceit, humankind sustains an impulse toward clarity, an urge for communion with the real and the true. This urge asserts itself in certain individual figures of *Dog Soldiers,* in certain incidental or background details of the narrative, and also in the Christian and Buddhist perspectives. In their totality, such expressions of the human pursuit of real seeing and true being in the novel constitute what may be designated as the theme of spiritual aspiration.

The quest for spiritual understanding manifests itself in recurrent allusions to religious concepts, artifacts, practices, doctrines, and so forth. Such allusions include references to the Bible, Saint Anthony, the Holy Ghost, the churches at My Lat and on Taylor Street in San Francisco, the plaster angel in the town square of Moroni, the former Jesuit monastery at El Incarnacion del Verbo with its carved facade depicting Christian and American Indian religious motifs, and with its improvised, eclectic altar within; references to Buddhist beliefs concerning form and the void, illusory manifestation, and the unity of all things, appear in the Prajnaparamita Mantra in Sanskrit, and spiritual societies such as "Those Who Are" and the Mexican Pentecostal cult. Such allusions remind the reader of an alternative perspective on existence and suggest the variety and persistence of human spiritual aspirations, even in a world of illusion and obsession, of vanity and violence.

Yet, at the same time, the world's neglect of spiritual values is also very much in evidence in the novel. Disregard for and decay of metaphysical ideals is suggested by details such as the use of Buddha figures and other sacred objects as mere decoration, the casual abandonment of Novena cards, a Catholic newspaper used for wrapping heroin, a framed tintype of Our Lady of Lourdes used to squash lizards, Holy-o's truncheon carved with Samoan gods, and the incongruous name of the corrupt Mexican policeman, Angel.

Not only spiritual ideals are neglected or corrupted in the novel. Every human dream or ideal is shown to have become debased or perverted. Such, after all, is the nature of a Fallen World where every redemptive impulse is subject to counteractive negative energies to check and nullify it. The novel's catalog of blighted dreams points to another central theme in *Dog Soldiers*: corruption.

Corruptibility is a nearly universal condition in *Dog Soldiers*—an attribute of individuals, groups, and societies. But mainly the central focus in this regard is on American society and the ways in which American ideals and aspirations are repeatedly failed or abandoned by their followers, undermined by human weakness and selfishness, or diverted to the service of wrong ends and unworthy purposes.

The opening chapters of the novel, though, present the venality and violence of Vietnamese society: ubiquitous prostitutes and thieves, a dishonest and ambitious military class, and vicious terrorists. There is Monsieur Colletti who has "taken eight pipes of opium every afternoon for forty years" (37); there is Colonel Tho, the original purveyor of the three kilos of heroin, who is described as having been "a very gung ho soldier at one time" (15); and there are the unknown terrorists who explode a bomb outside the tax office, not only killing innocent bystanders but, incidentally yet appropriately, smashing the carved personifications of Rectitude and Civic Virtue that adorn the facade of the building. Vietnam serves here as a sort of anteroom to the United States, preparing us for our encounter with corruption on a grand scale. With this connection, the exchange between Hicks and Converse in the seaman's service geedunk at My Lat becomes more pertinent:

> "You'd better be careful," Hicks told him. "It's gone funny in the states."
>> "It can't be funnier than here."
>> "Here everything's simple," Hicks said. "It's funnier there." (57)

The first indication of how things have "gone funny" in the United States is the marked decline of the Golden Gateway bar that has taken place during Hick's absence. The simple, traditional pleasures of the bar, such as its "good cheap Italian food" (78) and pool tables have been supplanted by the advent of topless dancers, lending to the place a sad and sordid air. Accordingly, the former clientele of hard-working merchant seamen has been replaced by escaped lunatics, prostitutes, perverts, jaded suburban thrill-seekers, drug dealers, undercover agents, and a contingent of sullen, menacing blacks.

"What a lot of shit this place is now" (79), Hicks remarks to the bartender, and his comment possesses a larger resonance, for, as we see, the Golden Gateway represents a sort of microcosm of the changes that are taking place across the nation, a kind of barometer of the new national mood. Things have indeed "gone funny": a new desperate hedonism and lack of restraint is ascending; there is a sense of incipient disintegration and a pervading atmosphere of danger.

Subsequent incidents in the novel confirm the ominous foretokening of the Golden Gateway bar: Mr. Roche's unfortunate encounter with the Gypsy Jokers, the activities of the vicious low-life freaks in Hicks's cabin, the searchlights installed on house lawns, the demented cries that repeatedly interrupt the filming at the Gardena Auditorium, the Quaalude laughter of the crowd at Quasi's (appropriately named, as the habitués seem to be but quasi-human), June's cynical statement that "what this country needs is protection" (179). All of these minor occurrences are signs of the rise of a new brash barbarism, the triumph of madness, baseness, and insatiable self-gratification over the ordinary social sanity, quotidian virtue, and relative self-restraint that formerly prevailed in the nation. Even the crass Eddie Peace is disconcerted and affronted by the voracious depravity of his new clientele, envisioning them as being covered with green fungus, the visible sign of their corruption, while Hicks imagines the new breed of American hedonists as "Martians" (202), seeing them with their frivolous and febrile appetites as an alien species.

Antheil exemplifies these malignant tendencies, and his career may be seen as a final travesty of the American ideal of the self-made man and the dream of material success. To the admiring Smitty, Antheil represents the embodiment of perfection and excellence, a living vindication of the free-enterprise system:

"He's the coolest," Smitty said. "Fuckin' guy's got bread stashed away, a beautiful home, chicks coming and going. They say the system don't work, man—don't tell that to Antheil." (236)

Sanctimonious and smug in his avarice, Antheil regards his achievements in a similarly noble light, seeing himself as a sort of contemporary heir to the tradition of Benjamin Franklin's *Way to Wealth*:

If you stuck with something . . . faced down every kind of pressure, refused to fold when the going got tough, outplayed all adversaries, and relied on your own determination and fortitude, then the bag of beans at the end of the rainbow might be yours after all. (340)

Not only the American Dream but the Aquarian Dream too is shown in the novel as having become corrupt. The millennial expectations of the counterculture—its quest for mystical enlightenment and for a new community founded upon human love—have disintegrated in very short order, and have left in the wake of their failure a lingering sense of mental and moral malaise. The violently psychotic Danskin's pursuit of Converse through Macy's Department Store, while "The Age of Aquarius" plays in the background, suggests the feeble impact that the ideals of the counterculture have had upon the conditions of life in the world. The triumph of human depravity over psychedelic transcendentalism is further underscored by the fate of the two teenage girls at Hicks's Black Canyon cabin. Seeking the romantic mystery and the expanded consciousness promised by the hip myths, they end up corpses, abused and then murdered.

The whole evolution of the counterculture was prefigured in miniature by the events at Dieter's mountain refuge in the salad days of "Those Who Are," before the cultivation of spirituality via psychedelic drugs became a fad. Dieter's wife, Christine, personified the unfolding of the movement: in the beginning exaltation, then madness. Similarly, the anecdotes concerning the gophers and the garden, and the fish at El Incarnacion del Verbo are parables of the human penchant for inflated expectations and their inevitable frustration. During "the time of peace and love and all that lives is holy" (219–20) that prevailed for a period among the members of the group, one of Dieter's disciples planted a vegetable garden, carefully enclosing it in chicken wire rather than poison the gophers who raided it continually. But in the face of persistent depredations on the part of the gophers, "In the end somebody got drunk . . . and came down here with a shotgun and blasted all the gophers they could find" (220). In a similar spirit, it was once thought by certain of Dieter's disciples that fishing was cruel, but with the passage of time it has transpired that "the people who objected to it most are all murderers now" (227).

The exploded dreams of the counterculture of the sixties parallels, in a way, the political idealism gone amiss of the American Communist Party of the thirties. Both movements represented millennial dreams that inspired the youth of their respective eras, and both succumbed to corruption, undermined from within by the kinds of human frailties that they had neglected to recognize or to take into account. Common to both Marxist utopianism and psychedelic revolution is the urge to transform the human condition in fundamental and radical ways, and also common is their signal failure to do so. In this regard, Marge ponders the parallels between herself and Dieter's son, Kjell, reflecting that "He was a child of Advance as she herself was—born to the Solution at the dawn of the New Age" (228). No measurable advance results from the strivings of the sixties and thirties generations. The New Age fails to arrive, and the world remains, as ever, obstinately defiant of and perversely unresponsive to solutions.

Marge is also struck by affinities of temperament and outlook between Dieter and her father, a similar air of certitude and conviction: "You're like my father—he's a Communist . . . So many people have it all figured out and they're all full of shit. It's sad" (230). Marge's father, Elmer Bender, was once a zealous party member, a contributor to the periodical *New Masses* and a volunteer in the Abraham Lincoln Brigade during the Spanish Civil War. But, like Dieter and most other dreamers in the novel, he has lived to betray his ideals. Elmer Bender is editor and publisher of various vulgar and cheaply imitative publications, including the coarse and gross *Nightbeat*. He even utilizes a nonunion printer to publish the torrents of lies and bad taste that he produces.

Elmer's alcoholic staff writer and former comrade-in-arms, R. Douglas Dalton, is another embodiment of disillusioned thirties idealism. Another veteran of the Lincoln Brigade, he recalls how, fighting against the Moors on the Jarama front, he thought at first, "this is like the *Chanson de Roland*" (132). But there was no glory, no chivalry: the Moors would pretend to surrender and "some of the fellas would let them come over and get a dagger in the gut for it" (132). Dalton himself was almost shot by his own side for cowardice. He now invents stories such as "Mad Hermit Rapes Coed Campers" for *Nightbeat,* and his youthful belief in Marx and history has long since given way to the alcoholic fatalism of Omar Khayyam.

Dog Soldiers shows humankind caught in a Fallen World, wavering and vacillating between selfishness and idealism, atavism and transcendence, corruption and redemption, vanity and clarity. The various characters embody both poles and points in between, while the great human endeavors and enterprises alluded to in the novel—the dreams of a just society or of spiritual awakening and deliverance—have consistently gone awry. Clearly, too, the novel insistently presents the brute atavistic tendencies of humanity, seen not only in the motivations and actions of the characters but also in the use of animal imagery.

Instances of such imagery include descriptions of the ARVN soldiers as being "nervous as rats" (35); the mooches' fingers "like blind predatory worms" (58) and "like arachnids on a decomposing log" (71); the "shark-eyed barmaids" of the Golden Gateway bar (78); Smitty's "undersea face" (157) and "undersea eyes" (235). Animal identity, the imagery reminds us, is a constant human potential. Or as Hicks remarks with regard to this unlovely aspect of man, "The big ones eat the little ones," and we remain but "a short hair from the dawn of creation" (164).

Yet if human beings in *Dog Soldiers* sometimes succumb to their animal nature, they are also at times seized quite unexpectedly by their spiritual nature, however much they may have tried to ignore or suppress it. Consider Smitty's dream, to which I referred earlier. Smitty dreams that he has kidnapped a man to hold for ransom but that somehow the man disappears. In an attempt to prove to the relatives of the kidnapped man that the man is still his captive and to provoke them into paying the ransom, Smitty is forced to cut off his own ear and mail it to them. But the ploy does not work, so Smitty is consequently obliged to cut off more and more of himself to mail to them, and yet more and more.

Smitty's dream is warning him that, far from gaining anything by his criminal activities, he is diminishing himself, forfeiting more and more of himself as he proceeds in his vain pursuit of illicit wealth. The dream shows the persistence of moral awareness even in so debased a person as Smitty. Smitty is, as it were, ambushed by his own higher, truer nature. Like the latent animal identity, a spiritual identity is a constant human potential.

Dog Soldiers is a novel of levels and resonances, intersections and interactions, paradoxes and ambiguities, and suggests the complexity of identity, experience, and existence itself. It is a dark and hard-boiled novel, yet ultimately affirmative. From the outset, the book unsettles us, showing us that behind the deceptively ordered, seemingly reasonable world whose reality most of us accept, there is a world of violence, irrationality, and radical instability, a world of malevolence and menace. At the same time, the novel reveals that within the ordinary seemingly virtuous citizen —the young mother, the intellectual, the stewardess, the lawyer— there are latent criminal capacities, unwholesome potentials for obsession and self-destruction. But, when we are perforce persuaded to accept the existence of such a raw and brutal reality and embrace the notion of so uncertain an identity in place of our former milder and more stable views of the world and ourselves, the author proceeds to undermine our new, neat conceptions as facile and superficial. Existence, Stone subversively suggests, is ultimately far different from the frenzy of appetite, the orgy of animality that it may appear to be, for the sensible, material world—together with all of its phenomena, including our consciousness—is an illusion, and the ultimate reality is spiritual and transcendental in character.

CHAPTER FOUR

A Flag for Sunrise

In a sense, all of Robert Stone's works interlock and overlap, reflecting each other, reverberating with each other, restating and reconsidering the same essential problems, together forming a unified oeuvre informed by a consistent, coherent vision. A particularly close affinity, however, exists between the two novels *Dog Soldiers* and *A Flag for Sunrise*,[1] which, though discrete and distinctive works, may be seen to share a common ground in their treatment of events and issues of contemporary American history in relation to ethical, existential concerns.

A significant link between the two novels is the Vietnam War. Although the war has been over for half-a-dozen years at the time of the events of *A Flag for Sunrise*, it is still very much alive in the minds and memories of certain characters, and is a recurrent motif in the narrative. Set in an imaginary Central American country named Tecan, a sort of amalgam of El Salvador and Nicaragua, *A Flag for Sunrise* concerns the specter of Vietnam as it haunts the American psyche and as it threatens to become truly revenant, resurrecting itself, as it were, in a new country. This ghost of the Vietnam War is embodied in Marty Nolan, a CIA agent who was once buried alive in Hué by the Viet Cong, and who has now "by some magic of Lazarus . . . found himself a new war and an enemy" (343).

Another link between the two novels is the similarity of their main characters, Converse and Frank Holliwell. Both men embody the spiritual aridity and moral torpor of their era. Both are without belief or faith, and without will or courage. Both have compromised and betrayed themselves, and both still aspire to effect some sort of radical change in their lives. Perplexed and ineffectual, unfulfilled yet unresigned, both men travel—half by sheer blunder, half by unconscious design—toward the dangerous edge of things, and toward the ultimate self-confrontation that awaits them there.

Holliwell's long and harrowing journey begins, seemingly altogether innocuously, with his acceptance of an invitation to deliver a scholarly address at a university in Central America, and his refusal at the same time to accept an informal assignment gathering information there for his old friend and classmate, CIA executive Marty Nolan. Yet in short order, despite his best intentions, Holliwell reverses his resolve in both of these matters, making of his university speech a drunken debacle, and ending by carrying out the mission proposed to him by Nolan.

Holliwell's contradictory and conflicting character is revealed through a series of trivial events over the course of the day on which he departs his comfortable home in upper state New York for New York City and a plane to Compostela, his Central American destination. Holliwell's lack of will or resolve is immediately evident in his indulgent drinking from morning to evening—a breach of his usually temperate habits—and in his resumption of cigarette smoking after a month's abstention. Holliwell retains sufficient sense of purpose and conscience to decline Marty Nolan's request that he gather information on Nolan's behalf in Tecan, but clearly Nolan senses his friend's lack of real conviction and declares his intention to repeat his request to Holliwell in the near future. Since Holliwell has in the past performed "favors" of a similar nature for Nolan in Vietnam, we might conclude that in this regard Nolan knows Holliwell better than Holliwell knows himself.

Holliwell ruefully reflects that he is "without beliefs, without hope—either for himself or for the world" (26), a state similar to Converse's disillusionment in *Dog Soldiers*. In addition, Nolan's ultimately successful temptation of Holliwell to spy for him parallels Converse's seduction by Charmian to smuggle heroin. Also like Converse, Holliwell profoundly desires belief: spiritual faith and moral commitment. Such a desire is evident when Holliwell is moved to weep twice on the day of his departure from his home. First, in the morning a bathetic and hopelessly corny religious country-and-western song on the car radio stirs the forty-year-old academic Holliwell to tears. And again, that evening, the memory of his boyhood friendship with an old ex-merchant marine, a Jewish Communist named Sy who held steadfastly to his ideals, makes Holliwell "feel like mourning, really like weeping" (30). In both incidents, Holliwell senses something lost or lacking in his life; both occasions are manifestations of his urgent but suppressed need for some meaning, some form of belief.

Similarly, Holliwell's sentimental sense of identification with the figure in a newspaper clipping that he carries with him—a prisoner who seeks communication by letter with someone female on the outside—suggests the alienated, constricted condition of some vital aspect of Holliwell's psyche, some neglected or rejected, imprisoned part of himself that seeks communion.

In this regard, Holliwell's dream while en route to Compostela—a variation, we are told, on a recurrent dream that he has been having for several years—reveals his unconscious evaluation of his life and his character. The house in the dream is a metaphor for Holliwell's self: it is dark and cold with only one lighted room (which he stands without) and no fire in the fireplace. His life, then, is one without heat or light, without passion or direction. The dream also depicts him as fearful and guilty about past and future involvement in the nefarious activities of the CIA, and equally afraid of official disapproval, of being excluded or stigmatized for not demonstrating his loyalty and acceptability. The dreams' predominant emotions of dread and uncertainty, along with its image of the imminence of a dog being shot, establish a connection between Holliwell and his alter ego, Pablo Tabor, whom Holliwell will ultimately encounter.

Holliwell's journey to Compostela and thence to Tecan at one level represents an interior journey, an encounter with places, persons, and situations that are externalizations or objectifications of aspects of his own psyche. In the course of his journey, the familiar external Holliwell—the academic, the family man—begins to break up more and more as the struggle between elemental forces within his psyche asserts itself with increasing frequency and intensity.

Holliwell's decision to go to Tecan and once there to visit the Catholic mission (as Nolan asked him to do) is prompted by a desire "to see people who believed in things and acted in the world according to what they believed" (101). Like the lonely prisoner in the newspaper clipping he carries, Holliwell seeks communion with those who are not imprisoned as he is by skepticism, cynicism, and unbelief. Holliwell's drunken speech at the University of Compostela is the first decisive sign of the process of self-subversion he is undergoing, the process portended by his earlier tears. Recognizing and despising the "circumlocutions" and "artfulness" (107) of his usual manner of academic address, Holliwell dispenses altogether with his prepared speech and instead delivers a spontaneous, honest, personal talk that reveals a rebellious, seditious streak in his character, a trait that he customarily conceals and defuses by careful irony.

A FLAG FOR SUNRISE

The deep dilemma of Holliwell's mind and spirit is his irreconcilably divided view of existence. On one hand, he is the prisoner of his own despair, his raw, bleak, profoundly pessimistic apprehension of the world. At the same time, he aspires ineluctably to believe in some transcendent goodness, in purity and purpose.

The landscape of Tecan, dominated by its dismal, malevolent volcanoes, objectifies Holliwell's gloomy view of life almost as if it were an internal landscape. To Holliwell, Tecan communicates "a troubling sense of the earth as nothing more than itself, of blind force and mortality. As mindlessly refuting of hope as a skull and bones. The landscape was a memento mori, the view ahead like a dead ocean floor" (157–58).

And, indeed, upon the ocean floor itself, out from the coast of Tecan where Holliwell goes scuba diving, he experiences a similar sense of life's essential, inevitable balefulness when he encounters some profoundly menacing force, presumably a shark:

> he saw the same shudder pass over all living things around him—a terror had struck the sea, an invisible shadow, a silence within a silence . . . Then Holliwell thought: It's out there. Fear overcame him: a chemical taste, a cold stone on the heart. (227)

For Holliwell, the ocean becomes a metaphor for the insidious nature of the world, which can on the surface appear attractive and even playful, but which is, in reality, a deadly and implacable trap. The deceitful, treacherous character of the world is to him like "a flower-painted car hauling corpses, a bright turban on a leper" (347). According to this dark and bleak perspective, all human endeavor is

futile and absurd, all notions of philosophy, metaphysics, and morality preposterously impertinent to the hopeless horror of the human
condition:

> The things people do don't add up to an edifying
> story. There aren't any morals to this confusion we're
> living in. I mean you can make yourself believe any
> sort of fable about it. They're all bullshit. (387)

Yet, notwithstanding Holliwell's inclination to emphasize the negative, destructive aspects of existence, he is also powerfully drawn
toward belief. This quality that he so desperately lacks and longs
for is objectified for him in the person of Justin, an American
devotionist nun who serves as a nurse at a Catholic mission on the
coast of Tecan. In one sense, Justin represents a lost aspect of
Holliwell, an element without which he is woefully incomplete.
The love that he conceives for her may be seen as the expression
of his imprisoned, darkling spirit's love for the liberating clarity
she embodies.

At their first meeting, Holliwell asks Justin what it is like for
her being a nun, and although the question is posed in a spirit of banter it is clearly of vital importance to Holliwell: he wants to know
what it is like to believe, he wants to know how to believe. Later, he
resolves that

> He would find out what it was she believed herself to
> be about over there under the wooden cross. He
> would find out what it was like for her; that was all he
> cared about. (296)

To Holliwell, Justin represents his salvation, healing for his harrowed soul:

> He wanted her white goodness, wanted a skin of it.
> He wanted to wash in it, to drink and drink and drink
> of it, salving the hangover thirst of his life, his war.
> (299)

Ultimately, however, Holliwell fails to obtain from Justin what he seeks. He makes love to her, but the union of flesh cannot provide the kind of communion that he really seeks, and her true meaning for him—"the beauty of inward certainties" (377)—eludes him. Inevitably then, without intending to, almost without knowing that he has done so, he betrays her to her enemies—out of weakness, out of fear, out of ignorance and the habit of compromise. He betrays her, believing it is in her own best interests, but precisely in so believing, he reveals to what degree he has misconstrued the meaning of her life and misconceived what her ultimate and true best interests (and his own) must be. Finally, Holliwell betrays her because he cannot comprehend any value beyond that of physical survival, any ethic beyond expediency. That is his fatal flaw, his failure.

Having embraced his despair and made a faith of it, Holliwell needs now only to act in ultimate accordance with that faith as Justin acts in ultimate accordance with hers. The final stage of Holliwell's journey brings the final fulfillment of the imperatives implicit in his point of view. Alone upon the sea in a small boat with Pablo Tabor, Holliwell is compelled to confront the inevitable and utmost consequences of the apprehensions and convictions by which he conducts his life.

From his first acquaintance with Pablo, Holliwell distrusts the young man, sensing in him "a nastiness, something foul" (420), yet also somehow familiar. Trapped with Pablo aboard their small craft, Holliwell realizes that he has reason to fear for his life and reflects that "[i]t was as though he had been cornered after a lifelong chase by his personal devil" (421). As their arduous voyage together continues day after day, Holliwell becomes increasingly convinced that the demented, erratic Pablo will very likely set upon him with murderous intent sooner or later. Holliwell, therefore, contrives to strike first.

Yet after Holliwell has fatally wounded Pablo and has heaved the dying man overboard, he looks into Pablo's face before it disappears beneath the waves and perceives in it none of "the shimmering evil" that had previously provoked in him such fear:

> The stricken features were like a child's . . . It was a brother's face, a son's, one's own. Anybody's face, just another victim of ignorance and fear. Just another one of us . . . (431)

Holliwell thinks, perhaps, that he has slain his personal devil or inward demon in the person of Pablo, but in so cruelly acting, he capitulates fully and finally to the darkness within himself. His mocking quotation from the last scene of Christopher Marlowe's *The Tragicall History of Doctor Faustus* suggests that, like Faustus, he is irrevocably damned. Holliwell's particular perdition takes the form of the dreadful knowledge that he has through murder forever forfeited his human status and has become a member in full of the merciless, predatory world of things, another ravenous creature in a world of meaningless mutual devouring:

> He, Holliwell, was things. There was nothing better.
> The absence of evil was the greatest horror. (437)

Holliwell's journey, then, represents a long descent into moral and metaphysical darkness. Like a grotesque caricature of a mythic hero or a knight errant, Holliwell bungles every trial, fails every test to which he is subjected in the course of his quest. The ordeals which he undergoes do not refine or ennoble him, but instead only call forth all that is latently base and weak in his character. He concludes his voyage bringing with him no boon, no elevating vision, but only his negative revelation of personal and universal emptiness, his dark message of history as mere fell rapacity, a frenzy of predatory feeding without end or purpose.

The journey of Pablo Tabor describes a similar downward curve. Pablo, a young American coast guardsman, flees what he feels to be the miserable, oppressive circumstances of his life, deserting wife and child, and travels to Central America in search of adventure and opportunity. He is (like Smitty in *Dog Soldiers*) a curious mixture of malevolence and innocence. Seething with suspicion, resentment, and rage, disposed to sudden violence, he is at the same time acutely vulnerable, capable of an almost childlike sincerity, and inclined to a kind of naive idealism and belief.

Pablo is afflicted by feelings of inferiority with respect to his mixed racial background, regarding himself as a "Gypsy mongrel . . . with poison in his blood" (124). He expresses his self-contempt through his loathing for dark-skinned people and his distrust of people in general, whom Pablo suspects are trying to "turn him around," to deceive him, insult him, and exploit him. Moreover, his innate paranoia is much exacerbated by his prodigious intake of amphetamines. His obsessive, drug-fueled sense of persecution inevitably leads to an explosion of murderous violence that results in the death of three people and ultimately his own death.

The potentially redemptive qualities that Pablo possesses—his gift for hope, his determination to find significance and enlightenment, his incongruous ingenuousness—are all inextricably interwoven with his grandiose compensatory fantasies and his self-aggrandizing delusions—yet, they are not to be dismissed or disregarded on that account. Pablo is genuinely concerned with certain essential existential questions, including why the world is as it is and what his own role in it is. Upon one occasion, when compelled at gunpoint to account for himself and his life, Pablo asserts, "Everybody's worth something . . . I mean everybody's life got some meaning to it. You know—there's a reason for people" (253). Similarly, upon a later occasion, when Holliwell has related to him the cruel fable of the buffalo and the scorpion, illustrating the hopeless, ruthless, and treacherous nature of life, Pablo protests, "It don't have to be like that" (430). Certainly, too, his love for his son is genuine, as is also the value he places on the innocence of children, or as he expresses it: "Kids are the only clean thing in this rotten fucked up world" (367).

"I got turned around, just turned around and around" (251), thus Pablo describes his life. This refrain recurs regularly in his speech and thought: part self-pity and part self-justification, part complaint, part lament, part explanation. And it is indeed an apt image of his life, for a feeling of ignominy has turned him away from the good, the true, and the morally right. Pablo is moving in the wrong direction, his will, and his motive energy is like a compass needle that has been reversed by an electrical storm. Navigating backwards, as it were, Pablo ultimately crosses the dusk line into darkness—relinquishing control to the "shadow" (321, 323) within him, committing black acts of murder—and becomes thereafter "night-sighted" (358) and a "night friend" (362), "the Darkness King" (359), attaining the final reversal of the mind and spirit.

Holliwell and Pablo have a strange kinship, as if they are connected to each other at some deep level of being, their separate odysseys paralleling each other and finally bringing them together. As mentioned earlier, Holliwell's dream of a dog about to be shot echoes Pablo's shooting of his dogs; while the dream about feeling different from and menaced by others that Holliwell recounts to Pablo just previous to killing him is, as Pablo recognizes it, a precise depiction of Pablo's own secret shame and fear. (Ironically, the two men are never closer to a sympathetic understanding and acceptance of each other than at this moment just before the ultimate act of misunderstanding and antipathy.) Furthermore, through addiction to pills or liquor, both men gradually undermine themselves, relinquishing control of their lives to the "shadow" within and capitulating to what is weakest and worst inside them, leading both men inevitably to commit murder. Perhaps their lives may have potentially complemented each other: the best in Pablo—his courage and his capacity for belief—might have helped to redeem Holliwell, while Holliwell's intelligence and moral insight might have served to help guide Pablo. But alone together in their boat they fail to discover either their affinity or their mutual need, and act instead out of their most ignoble delusions, their creaturehood, with tragic results for both of them: Pablo's death and Holliwell's death-in-life—the "Abridgment of Hope" (430, 439) for both men.

In contrast to Holliwell and Pablo, Justin acts out of strength and courage, compassion and humility, and is refined by her actions, achieving in the end a sort of sainthood. She is not without her human faults and weaknesses—she is fearful, experiences profound doubts, is capable of pettiness, and subject to temptation—but she possesses the will to overcome, to rise above her defects, and to direct her energies toward the service of noble ends. Justin's struggle to realize her higher self is suggested by her double name: her given name is May Feeney; her chosen religious name is Justin. Although at times in the novel she becomes discouraged and disillusioned, expressing her intention to renounce her vows and return to being May Feeney, in the end Justin lives up to her true name.

At the beginning of the novel, Justin has reached a point where she no longer knows if or in what she believes. She has begun to face an incipient, insidious despair, a sense of personal and universal futility. At the same time, though, despite a certain surface cynicism and irreverence with regard to the dogma and the hierarchy of her church, she continues to respond emotionally to the most basic and traditional symbol of her faith—the figure of Christ in the procession at Puerto Alvarado—and is striving toward a more humanistic vision of divinity: a vision of God as immanent in humankind, especially in the human pursuit of social justice, and God as the motive and goal of history.

Still, Justin's commitment to the Tecanecan revolution is, without her knowing it, a mode of self-abnegation and self-transcendence. Justin prays to be useful, worthy to serve, and to be transformed and purged of imperfections, merging in her prayers revolution and transfiguration:

> To do penance and to amend my life, amen. To struggle unceasingly in the name of history. Gimme a flag, gimme a drum roll. I'm gonna be there on that morning, yes I am. And it won't be the me you think you see. It'll be the worthy revolutionary twice-born me. The objective historical unceasingly struggling me. The good me. (264)

Justin, though, is in no way guilty of vanity, posturing, or dilettantism in her involvement in the Tecanecan liberation movement. When she believes that she may inadvertently be endangering a vital operation of the revolution by having attracted to herself the notice of Lt. Campos of the Tecan Guardia Nacional, she does not hesitate to place the interests of the movement above her own ardent desire to be a part of it, even though the idea of not serving as an active participant is bitterly disappointing to her. This capacity for self-sacrifice is demonstrated to a higher degree when Justin takes it upon herself to act as a decoy, diverting the attentions of Campos and his allies to herself so that other revolutionary operations can proceed undetected.

Holliwell's brief role in Justin's life is as a tempter, seeking to entice her away from the fulfillment of her duty and her destiny with love and sex, practicality and reason. For a time he seems to enjoy some success in his endeavor, yet just following what should have been his moment of triumph—his deflowering of her—he loses her to her faith and her vocation: Justin leaves the room to bathe and returns wearing a version of the habit that she had intended to abandon. Later, Holliwell essays other forms of temptation, attempting to dissuade her from assisting the revolutionaries, to persuade her of the danger, the futility, and the utter meaningless of her chosen cause. In the end, though, none of Holliwell's seductions or arguments prevail against Justin's simple strength and compelling desire to serve God in humankind.

The revolution has an almost alchemical effect on Justin, calling forth in her those qualities of dedication, bravery, and childlike enthusiasm that had previously been thwarted in her life and were beginning to turn to cynicism and despair. The final phase of her transformation occurs during her dreadful martyrdom, when at last in her extremity she achieves contact with divinity, yielding to God her will and identity, and becoming fully and truly, as she says, "the handmaid of the Lord" (418).

Although the novel does not explicitly make the connection, the purple flowers that bloom suddenly after Justin's death on the ancient site near the mission where she served may be seen as an emblem of Justin's final refinement in Christ and of the subtle purifying effect such acts of sacrifice and love have upon the world. The flowers, significantly morning-glory, are noticed by Justin's former colleague, Father Egan:

> In the days since the battle, the flowers had seemed to spring from their pods almost as he watched. Their odor was heavy and sweet; it hung like a Mystery over the clearing and the surrounding forest. (436)

Father Egan also develops spiritually. At the beginning of the narrative he is drinking heavily, and his faith seems to him to be "moribund" (4). He is writing a heterodox theological work, rewriting the manuscript for the seventh time, as if unable to deliver himself of the book. His subsequent growth and unfolding seem to be stimulated by the "congregation" that he acquires for his heretical sermons: a motley collection of North American dropouts, dopers, and wanderers who gather nightly at the site of the ancient religious monuments near the mission. The communication of his ideas to a living human audience, rather than formulating them in solitude on paper, catalyzes in him greater clarity of thought and feeling.

Both on the intellectual and practical levels, Father Egan attempts to redeem light from darkness. His sermons constitute a synthesis of elements of gnosticism, Neoplatonism, Christianity, and Buddhism, whose central theme is the affirmation of the mystical presence of the brightness of the eternal Living God in the darkness of the temporal, material world. At the same time, Father Egan attempts to enlighten the minds of dangerous, murderous men such the mad Mennonite, Weitling, Lt. Campos, and Pablo, to dissuade them from committing further crimes.

By the end of the novel, Father Egan has gained a deeper insight into and a greater acceptance of the mystery of existence:

> Egan wondered what made him feel so happy at times
> . . . His moments were never dull since he had come
> to occupy them one by one. Something was always
> happening and he passed many of the daylight hours
> without a drink. (437)

Father Egan's more relaxed attitude toward life and death, and calmer, more compassionate wisdom can be seen when he meets with Lt. Campos at the end of the novel. Whereas in the opening encounter between the two men it was clearly Campos who dominated, in the concluding meeting the roles are reversed. Father Egan has succeeded in reviving his moribund faith, and regardless of the ultimate fate of his manuscript, whether he completes it or not, whether it is published or not, he has communicated a vital spiritual-humanist message to the world.

Of the other characters in the novel to whose thoughts we are privy only one other is unselfish and seeks to do good: Don Sebastian, also called Aguirre. In contrast to the spiritual-humanist witness of Justin and Father Egan, Aguirre embraces a socialist-humanist vision. A dedicated Marxian revolutionary of many years, Aguirre believes in history, which he conceives in anthropomorphic terms, as a sort of supernatural guiding force, almost as a God. Aguirre is committed, efficient, prudent, acute, discerning, and indefatigable in his service to the revolution, impatient with sentimentality, cynicism, or self-indulgence in any form. He has fashioned himself as an implement of history, subduing in himself any and every weakness, illusion, scruple, or qualm that could impede him in this regard.

But precisely in so doing, Aguirre has suffocated within himself whatever compassion might originally have motivated his dream of social justice and human dignity. In the single-minded service of his cause, he has dehumanized himself, divesting himself of conscience, empathy, and most certainly love. His Marxian ideals are cold abstractions, like so many mathematical formulas and equations. The practical consequence of Aguirre's stern, utilitarian approach to human liberation is that the Tecanecan revolution to which he has been midwife must inevitably end in a Stalinist-style tyranny: the man whom Aguirre has chosen to lead the revolution—the ruthless and self-righteous Emilio Ortega Curtis—is the very type of an aspiring despot.

In this way, Aguirre's devoted self-sacrifice and dogmatic altruism is ultimately self-defeating. To replace a heartless political system with another heartless political system is surely an exercise in futility. In contrast to the quests of Justin and Father Egan, who each succeed in making some modest contribution toward human betterment, the extensive and decisive transformation of society intended by Aguirre can only end by maintaining or even increasing the sum of human suffering.

Emilio Ortega Curtis, the future dictator of Tecan, does not alone embody the peculiar human tendency to be duplicitous, calculating, and brutal, all in the furtherance of a good cause. Marty Nolan and Ralph Heath, for example, are cut from the same cloth as Ortega, although, quite incidentally, the ideology that they embrace is antithetical to his.

For all of Nolan's urbane manner and seeming practicality, there is something "faintly gross" and "unwholesome" (19) about him, a suggestion of things sinister. He misleads and exploits the trust and good will of his friend Holliwell, and his nefarious schemes—concocted over lunch in elegant restaurants or in the air-conditioned comfort of his office at Langley—cause people in faraway, miserable little countries to suffer and die. Similarly, Heath, with his hearty, simplistic pronouncements concerning human dignity, self-respect, and civilization, is a self-serving, sanctimonious scoundrel, drawing handsome fees in return for his efforts on behalf of international business interests, while simultaneously indulging his secretly savored role as "the wrath of God" (402) by casually disposing of those whom he believes to be evil.

Ortega, Nolan, and Heath share a deep-seated, unwavering conviction of the absolute, infallible rightness of their judgments and actions. They believe that by the authority of history or of God, they have been ordained or appointed to correct the deficiencies of the world.

There is a disturbing likeness between such men as Ortega, Nolan, and Heath—all no doubt sound of reason and well adjusted according to the conventional standards of mental health—and the homicidal psychotics Campos and Weitling: they all share a common capacity to justify their most atrocious deeds in the name of the end that they believe themselves to be serving. Weitling believes that his murders preserve the world and will bring about an age of beauty and plenty for humankind. The demented millennial visions that motivate his crimes are, as Father Egan observes, scarcely different from those used to justify the assassinations, revolutions, and purges practiced by political utopians and ideologues. Campos, too, sees himself as a guardian of civilized proprieties and order. Ironically and tragically, the unspeakable deeds of Campos and Weitling are in one sense but a more naked, less sophisticated, and, numerically speaking, even less destructive version of those actions undertaken or planned by Ortega, Nolan, and Heath——their calm, orderly, ideologically motivated, and, therefore, sane murders.

The prominent animal imagery in the novel further reveals humans as creatures predominantly driven by selfish appetite and disposed to injure and exploit others for their own gain. The most conspicuous and recurrent of such images are of sharks and primates. The shark motif is introduced in the first chapter when Father Egan performs a burial at sea of one of Campos's victims, while near his boat two bonitos jump to avoid a shark. Here, the image of the shark suggests the vicious, voracious nature of the world. The motif attains its fullest, most ominous metaphoric power during the scene of Holliwell's undersea dive, when he senses the presence of the shark. On this occasion, the shark takes on the significance of universal evil, representing the embodiment of a malevolent cosmic force. Later in the novel, the shark metaphor is associated with the kind of self-righteous murder practiced by the competing parties in geopolitical affairs. Explaining his sense of mission to Holliwell, Heath appropriately likens himself to a shark: "I'm the shark on the bottom of the lagoon. You have to sink a damn long way before you get to me. When you do, I'm waiting" (402).

Later still, Holliwell, in killing Pablo, assumes the role of shark, realizing afterward that by his act of murder he has affirmed that there is no human value, no meaning in life beyond sheer physical survival, which must of necessity be purchased by the slaughter of others. Half-delirious, half in shock at his bloody deed, Holliwell believes that he overhears and understands a conversation between two sharks who meet on their way to a feeding frenzy:

"'What is there?' the shark asked a companion.
'Just us,' the other shark said." (432)

Below the sea or upon the land, for animal or for human, the law of predation is the same; for individuals, for groups, and for nations, the big ones eat the little ones, the stronger devour the weaker, and are themselves devoured in a universal frenzy of cannibal feeding.

The primate motif is introduced in chapter 2 when Nolan comments on the primitive, animalistic foundations of human conduct: "Just pick up the *Times* on any given day and you've got a catalogue of ape behavior. Strip away the slogans and excuses and verbiage, the so-called ideology, and you're reading about what one pack of chimpanzees did to another" (26). In resonance with this characterization of human affairs, the phrase "bad monkey" is recurrent in the text, used by the children of Tecan as an epithet and used by Weitling in reference to himself. Similarly, after Pablo has slain his employers, the Callahans, he becomes a "dirty monkey" (326) in the eyes of Negus, the surviving member of the crew whom Pablo subsequently murders in cold blood. Campos is seen as "simian" (283) by Justin, while Weitling is seen as a "killer ape" (367) by Pablo.

Instances of predatory behavior figure prominently in the novel, as do animal similes and metaphors. The sea, with its "shadowed deeps, predatory eyes" (41), its barracuda and sharks, is the novel's central symbol of the essential conditions of pitiless existence. The scene in which basket loads of shrimp and other creatures are hauled up from the depths of the sea by Pablo and Deedee Callahan is a vivid metaphor for life in the ravening world:

> Before them, under the bright lights, was a living
> creeping jambalaya, a rapine of darkness and death. In
> thousands, creatures of hallucination—shelled, hooded,
> fifty-legged and six-eyed—clawed, writhed, flapped
> or devoured their way through the mass of their fellow
> captives, the predators and the prey together, over-
> thrown and blinded, scuttling after their lost accus-
> tomed world. (311)

Rapacity, predation, and viciousness abound in *A Flag for Sunrise*. Young ghetto "animals" (29) in New York City rob and kill a harm-less, defenseless old man. In Compostela two older armed Indian boys chase a younger shoeshine boy down the street to extort his dollar from him. At the border between Compostela and Tecan a crowd of young boys amuse themselves by stoning to death a cow that has become stuck in the mud. Tecanecan teenagers huddle together in the darkness "like predators" (54). Naftali, a feared and cold-hearted international criminal, "hawk-faced" (247) and with "predatory eyes" (250), was himself as a child the victim of savage predators: the Nazis. The "rodential" (271) Buddy, a small-time American hood, tells tales of snuff films made with abducted children. Treachery and theft. Torture and murder. Like the entrapped creatures of the deep described above, human beings claw and devour their way "through the mass of their fellow captives."

In opposition to the motifs of animalism and predation, however, stand the motifs of flag and jewel—images that suggest high purpose and spiritual aspiration. The flag image is introduced in chapter three during a conversation between Sister Mary Joseph and Father Egan, but only later in the novel does it acquire its full metaphorical significance as an emblem of elevated purpose: when we encounter it in Justin's inner monologue (264), and again when she quotes a poem by Emily Dickinson, "Sunrise—Hast thou a flag for me?" (372)

Justin finds her flag in the Tecanecan revolution, or more precisely in the human hope and mercy that she believes is embodied in the revolution. Justin profoundly needs and ardently desires a commitment to something beyond herself, to some worthy ideal, some tangible goal and purpose that she can serve, and the revolution meets these needs and provides her with the flag she requires.

Others in the novel seek and find their flags or feel the lack of them. For Tom Zecca, the U.S. military attaché in Tecan, it is the concept of duty and honor. For the Tecanecan revolutionaries—the communists, the moderates, and the idealists alike—it is the dream of liberty and justice. In every case, finding a flag requires of the individual a kind of Kierkegaardian "leap of faith," an existential act of will and commitment, or as Justin puts it, "You've got to make the jump . . . toward man or history, the future—call it whatever . . ." (132).

By making such a jump and serving the chosen flag, the characters are ennobled. The flag represents in this sense a vehicle of self-refinement, self-realization. Clearly, this is the case for Justin, and also for the former brothel bookkeeper who becomes an insurrectionist commander in the Tecanecan revolution and discovers in the process qualities of courage and eloquence within himself, attaining a sense of freedom and true identity. The effect of never finding a flag to serve strikes Holliwell, who must recognize that he is finally no other and no better than "things," and also hits Pablo, who must ask of himself and others "What's the use of me?"

The recurrent image of the jewel symbolizes a state of being beyond the ignorance, darkness, plundering, and violence of the mortal world. The jewel, as Father Egan explains, represents the mysterious presence of the eternal in the temporal, the redeeming presence of divinity in mere matter.

But, as we see in the novel, the world is far more interested in acquiring tangible jewels than in cultivating or celebrating the jewel within. Naftali, Pablo, the Callahans, Negus, and the "contractors," all strive relentlessly to possess diamonds and emeralds, neglecting even to consider the precious Jewel within themselves. Similarly, when Holliwell finds Naftali's large diamond, he fails to recognize it for what it is and casts it overboard. His casual, imperceptive act represents a concise allegory of humankind's perennial disregard for and dismissal of spiritual values.

Closely related to the opposition of animalism and predation on the one hand, and the motifs of the flag and the jewel on the other, is the motif of darkness and light, night and morning. This motif, introduced by the title, is central to the novel's meaning. The condition of darkness and night is a metaphor for a state of being and a state of mind in which the law of the jungle prevails, in which selfishness, cynicism, cruelty, and complacency reign supreme, and in which humankind is devoid of moral or spiritual vision. Light and morning represent the transcendence of this primitive state, and constitute a condition of spiritual insight, the apprehension of the real and the true, the eternal and the divine that exist beyond the ignorance and illusion of the finite, material world. The contrast of light and darkness are set forth in an early scene when Justin attends a religious festival in a small town near her mission. The light of the carnival machines is transfiguring: "The light there was fantastical, compounded of rainbow colors" (54), while beyond the light the human "predators" huddle together.

Of the characters of the novel, only Justin and Father Egan succeed in making the journey out of darkness and into light, through night to sunrise. Pablo and Holliwell, together with many others, remain lost in darkness.

Whether we see darkness or light depends upon our eye, which is identical with our "I," or state of our consciousness. We perceive according to who or, more accurately, how we are. This idea is conveyed in the novel by the eye motif or the theme of vision. Father Egan expresses this reciprocal relationship of the eye with the world, the "I" with God, "The eye you see him with is the same eye with which he sees you" (333). In contrast, Ortega serves as a spokesman for the narrow, distorted perception of ordinary consciousness, the complacent blindness of the ego-mind, when he cautions against introspection: "Look too long into yourself and you won't know whom you're seeing" (202).

Sunglasses function in the novel as metaphors for restricted perception. The "silvered" (39), "reflecting" (153), "one-way" (433) sunglasses characteristically worn by Lt. Campos and much favored by the other Guardia troops are an outward sign of an unwillingness and inability to achieve a reciprocal relationship with reality: everything must be one way only; the world and others are viewed exclusively from the narrow, self-protective perspective of the isolated ego. Likewise, Holliwell's sunglasses suggest his circumscribed vision, his light-resistant view of the world. Significantly, he retains his sunglasses through all of his misadventures, indicating the unaltered, static character of his mind and his mode of vision:

> Holliwell felt for his sunglasses and found them in his
> shirt pocket. Miraculously, absurdly, he had preserved
> them unbroken. (417)

Another aspect of the theme of vision is the motif of misapprehension, including illusion and delusion, subterfuge and self-deception. Throughout the novel, we are made aware of the disparity between appearance and reality, between conception and fact, between self-image and the actual role or identity of an individual.

Illusion, presented as opposing ideologies, factions and individuals that engage in stratagems of concealment and deception, is virtually the guiding principle of human affairs in the novel. The CIA agent who acted as advisor to the president of Tecan seemed, we are told, "a foolish, trivial man, almost likeable," but he knew, in fact, "a great deal about who disappeared and why" (51). The hearty crowd of "contractors" and "merchants" who gather in Tecan as if on holiday or business just prior to the revolution prove to be counter-revolutionary agents. Oscar Ocampo and Hector Morelos seem to be actively working for the revolution, but are, in fact, defectors and spies. Their comrades pretend to trust them, but in reality, plan their demise. Bob Cole, an American journalist genuinely sympathetic to the Tecanecan revolution, is thought by the revolutionaries to be a spy and is therefore killed by them. Justin, whose role in the revolution is really quite insignificant, is nevertheless believed by the CIA and the Guardia to be a major figure in the movement. Both sides are deceived by their preconceptions and their expectations, and the illusion is mutual.

Self-deception is also a general condition in the novel. The budding tyrant Ortega regards himself as a potential benefactor of his people, chosen by history for his prominent role. Pablo, too, believes himself to be among the elect of the world. "There's a process," he asserts, "and I'm in the middle of it. A lot of stuff I do is meant to be" (423). And, "everything that happened, man, happened for a purpose. To teach me. So I could learn" (425). In reality, of course, he merely is projecting his infantile egotism out onto the universe, still seeing himself as the center of creation. Holliwell, too, deceives himself, though in a different manner from the delusions of grandeur in which Ortega and Pablo indulge. Despite all of his intentions to the contrary, Holliwell serves as Nolan's agent. Despite his professed devotion to Justin, he betrays her. And despite his conception of himself as a civilized, liberal, honorable man, he cruelly slays Pablo.

In an ultimate sense, too, humankind labors under a fundamental misapprehension of the reality of identity and the phenomenal world, for as Father Egan affirms, "Everything's all right. In spite of what it seems" (292). The world of suffering and death, the temporal, material order is but an illusion, a vast misapprehension, and in truth the only reality is the light and the joy of eternal being in God.

The evolution of the ancient religious site near the mission suggests that the world will ultimately be redeemed from illusion and humankind will be delivered finally from the nightmare of false, fragmented consciousness and from the fears and pains of material existence. The site, a clearing where three carved stelae stand, was in ancient times a place of human sacrifice, and still retains an aura of blood and death. The soil there is infertile, as if accursed. Upon the stelae are carved the face of a fanged cat, the rattles of a snake, and the figure of a lizard. The stelae seem to represent man's worship of his own animal nature, the deification of the basest, cruelest human attributes.

Significantly, though, it is upon this site that the modern seekers and pilgrims congregate, a new nonviolent sect in quest of spiritual enlightenment. It is here, too, that Father Egan preaches his message of deliverance and liberation, and it is here that he works to redeem Weitling from the darkness that possesses him. And, finally, it is here that the morning-glory flowers bloom after Justin's martyrdom.

The change in the site's character, its slow refinement through the centuries implies a parallel evolution of human spiritual consciousness: an advance from primitive blood rites to a religious orientation informed by compassion and hope of redemption. The blossoming of the morning-glory flowers prefigure ultimate spiritual victory—the end of night on earth, the coming of morning; the end of suffering and death, and the advent of eternal beauty and glory.

In the meantime, however, and until the millennium, there are only minor triumphs, such as Justin's transfiguration, while darkest night remains and "the rule of plunder and violence" (375) persists. The reign of selfishness and viciousness in this world and the effects of human predation within societies and between nations represent the social and political theme of *A Flag for Sunrise*.

Throughout the novel, there are depictions of the unjust, unjustifiable contrasts between rich and poor. The staggering social contradictions can be seen in Compostela and Tecan, with their comfortable suburbs (carefully barricaded and police patrolled) inhabited by government officials and professionals, and the endless shanty towns and slums of these countries, their squalid rural villages, all crowded with the miserable and the desperate. The already powerful and privileged clique (as in Tecan), in its insatiable greed and for its own further enrichment, deprives the poor of even a meager subsistence.

The novel also addresses the complicity of the United States in causing or in maintaining some of the world's misery, resulting from deliberate policy in which human misery is a calculated factor. Marty Nolan characterizes the Tecanecan regime as "murderous troglodytes" and acknowledges that "we put them in" (23) and that we maintain them in power, but at the same time justifies such undemocratic and inhumane practices in the name of geopolitical realpolitik, ultimate ends, and other abstractions. Similarly, Tom Zecca, the U.S. military attaché to Tecan and a quintessential American, clearly recognizes the unscrupulousness and despicableness of the governing clique of Tecan which he helps support, yet in essence, Pilate-like, he washes his hands of the situation and its appalling human consequences, choosing not to act upon the knowledge that he possesses.

Lago Azul Lodge also takes part in the American complicity in human misery. The lodge is owned by Global Fishfinders; this

American company caters to rich sportsmen, flying them from the United States to specially built lodges in Central America where they can fish and hunt the local game. With complete contempt for local history and sensibilities, Global Fishfinders renames the lake they purchase, and with utter disregard for the local economy and ecology, they stock the lake with fish imported from the United States, largemouths which quickly devour "every native species in the lake" (145), thus resulting in the extinction of the lake's unique bird life and leading ultimately to the ruin and starvation of the local Indian fishermen. The incident constitutes a virtual parable of callous exploitation and international predation.

A Flag for Sunrise encompasses multiple dimensions—psychological, political, moral, metaphysical—uniting them in a cohesive design that is at once a comprehensive picture of our present age and a penetrating analysis of its issues and attitudes, obsessions and contradictions. At the same time, a texture of literary allusion lends to the characters and incidents of the novel a wider reference and a deeper resonance.

Apart from allusions to T. S. Eliot, W. B. Yeats, Christopher Marlowe, William Blake, and Emily Dickinson, certain characters and situations in the novel parallel William Shakespeare's *The Tempest*.[2] Father Egan mirrors the figure of Prospero in that both share the vision that the whole fabric of material reality is but an illusion that will in the end "dissolve, And . . . Leave not a rack behind" (*Tempest* 4.1.155–56), and in that both renounce their respective powers—magic and priestcraft—and instead fasten their hopes of salvation upon Divine Mercy and mutual human forgiveness. The character of May/Justin parallels both Miranda and Ariel, while both Weitling and Campos are Caliban figures. Holliwell plays the role of a failed Fernando, almost at times closer to Stephano, the drunken butler. The Shakespearean parallel contributes to the novel an archetypal dimension, a sense of the timelessness and universality of the events and of the persons who enact them, and also suggests the ultimately illusory character of identity, history, and existence itself: "we are such stuff as dreams are made on" (*Tempest* 4.1.156–57), Prospero declares. This is an insight with which Father Egan would surely concur.

A Flag for Sunrise is a gripping, disturbing novel, representing man at his worst and life at its most hopeless, yet also affirming what is worthiest and most hopeful in human existence.

CHAPTER FIVE

Children of Light

Children of Light[1] is both the shortest of Robert Stone's novels and the simplest in design: there are only two main characters and very little action of a dramatic nature. Yet despite the relative conciseness of the book, it is full of depth and complexity; and despite the novel's uncharacteristic lack of suspense, violent action, political or criminal intrigue, it deals with quintessential Stone concerns, including the themes of reality, identity, perception, self-betrayal, and self-transcendence, and the theme of America.

Gordon Walker, the principal narrative focus of the novel, is a familiar kind of Stone protagonist: dissipated, desperate, a man in pursuit of a dream, and pursued in turn by fear and death. As the novel opens, the middle-aged Walker is in a state of crisis: his wife left him recently and he has since been on an extended binge of alcohol and drugs; he sees his life as irredeemably wasted, and the state of his physical and mental health is extremely precarious.

Yet rather than confronting his problems or amending his life, Walker indulges in elaborate tactics of evasion. Significantly, Walker carefully avoids the sight of himself naked in the bathroom mirror; he does not wish to acknowledge the true condition of his life. And when a mood of desolation threatens to overwhelm him, he skillfully evades it by assuming a role. To keep fear and self-recognition at bay, he takes valium, alcohol, and liberal doses of cocaine; but as a seasoned "survivor," adept at how to endure and resourceful with regard to "what it was that got you through" (9), Walker is well aware that such remedies are only temporary and limited in their effect, and that what he acutely requires is a reason to survive, a plan, a dream.

Walker's saving dream, which he suddenly seizes upon, is of his former love, the actress Lu Anne Bourgeois. He determines to visit her on location in Baja, California, where she is at work on a film. His decision to do so—motivated by his own immediate need to continue to flee rather than to face up to his problems—is a crucial one:

> His business now was to save himself and his marriage, restore his equilibrium. What we need here is less craziness, he told himself, not more.
>
> Then he thought: a dream is what I need. Fire, motion, risk. (13)

Walker is fleeing the disordered stagnation and sterility of his life. Originally, he intended to be a playwright, but after an initial fiasco with the theater, he settled for writing film scripts for the Hollywood studios and taking an occasional acting job. In this way, he has forsaken his gift, betrayed his dreams for a life of relative ease and self-indulgence. Dreams have now become "business" (8) to Walker; he exploits them for commercial purposes. He has become a collaborator in the manufacture of tawdry, trivial illusions for the American public. And his self-destructive behavior expresses his contempt for his self-betrayal and his complicity in perpetuating meretriciousness.

The only serious work that Walker has accomplished is his screen adaptation of Kate Chopin's novel *The Awakening*, a project undertaken upon his own initiative, a labor of love inspired by Lu Anne. Indeed, this is the very script that is being filmed in Baja, with Lu Anne in the role of the principal character, Edna Pontellier.

In a fleeting moment just before Walker arrives on the film location at Bahia Honda, he views through binoculars the distant enactment for the camera of a scene from his script, and he feels himself to be "at the point of understanding the process in which his life was bound" (129). But the instant of imminent insight slips away and Walker strives futilely to substitute for it with cocaine. The incident recapitulates in brief the pattern of his life: the vain attempt to replace authentic and meaningful endeavor with the false excitement of artificial stimulants.

Walker's presence on the Bahia Honda locations proves decisively disruptive to the filming of *The Awakening*. His cocaine exacerbates the schizophrenic tendencies of Lu Anne and, in combination with the resumption of their turbulent love affair, accelerates her mental decline. Walker creates a scandal on the set by incautiously allowing himself and Lu Anne to be photographed in a most compromising manner by a blackmailer, and he is later involved in a drunken fistfight with a visiting journalist. He accompanies Lu Anne on her mad flight from the film location, and he fails to save her when she attempts suicide.

In a sense, Walker may have unwittingly willed all that happens in Baja out of a perverse need to destroy the very thing and the very person most meaningful to him. They represent a challenge and a reproach to his weaker self—the self-indulgent, self-gratifying aspect of his personality to which he has capitulated. Thus, Walker survives at the expense of Lu Anne's death. Earlier, Jon Axelrod remarks to Walker, with reference to the blackmail photograph, "You look like a vampire" (187), and there is a metaphoric truth to his observation.

A similar perception of Walker's parasitic survival motivates the pointed mockery and overt insult by Shelley Pearce in the final scene of the novel, when after taunting him about his apparent insensitivity, she spills a glass of water into his lap. Lu Anne is dead, and without her the film of *The Awakening* is a dead loss, but Walker has managed to emerge from the tragic debacle at Baja renewed and redeemed in physical, emotional, and economic terms. He has given up drinking, and is in the process of restoring himself to health; his wife has returned to him, and he is again applying himself to his lucrative trade as a script writer. Significantly, it was not a heart attack, as he believed, that prevented him from rescuing Lu Anne, but a case of hepatitis. Evidently, in Walker's case the heart is not really so vulnerable an organ as he would prefer to think.

Perhaps the most pertinent metaphor for Walker's condition of mind and spirit is the position in which he finds himself during the storm atop Mount Carmel, when he seeks shelter within a building constructed as a film prop. The entrance to the structure consists of a massive-looking but actually quite flimsy outer door and, behind that, a solid and substantial door, secured with a padlock. Walker is able to break through the outer door with ease, but unable to open and enter through the inner door. Thus, while the storm rages around him, "Walker huddled in the sheltered space between the false door and the true one" (238).

This image may be understood on a figurative level as a representation of Walker's limited power of insight. While he is probably capable of seeing through the falsehood and fraud of the ordinary, everyday world, he acutely lacks the ability to see through the material world itself, to perceive its essential vanity and ultimate insubstantiality in relation to the ineluctable reality of the spirit. His aptitude for breaking down the false door while remaining unable (or unwilling even to attempt) to open the true door, affords him but scant comfort, and inclines him toward cynicism and pessimism. He remains, as it were, in an antechamber of life, huddled there like a fetus, not fully or truly born.

Walker's counterpart in the novel is Lu Anne. Unlike Walker who is partial and incomplete, Lu Anne is self-divided. Also in contrast to Walker, she is a dedicated artist, willing to put her very life at risk for the sake of her art, as she does when, against medical advice, she discontinues the medication that holds her schizophrenia in check, in order to perform effectively as an actress. Yet, if she is in this regard capable of courage and determination, she is also fragile and vulnerable in the extreme. Her illness has made of her an embodiment of human duality: creative and destructive, joyous and depressed, hopeful and fearful, sociable and isolated, reverent and blasphemous, possessed both by demons and by angels. As Walker observes she has "two speeds: Bad Lu Anne and Saint Lu Anne. Bad Lu Anne was not in fact malign, but formidable and sometimes terrifying" (197).

At another level, though, Lu Anne's affliction constitutes a method of inquiry into the nature of identity and reality. Impelled by her illness and by its attendant gift, her talent as an actress, Lu Anne searches for her true self among the many roles she assumes: her role as the actress Lee Verger, her various stage and film roles, including especially Rosalind in Shakespeare's *As You Like It* and Edna Pontellier in the screen version of Kate Chopin's novel *The Awakening*, and also in the roles that she enacts in her madness, including Christ, Eve, and Lear mad on the heath. Even her death fits into a role, paralleling the fictional suicide of Edna Pontellier, and later being compared by Shelley Pearce to the drowning of Ophelia in *Hamlet*.

Yet, if she is sometimes bewildered or overwhelmed by her myriad roles, Lu Anne also discovers in each of them something of herself, attaining a sense of the potentials and poles that she encompasses. Moreover, she is the only character of *Children of Light* who seeks an identity or reality beyond the superficial and the expedient; all of the other figures hastily and complacently accept the world and themselves at face value.

Lu Anne's mental affliction has brought her nearer than any other character in the novel to the ultimate terms of existence. Thoroughly acquainted with the sorrow and terror of life, and imbued with the desperate hope and faith born of such harrowing experience, Lu Anne has gained a sense of the numinous, a sense of contact with a dimension of spiritual reality. This quality of mystical insight is most clearly manifest in the novel's climactic scene on Mount Carmel in which Lu Anne improvises a ritual of penance and purification, a ceremony of renewal and rebirth.

In view of Lu Anne's capacity for reverence, belief, and ecstatic communication with the ineffable, why then does she commit suicide? Since we see her final act from Walker's narrative point of view and are not privileged to know her thoughts at the time, we can only speculate. And yet her death is the event toward which the novel has been inevitably moving: its motivations and its implications constituting central elements in the pattern of the action. But there is not, perhaps, an unequivocal answer to the questions raised by Lu Anne's suicide, an act which seems to possess qualities both of defeat and of affirmation.

Certainly, at one level, like Geraldine in *A Hall of Mirrors*, Lu Anne is a victim, driven to death by the passive betrayal of those whom she loves (Lionel and Walker), and by the unrelenting torment and sheer sordidness of life—a woman too sensitive, too vulnerable, too good, to live in a cruel and selfish world. In this sense, Walker's observation of the planet Venus in the constellation Taurus in the predawn sky of the day of Lu Anne's death is an appropriate omen:

love and beauty trampled under the hooves or impaled upon the horns of the brute bull—the victory of the harsh, stern system of things over tenderness and grace. In this sense, too, we understand the implicit comparisons made by Walker and by Shelley Pearce of Lu Anne to Ophelia: both figures are innocents whose minds are poisoned by madness; both are child-like souls who are overwhelmed and destroyed by the ambitions and machinations of others.

In another sense, though, like Justin in *A Flag for Sunrise*, Lu Anne is a willing martyr and her suicide an act of self-immolation. After her ritual of purification atop Mount Carmel, Lu Anne believes that she has been given "permission" (239) to die. She has been cleansed by the rain and has beheld the rainbow, the symbol of God's covenant, and the last we see of her, "The light gave her an aura of faint rainbows" (252). The image suggests affirmation and fulfillment, rather than defeat.

Also, like Edna Pontellier, with whose fictional character her own identity is so intertwined, and whose suicide is a model for her own, Lu Anne is impelled by "immortal longings" (120)—indeed, saying as much herself before entering the water (251). Like Edna Pontellier (as interpreted in Walker's directorial note to his screen version of the novel) perhaps Lu Anne, too, *"senses a freedom the scope of which she has never known. [And] . . . has come beyond despair to a kind of exaltation"* (120). Considered in this perspective, her death is an act of self-affirmation, the consummation of her quest for selfhood, wholeness, and spiritual liberation. Such an interpretation is given support by Lu Anne's declarations to Walker just before her suicide: "It's my birthday" (250), and "This is the last of the Gestae Francorum" (251).

The dual nature of Lu Anne's suicide is in keeping with the dividedness of her personality as suggested by her mental condition and by her two names, Lu Anne Bourgeois and Lee Verger. Her given name suggests complacency and mediocrity, while her stage name suggests one who seeks extremes, who is drawn toward the brink or the threshold, toward the dangerous edge of things. She develops in the novel from a "bourgeois" condition—wife, mother, respected actress—to a condition on the dangerous edge of things: naked, bleeding penitent, sacrificial offering forcing the bounds and borders of the spirit, and implacably at the verge.

Indeed, in its simplest terms, the novel could be said to concern two characters who embody two attitudes toward life: a "walker" and a "verger." The former is pedestrian, lacking in imagination, cautiously adhering to the commonplace; the latter is impelled to move and to exceed, to be in a state of transition or change. Both characters live up to their names. Walker's instincts are ultimately for survival. He tends to seek enclosure, safety; he cultivates despair as a refuge from life. Lu Anne's deepest instincts are for self-sacrifice. She is driven to expose herself to the worst, and in her heart she cherishes hope and belief.

Lu Anne's self-sacrificing devotion to her art, her spirited resistance to despair and the demonic, and her anguished pursuit of belief have no equal in *Children of Light*. The other characters of the novel are variations on the "walker" type, people who have capitulated to caution or to comfort, or who remain confined in their anger, lust, or vanity.

The novelist Bronwen is the first example in the novel of this kind of stuntedness of spirit. A talented and successful author, she is a failure both as an artist and as a human being. Despite the wit and originality of her novels, her writing—like her life—has been "honed smooth by early success and the best of California" (7). And, despite all her privileges and external graces, inwardly she is "cold hearted, a spiky complex of defenses mined with vaults of childish venom and hastily buried fears" (7).

Dongan Lowndes, another talented writer, has also been faithless and disloyal to his vocation, forsaking fiction for journalism of a dubious nature. Like Bronwen, his inability to create something of human consequence, something beyond the merely witty and supercilious, is closely allied to his inadequacies as a person: he is vicious and slyly disparaging, manipulative and duplicitous. As Walker skillfully sums him up:

> He can write the birds out of the trees, this guy. The good fairies brought him insight and invention and sound. But the bad fairy took his balls away . . . So here he is. He's got all this great stuff going for him. He's a first class writer and a fourth rate human being. He doesn't have the confidence or the manliness to manage his own talent. He doesn't have the balls. (218)

If Dongan Lowndes lacks balls, as it were, then the Drogues—old Walter Drogue, Walter the Younger, and his wife Patty—lack heart. Glib and caustic, lacking acutely in insight and empathy, yet conspicuously successful and respected in the field of making motion pictures, they represent the very quintessence of that self-important superficiality, that strain of smug vulgarity that has traditionally been associated with Hollywood. Moreover, the lechery of old Drogue is grotesque and obscene, while the crude sexual obsessions of his son are repellent even to the father; their fixations serve in both cases as an index of the perpetual adolescence of their minds. The "overripe sweet odor" (60) associated with their well-appointed director's compound at Bahia Honda is the odor of corruption.

However obvious their deficiencies and derelictions may be to other observers, the secondary characters described above seem quite oblivious to their own failings. But there are a number of other figures in the novel who, like Walker, are uneasily aware that they have betrayed their dreams and ideals and have sold themselves for safe and sumptuous living.

Lu Anne's husband, Lionel, a South African born psychiatrist with a lucrative practice in Los Angeles, feels a certain guilt and self-contempt for choosing to abandon his troubled native land for the comfortable and affluent life of "a Hollywood shrink" (50); he contrasts himself in his thoughts to his friends who have remained in South Africa and become politically involved, actively engaged in the struggle there for human rights. Lionel feels a keener sense of guilt and self-loathing, though, at his act of abandoning Lu Anne to her fate when he takes leave of her at Bahia Honda, leaving her in her precarious mental state to the mercy of the Drogues:

> She had called him her knight and he was leaving her
> to them. He was numbed with his own betrayal . . . He
> loved her. But her madness was too much for him. It
> was stronger than he was . . . (60–61)

Later, at the memorial service for Lu Anne, Shelley Pearce notes with bitterness how relieved Lionel looks.

Dr. Siriwai, like Lionel and Walker, also betrays his dream. Intending originally to use his medical education for the benefit of the rural poor in his native India, he has become a wealthy charlatan, growing rich first from his generous prescriptions for drugs to his Hollywood clientele, and later by exploiting the hopes of terminally ill wealthy patients at his clinic in Mexico. Significantly, many of his teeth are gold, as if to suggest the nature of the transformation he has undergone, the bargain he has made. Dr. Siriwai recognizes his self-betrayal, but like Walker and others in the novel, he has accommodated himself to it. In a moment of candor, though, the doctor acknowledges to Walker that he knows what he has forfeited, and by implication what they both have forfeited:

> "Look at me," Dr. Siriwai said, "you'd think I was well situated. I might envy myself from the outside looking in but little I'd know about it. I'm more than sixty-five, Gordon. According to the Vedas I should be free. I should return to the mountains, free as a mountain bird to meditate, and think about it all from morning to night. But I can't you see . . . Because I failed where you failed, Gordon. Failed to do the job . . . I went for the big bucks and the bright lights just as you did." (106–7)

Similarly, the Mexican painter, Maldonado, has also sold his passion and his vision for gold and reputation. The members of the film colony avidly collect his work, and his paintings, prints, and designs are successfully marketed in the United States by "a very prestigious department store" (214). Disarmed by the directness and simplicity of Lu Anne's question as to whether he is a good painter, Maldonado admits that he is not. He began his career painting in a "realistic and political" (213) manner, motivated by rage and compassion, but he has since evolved into a merely decorative painter whose innocuous, expensive designs grace the homes of the American upper middle class, and are soon to be "stamped on every shower curtain in America. In every swimming pool, jacuzzi and bathtub" (214). Maldonado is ruefully aware that he has violated the very notions of inspiration and integrity in art, and that his art and his life are based upon self-betrayal and falsehood: "Because I lie so well in your language, and because I listen so well to lies, I'm successful" (214).

In a corresponding manner, though in quite another field of endeavor, Quinn—a former movie stuntman currently supporting himself as a drug dealer—also feels the loss of the boldness and daring that were once the source of vitality and integrity in his life. Watching with admiration two young hang gliders, he remarks to Walker, "That's the way to do your life, Gordo. Look the gray rat in the eye" (71). Quinn laments the contemptible timidity that overtakes us with age, the forfeiture of honor and honesty to our desperate, despicable will to survive at any price, and the insidious attachment to security and creature comforts that serves to bind us to adventureless, vapid lives:

> There's a couple of hundred goddam things I should do. But I don't know which, the way things are. I don't want to be broke no more Gordon, I ain't used to it. (75)

For Quinn, as for Walker and others in the novel, drugs have become the substitute for dreams, comfort the substitute for challenge and achievement, and survival the substitute for authentic life.

Shameful concessions are also made by the younger and as yet unestablished figures in the novel, including the actress Joy McIntyre, stunt coordinator Billy Bly, and assistant movie agent Shelley Pearce. The former two have both traded their sexual favors for money and for career advances, and both feel defiled and violated by having done so. Joy weeps in the darkness after her sexual liaison with old Walter Drogue and attempts to repress her sense of shame, while Billy remarks of his experiences along the same line: "it's ugly as catshit . . . It's dirty and scary. It smells" (162). And Shelley, for all her moral indignation at Walker for his complicity in Lu Anne's death, in the end prostitutes herself in another and no less odious manner, retracting her censure of Walker for the sake of taking him on as a client in her newly formed agency—in short, selling her conscience for gold.

With the exception of Lu Anne, all of the other characters of *Children of Light* have concluded a kind of Faustian bargain, gaining for themselves a degree of economic security or status and acclaim in their field, at the cost of their imagination, integrity, and identity. Moreover, in relation to others, each of the characters has failed signally to live according to that fundamental code that Walker names "the terms of the heart," that is "love, caring, loyalty" (7).

Stone's novel portrays contemporary American life as emotionally, spiritually, and intellectually sterile, and contemporary Americans as deceived and self-deceiving. The novel conveys how readily we relinquish our dreams and ideals, how easily we yield the deepest inclinations of our minds and hearts, trading them for trifles and

for trash, and how desperately thereafter we dissemble from ourselves the knowledge of our perfidy, our ignominy, our inward ruin.

The collective loss of innocence and grace is also reflected in the
novel in the transformation of the American landscape, its despolia-
tion by the forces of cupidity and insipidity. As Walker drives south
en route to Baja, through the Orange County rush hour traffic, he
notes the last besieged vestiges of the original American landscape
and the relentless unfolding of the new America:

> He passed mile upon mile of development divided into
> units by redwood fencing and bougainvillea, mock vil-
> lages centered on a supermarket and a Bob's Big Boy.
> Every half mile or so a patch of stripped, empty acreage
> awaited the builders and better times.
>
> On his right, through some realtor's stratagem, the
> land was unimproved. Herefords grazed in fields of yel-
> low grass, wildflowers and manzanita flourished. From
> somewhere came the smell of orange trees . . .The near-
> est groves were miles away now.
>
> . . . For a few miles, it was all suburban maritime;
> there were condominiums with marinas, dive shops, sea
> food restaurants. Further down the Herefords wandered
> among undulating oil well pumps, a landscape of tax
> deductions. (20–21)

The ironically named beach town of San Epifanio is a sort of
metaphor for the American condition: the impersonal menace and
casual anomie of the young; the littered and uriniferous park; the
counterfeit heartiness and forced gaiety of the Miramar Lounge with

its undercurrent of barely suppressed despair and animosity; the apotheosis of affectation in the person of one grotesque middle-aged Casanova "so false as to seem scarcely human" (37), who yet succeeds in his wooing of a young woman at the bar (a very allegory of imperceptiveness); the pathetic pastel decor and soft lighting of the San Epifanio Beach Hotel hiding from view "the rust, the mildew, and the foraging resident rats" (45). The images convey a sense of pervasive estrangement, isolation, imposture, and disintegration, comprising an anti-epiphany, or an epiphany of the infernal.

The loss of national and cultural vision implied by such a condition is connected to a more general and literal loss of vision that is a dominant theme of the novel: failure to discern the true from the spurious, substance from illusion, reality from reflection.

In *Children of Light*, the numerous instances of mistaken and distorted perception suggest how personal prepossessions and predilections of temper and experience impede awareness or understanding of the nature of the world, of others, and even of ourselves. The general background of the novel is, of course, the cinema, whose business it is to create illusions. The "sinister magic" (87) of this enterprise is exemplified by the film set for *The Awakening* at Bahia Honda, where late nineteenth-century Louisiana is recreated in detail in late twentieth-century Mexico. Walker and Lu Anne exemplify the potential for delusion inherent in a profession that is based on illusion. Both at times confuse their own identities with those of the characters they have enacted or are enacting. Indeed, at one point, Lu Anne is provoked by such experiences to reflect upon the elusive nature of identity and reality: "What's happening here? Who are we and what are we playing at? Where does one thing leave off and the other stuff commence?" (121). Her earnest questions possess pertinence and resonance and represent the central issues of the novel.

A recurrent motif in the novel is the media of vision, including binoculars, film cameras, photographs, mirrors, reflections in glass windows—all varying means of apprehending the real, each representing both an extension and a limitation of vision. The primary and ultimate mode of vision, though, remains the human eye, and what it perceives is determined in large measure by the mind behind the eye: we see according to who we are. Thus, Dongan Lowndes with his "contaminated eyes" (79), his "fecal eyes" (204), sees only filth and shit, as it were, while Lu Anne with her "secret eyes" (123, 235) sees the hidden, invisible levels of reality: the dark and terrible, and the divine.

Walker, though usually keenly perceptive, is sometimes deceived by appearances in crucial matters, as when twice he mistakes Lu Anne's stand-in, Joy, for Lu Anne herself, and when on one occasion he mistakes the mirror image of another man's face for his own reflection. Given this tendency and his innate cynicism, it is inevitable that he should dispute with Lu Anne the character and meaning of their experiences on Mount Carmel.

For Lu Anne, Mount Carmel parallels its namesake, which was used in the mystical treatise of Saint John of the Cross as a metaphor for the spirit's torturous ascent to God. To Walker, though, it is merely a mountain, a mound of earth and stone. "It's holy ground" (233), Lu Anne declares, treating it as such, while to pragmatic, prosaic Walker, "It's fake" (233) and "It's nowhere" (235). Accordingly, their perceptions of the events that take place there are irreconcilably divergent. To Lu Anne the rain is cleansing, betokening renewal and rebirth; to Walker it is merely a nuisance to be avoided. To Lu Anne the rainbow is a sign; to Walker an occasion for sarcasm. To Lu Anne the appearance of the wild pigs is a synchronous, significant event, an answer to her query concerning the existence of mercy in the world; to Walker the event is simply a meaningless coincidence. Even the pig shit is seen by Lu Anne as being metaphoric, while to Walker it is no more than what it appears to be.

Walker apprehends the world through reason and practical convenience. He perceives the material world and no more than that; indeed, he denies the existence of anything beyond physical reality. Lu Anne sees the world through the transfiguring power of her imagination, by which she sees into or beyond physical reality to the spiritual dimension of existence, the essential underlying principle of being. At its deepest level the novel is a dialogue between these two ways of seeing and the imperatives implicit in each: survival contra transcendence.

The opposition of perspectives and values enacted between Lu Anne and Walker takes place within a context of recurrent antithetical images of light and of water, suggesting the realm of the numinous and that of the material world, respectively. These contending images, which represent the ultimate poles of the novel, are introduced in the opening sentence, developed in the opening scene, and are then further developed intermittently in the scenes that follow.

The first section of the novel establishes a subtle tension between images of water and light. Walker wakes in the opening scene of the novel to a gleaming, "resplendent" morning, "a shimmering sky, dappled with promise" (3), but first he curses the light, then seeks to evade it, locking himself in the bathroom "against the fulsomeness of the morning" (4). At the same time, he is immediately attracted to water, first drinking long and deeply from the kitchen tap and rubbing his face with water, then seeking to calm his nerves by taking a shower.

Already, however, the element of water begins to accumulate associations with sickness, ruin, and fear, as Walker vomits in the shower, experiencing there a sense of desolation, followed by "a wave of regret" (4)—the very vehicle of the metaphor in this instance being aqueous in nature. Subsequently, water becomes associated with death and stagnation, terror and horror. In the swimming pool outside Walker's apartment, "Dead leaves floated on the surface of the dark green water" (9). The surface of the pool is "still" (10) while the water in the swimming pool at the San Epifanio Beach Hotel is "motionless" (45). The latter pool is also the site of a particularly intense anxiety attack for Walker, and the pool water provokes in him sensations of revulsion: "It seemed foul, slimy over his ankles. He thought it smelled of catpiss and ammonia" (45).

Appropriately, in this regard, the first time we encounter the egotistical, materialistic Drogues, they are "sitting chest deep" (51) in a whirlpool bath. Significantly, too, a favorite expression of Young Drogue, suggesting his aggressive megalomania, is "I can swallow that asshole with a glass of water" (19, 59). Water is, of course, the element that destroys Lu Anne. And water figures prominently in the final scene of the novel, the funeral banquet, following the memorial service for Lu Anne: Walker is drinking Perrier mineral water now, and when Shelley Pearce wishes to insult him for his complicity in Lu Anne's death she spills his drink into his lap. Her gesture of contempt carries a deeper symbolic resonance, suggesting that water has finally and unequivocally become Walker's element, that through his weakness and his selfishness he has become inextricably bound up with the material world and all its illusions, vain pursuits, and inevitable corruption.

The motif of light and its associations with spirituality are suggested by the title of the novel, which is drawn from Saint Paul's *First Epistle to the Thessalonians* (5:5–8): "Ye are all the children of light, and the children of the day: we are not of the night, nor of darkness. Therefore, let us not sleep, as do others, but let us watch and be sober. For they that sleep sleep in the night, and they that are drunk are drunk in the night. But let us, who are of the day, be sober, putting on the breastplate of faith and love, and, for a helmet, the hope of salvation." Clearly, almost without exception, the characters of *Children of Light* fail to heed this injunction and fail to maintain their identity as children of light. The sleep of materialism and egotism and the intoxication of drugs, alcohol, and sensuality affects nearly all of the characters, who also fail in terms of faith, love, and hope of salvation. Moreover, the very enterprise of making motion pictures for money, for personal glory, and for the trivial distraction of others, is, at it were, a sin against the light, a misuse of light, or as Walker says of them, "There are people at this table who can vulgarize pure light" (213).

Lu Anne is the sole character of the novel associated with light. We first encounter her "looking into the afterglow of sunset" (23). Later, during her holy frenzy atop Mount Carmel, she appears in a sort of nimbus, "all lights, sparkles, pinwheels" (237). And, we last see her with "an aura of faint rainbows" (252) around her, just before she swims westward into the Pacific toward the fading, faraway light of the setting sun.

Throughout the novel, Lu Anne's inward course remains the same, the one she aims for when she and Walker flee the film location at Bahia Honda:

"Are you going to tell me where we're going?" (Walker asked.)

"Morning," she said soberly. "We're going to where it's morning." (222)

Throughout the novel, her inward struggle also remains the same: to redeem light from darkness, to save from the dark hegemony of madness, fear, and despair, the brightness of innocence and integrity, courage, belief, and love.

Children of Light attempts and achieves a number of things. It is, in part, a novel of manners, a depiction of a self-serving domain of American life and of the self-deceiving people who comprise and perpetuate it. Using the film industry as a metaphor, the novel also constitutes an ironic and critical commentary upon contemporary American values and illusions. More than this, though, *Children of Light* is an acute psychological portrait, a careful and exact rendering of a man who, despite his considerable powers of perception and self-analysis, is hopelessly out of contact with his real motives and his deepest and inmost identity. And, finally, the novel deals with the fundamental existential issues: the quests for selfhood and for spirituality. All of these levels of meaning in the novel are united as mutually reflexive dimensions of a single central conflict: the counterfeit versus the real.

CHAPTER SIX

Outerbridge Reach

In *Outerbridge Reach,*[1] all of Stone's gifts for characterization, description, tension, action, and poetic suggestiveness reach their fullest expression in a spacious and richly textured work. Centered upon the fundamental question of the nature of truth and its relation to human experience, the novel focuses upon three contemporary Americans, the character and condition of whose lives are radically and irrevocably altered by their separate encounters with unsuspected and unsettling truths.

Of the three chief characters of *Outerbridge Reach*, Owen Browne is given the most narrative attention. At the outset of the novel, Browne is a man of about forty-two years of age, happily married, the father of a teenage daughter, a highly paid writer of promotional material for a recreational boat dealership, but feels a vague yet persistent sense of discontent and disappointment with his life, a sense of being somehow "in rebellion against things" (11). Browne's obscure, undefined sensations—part guilt, part regret, part anger—serve as catalysts for all the complex events that follow in the novel.

At the outset of the novel, Browne does not yet perceive that ultimately he is in rebellion against himself, against the false identity that he has accepted as his own, against all the illusions and deceptions of his life. Significantly, the book that Browne is reading during his leisure time is Captain John Wood's *To the Source of the Oxus,* a title that presages Browne's own later voyage of exploration to the source of his own being and identity.

Browne's malaise and moodiness are manifestations of what has popularly become known as a "mid-life crisis," a problem also faced by his two friends and former Annapolis classmates, Ward and Fedorov, both of whom have after twenty years of service taken early retirement from their careers in the navy. Fedorov is on his way down, sinking into alcoholism, while Ward is about to embark on a new career, planning to attend a seminary and to be ordained as a minister. Browne is caught somewhere between the options represented by his two friends, between self-destruction and self-realization, and his eventual transformation involves elements of both of these.

Browne yearns to serve worthy ideals in a world in which such ideals have been compromised and sullied, if not obviated altogether. Rather than recognize the imperfect and even corrupted character of the causes he serves, Browne instead evades or represses such knowledge, becoming willfully self-deceived, lending himself to the perpetration of falsehood. He is a sort of modern knight manqué (significantly, his boat is named *Parsifal II*), striving to maintain a personal code of truth and honor in a world of ambiguity and mendacity, of venality and frantic greed.

The 1930s blues and swing music that Browne enjoys suggests his allegiance to the values and sentiments of a simpler, more innocent America. Browne is an anachronism in the America of the 1980s, mourning the loss of American optimism and idealism—offended and puzzled, for example, by his daughter's use of obscene language, appalled by the drug culture of the cities, by the lack of ethics in the business community, by the cynicism and negligence and general lack of restraint and responsibility that characterize contemporary American life.

Browne's personal code of values manifests itself in several small but significant ways. His refusal "to dissemble heartiness" (65) at business meetings has led to his relative isolation within the power structure of the firm in which he is employed. Similarly, he also declines to promote company products that he knows are of inferior quality, as in the case of the Highlander Forty-five boat, "which from his own experience Browne knew was badly made" (85). He becomes "angry and revolted" (87) by evidence of the new promiscuity, and he later refuses to pose for publicity shots that do not represent his actual beliefs, as when he will not cooperate in the plan to photograph him "in prayerful meditation in the chapel at the Seaman's Welfare Association" (198).

Browne's deepest instincts are to serve something beyond mere self, to contribute to a noble cause and further a worthy end: "he was tired of living for himself and those who were him by extension. It was impossible, he thought. Empty and impossible. He wanted more" (45).

Yet, paradoxically, even Browne's yearning to transcend the limits of the ego, his desire to ease "the burden of self" (45), as he phrases it, expresses itself in a rather egotistical manner. Browne is unwilling to heed the simple, humble advice of his friend Ward who enjoins him: "Value your life . . . Value your family" (155). Instead, Browne insists upon undertaking something dangerous, dramatic, and glamorous, enrolling himself in the solo around-the-world voyage competition, seeing the race as a chance to redeem his life from what he sees as its "pedestrian and dishonorable" (154) character. In truth, his participation in the race represents more an evasion of than a confrontation with the existential issues of his life.

Thus, Browne's fatal flaw may be his blindness to the obvious: a romantic egotism that distracts him from perceiving and addressing his real problems and duties, and that also sustains his unquestioning acceptance of the kind of ideals with which he has been instilled, ideals of heroic struggle and righteous, meritorious victory. This failure to examine the principles and premises by which he lives is epitomized metaphorically by his credulous and uninformed conviction that the Altan Forty boat—the boat in which he intends to circumnavigate the globe—is "sound . . . beautiful . . . and something to be proud of " (68) and is a product worthy of being "regarded highly" (85). Browne seems to be virtually alone in not perceiving (as do Riggs-Bowen, Crawford, and Finelli, for example) that the Altan Forty is shoddy and unseaworthy, that it is, in fact, a "piece of shit" (177).

Browne's peculiar blindness, his inability to discern or to judge certain essential circumstances, events, or situations, extends also to his conception of his own identity. There are aspects of his character which he has suppressed or neglected, ignoring or restraining them while he pursued his career goals and performed his life's roles as dutiful son, naval cadet and commissioned officer, husband, father, and family provider. Now, in middle age, these disregarded, disinherited portions of Browne's psyche begin to oppose the functional, partial, external identity that Browne has complacently come to accept as the totality of his self.

The earliest signs of the gathering of subversive energies in Browne's psyche are his general sense of unease and his moodiness: his sleeplessness and his troubling dreams, his aimlessness and impulsiveness, his sudden seizures of fear and anger, his nostalgic yearnings and reveries, and his violent fantasies. His decision to undertake the around-the-world voyage is a direct consequence of this growing inner disturbance and discontent, but instead of relieving or eliminating this condition, the dramatic determination sparks further changes in his disposition. He begins to weep at night in his dreams, and he begins to tell lies. Browne's lies are harmless enough in themselves, merely boasts of solo voyages which he has not, in fact, undertaken, but given the degree of his commitment to truth and the scrupulousness of his personal integrity, the lies suggest some profoundly subversive agency within him beginning to manifest itself more forcefully.

Another manifestation of those antithetical, adversarial energies below the threshold of Browne's conscious awareness is his proneness to accidents. This tendency culminates in the ominous and very telling occurrence when Browne loses his balance on the dock the morning of his departure upon his long voyage. His leg slides off the end of the dock and into the murky water where it is cut on "a rusted and jagged-edged half chock, a foot and a half or so below the water line" (192). At a literal level this event is significant to the story in that it results in an infection with accompanying fever that serves to introduce Browne to the realm of hallucination and counter-reality. At a metaphorical level the act of slipping on the dock suggests that the balance that Browne has lost is more than merely physical and more than just temporary. He has lost his precariously maintained inner balance, and from this point forward, he will no longer be capable of sustaining control of his unconscious mind. The inward balance of power is now shifting. Significantly, too, Browne is wounded by what lies below the surface of the water, just as it is what has lain beneath the surface of his conscious mind that will now inflict harm upon him, wounding and infecting his reason and his ego identity.

Already forty-eight hours and two hundred miles into his voyage, Browne recognizes that inwardly he has entered "a zone of transit between his lost world and the one beginning to take hold" (215–16). His formerly stable, seemingly solid land-identity is now steadily giving way to a fluid, protean, unpredictable sea-identity; his conscious mind is being overturned by his unconscious. Significantly, his boat's compass becomes shifty, "as though some countermagnetic force were in the air" (221). At the same time, his inner psychic vision begins to achieve dominance over his physical vision. Passing a small Cape Verdean island one day in the early afternoon, the image persists in his inner vision through the hours of the night: "His mind's eye refused to give up the image of the black and green island . . . The image of the island stayed with him relentlessly until he could almost see it, glowing out on the dark ocean" (221–22).

Crossing the equator, Browne crosses an inward equator as well, entering the nether hemisphere of his mind, where internal and external experiences interpenetrate and interact, connect and correspond, and where events occur according to a new and occult causality. The visible result of this new condition of mind is a series of synchronous occurrences, such as the radio pronouncing pertinent messages, omens, and warnings, the coincidence of a cloud passing in the sky above the boat and a shark passing in the water below, the appearance at appropriate moments of a stormy petrel, and the dream of an ominous gray sky just prior to the actual appearance of precisely such a sky.

The biblical story of Jacob and Esau that Browne hears on a religious radio station is, in symbolic terms, his own story: the figure of Jacob may be seen to correspond to Owen's external self, the competent, assured, successful person whom he has taken himself to be; while Esau may be seen as Owen's other self, the rejected, neglected self whose rights were usurped by the cunning ego personality.

The increasingly vivid presence of Owen's father in his thoughts, reveries, and dreams during the voyage suggests that Owen's psychological conflict has its roots in his uneasy, ambivalent relationship to his father, and particularly in his childhood desire to live up to his father's expectations of him, a desire which later came to direct the course of his life. Owen's dream of swimming illustrates the character of his relationship to his father.

In that dream, Owen can barely keep his head above water, while at the same time he is paddling away from a turmoil in the water behind him. His father, "drunk and enraged" (287), shouts at him in an angry voice. Clearly, the dream metaphorically describes the state of Owen's inner life: his sense of the extreme precariousness and dangerous vulnerability of his condition, together with his sense of being driven and pursued by his disapproving father.

The disintegration of Browne's accustomed identity and the growing influence of his shadow self proceed by small shifts and subtle displacements—a lie about the weather in a radio conversation with Anne, the unfamiliarity of his own face in the mirror, his ceasing to read, a sense of altered personal rhythm—until during the tempest that strains and wracks his boat, doing likewise to his mind, Browne realizes suddenly the falseness of his conscious identity: "He had been trying to be someone else. He had never really wanted any of it . . . It had all been pretending, he thought, as far back as memory" (302).

The failure of the boat's masthead light after the storm corresponds to the extinguishing of his old identity. Shortly after this event, Browne sights the "upside-down island" (311) in the distance, an externalization of his now inverted identity, an outward and visible sign of the ascendancy in his mind of his underself, his latent unconscious identity.

The renaming of his craft and his landfall on the Island of Invisibility complete Browne's inner transformation, while the removal from his boat of the transponder (by means of which his position can be ascertained by outside parties) represents a decisive repudiation of the familiar, conventional world with its fixed patterns of measurement and value. Alone upon a desolate, uncharted island and feeling "distinctly in rebellion" (331), Browne begins "fashioning a counterworld in which to locate his improved self" (346). This new self feels liberated from the constraints of commonplace notions of truth, for Browne has realized the extent to which he has served untruth in his life, both as a naval information officer with the Joint Public Affairs Office in Vietnam, and later as a writer of advertising copy for the Altan Marine Corporation. Thus, Browne's imaginary counterworld takes the form of marking false positions on his map and entering them into his log, together with suitable, credible-sounding, though fictitious, entries. In the beginning, doing so represents an act of rebellion and a kind of affirmation of his antiself, his shadow identity. But the act of reporting his false position via radio, claiming a forward position in the around-the-world race, violates his own most deeply held and dearly cherished beliefs, and constitutes an act of ultimate transgression against his own spirit.

Having placed himself utterly outside of the established patterns, Browne finds himself adrift in a world of "singularities," a realm in which "no one action or thought connected certainly with any other and no one word had a fixed meaning" (371). This counterworld proves as barren and sterile a place as its external counterparts, the desolate island and the empty sea.

Browne has become a sort of modern parallel to the legendary Flying Dutchman, unable to return home from his voyage because of his grave transgressions, doomed to sail the seas until he is redeemed. There is a parallel here, too, to the figure of Harold Krebs in Ernest Hemingway's short story "Soldier's Home."[2] Like Browne, Krebs's extreme experiences (in the war) sunder him from the familiar, comfortable but constricting pattern of reality that he unquestioningly shared with his community, his parents and his peers. And like Browne, Krebs transgresses against his own deepest beliefs by telling lies.

Caught between the unsatisfactoriness of his former life, to which he could not now return even if he wished to do so, and the intolerableness of his present life, a life of lies and ultimate isolation, Browne redeems himself in the only manner he can conceive: ending his life by drowning himself. In the spirit in which it is undertaken, Browne's suicide is a brave act, even a noble act, one that repudiates all compromise and betrayal, all selfishness and weakness. After a lifetime of self-deception and the deception of others (as information officer, as advertising copywriter, and as mendacious boat race contestant) Browne realizes how profoundly important and absolutely vital the truth is to him: "God, he thought, it's truth I love and always have. The truth's my bride, my first and greatest love"

(383). Only, Browne believes, by an act of sacrifice can he achieve atonement with the truth.

Browne is another of those figures whom we so frequently encounter in the fiction of Robert Stone, persons impelled by psychic necessity, by some inward flaw or spiritual malaise, to seek extremes of experience, to search out the dangerous edge of things in the hope of making themselves sound or whole again. Browne's quest is, as he defines it, "To find the edge on which the interior met the exterior space" (249). His "need," he discovers, is to be at "the edge of things" (276). Or, as he remarks in another context, "You had to come a long way . . . to the margins of the world, to get the message straight" (287). The process that Browne undergoes in the course of his quest is a sort of dark night of the soul, a fearful purification: a stripping away of illusions, an expunging of faults and errors, and a final surrender to truth.

Ironically, the only other figure in the novel who is capable of understanding or appreciating the heroic character of Browne's final act is the cynical filmmaker, Ron Strickland. Strickland, despite his contempt for Browne's naive idealism, notes that Browne has "the eyes of a poet" (110). And so, fittingly after all perhaps, it falls to Strickland to deliver Browne's eulogy:

> In a way he was a true hero . . . Not as some hyped-up overachiever but as an ordinary man . . . You know, his problem was really his honesty. Some men would have faked it and spent the rest of their lives laughing. Not our Mr. Browne . . . He wasn't a great sailor. But he was an honest man in the end. (391)

Strickland is Browne's antithesis in the novel: iconoclastic, trenchant, and sardonic, while Browne is idealistic and traditionalistic. Strickland tends to be impulsive, extravagant, possessed of an artist's temperament, while Browne is sterner, steadier, and more commonplace. Yet both men share an unknown, latent aspect of their character, an aspect quite opposite and adversarial to their conscious, surface identities, and one that manifests itself in their lives with increasing and irresistible insistence.

Strickland is a kind of perceptual commando, adept at making deft, devastating raids on human hypocrisy—operating alone behind enemy lines, as it were, sabotaging the spurious, self-serving appearances of particular individuals, programs, and regimes. The method of his art is to provide his subjects with a seemingly impartial or sympathetic forum in which to explain themselves, a forum in which they will—as an inevitable consequence of their vanity and their shallowness—disclose and discredit themselves. Strickland's personal and artistic concern is, as he expresses it, "The difference between what people say they're doing and what's really going on" (19).

Yet however well-suited his mocking, suspicious mind and his keen sense of irony may be to his chosen mission, these qualities do not in any way contribute to his moral character, nor to his wholeness or appeal as a human being. Strickland has in his makeup elements of the callous, the misanthropic, and the vengeful that are distinctly unpleasant and that tend to make him a one-dimensional man, possessing but a partial, limited understanding of the truth he claims to serve.

We perceive this disagreeable aspect of Strickland's character already the first time that we encounter him in the novel, when in order to prove to a friend a point concerning the sexual hypocrisy of a revolutionary minister of state in a socialist Central American country, Strickland wounds the feelings of a naive and idealistic young woman, causing her to weep, then trying to seduce her himself. Another telling, if relatively trivial, incident occurs upon his return to New York City when "approached by a lost soul who had been begging from passing cars with a Styrofoam cup" (28), Strickland fills the man's cup with his Central American small change. It is a gratuitously unkind, contemptuous, and sarcastic gesture.

Similarly, when Strickland's companion, the prostitute Pamela, in a mood of desolation and desperation seeks solace from him, he declines to offer her any gesture of human consolation or comfort. Still later in the novel, Strickland allows Anne Browne and her daughter, Maggie, to be exposed to public humiliation simply in order that he may make his film about Owen Browne.

Seeing the world exclusively in terms of the deceivers and the deceived, Strickland despises fatuousness and gullibility, earnestness, and idealism in any form. He does not believe in love, only in appetites and self-interest. He does not believe in noble causes and high principles, but only in universal pretension and self-promotion, dupery and self-deception, cowardice and ignobleness.

Nor is Strickland above engaging in some deceptions of his own, all, as he insists, in the pursuit of truth. Repeatedly, he exploits the trust of other people, seducing them, inducing them to perform for him, to reveal themselves. He employs his "easy, amiable smile" (17), his stutter, even semi-disguises such as his nautical outfit, in an attempt to disarm others, to deceive them, to "make them spread, make them dance" (83) for him. Likewise, in the actual composition of his films, the cutting and editing, the matching of sound to visual image, Strickland feels no qualms in engaging in "a limited degree of deception . . . in a good cause" (397). He even feels justified in the outright theft of material from the woman whom he purports to love.

Significantly, the imagery most frequently applied to or associated with Strickland in the text is that of a phallus or a snake. Anne, in particular, conceives of Strickland in these terms:

> Thinking about him, she could picture a snake slithering across bright green grass toward a dark cistern. (144)
>
> The image of Strickland as a prick, as something literally phallic, was one she could not somehow put aside. (254)
>
> He looks phallic, she thought. Yes, a prick, a snake. (304)

Clive Anayagam, a television producer, also remarks on the metaphoric likeness between the cold, acute vision of Strickland's film work and the act of sexual penetration:

> "You have a penetrating vision," Anayagam said. "You're a veritable fucker." (325)

Taking the metaphor further, Anayagam suggests that Strickland's penetration of his subjects constitutes a form of violation, a kind of rape.

Strickland's vision, it is implied, is as malignant as a serpent's venom, as loveless as a rape.

In this regard, it is also significant that Strickland's favorite and customary bet at the dice table is "snake eyes" (272). During his visit with Anne to a casino in Atlantic City, it proves to be a winning bet for him, but his winnings mean nothing to him. He ends by literally scattering into the darkness the money he has won.

This incident encapsulates Strickland's condition. In metaphoric terms, Strickland possesses a pair of "snake eyes," that is his habitual negative vision of others, of life and the world. He has, as it were, staked his life on his snake eyes, gambling that his mode of perceiving human behavior and motivation and the events of the world represents the true, clear way of seeing, that he sees things as they are. In so believing and in having ventured accordingly, Strickland has won a comfortable livelihood, a glamorous and stimulating life, and a certain reputation and status. He is discovering, however, that all that he has gained is without meaning for him. Real meaning and satisfaction elude him.

Strickland also on some occasions suspects that his perspective, his perception, his bleak, brutal vision of the world as a Hobbesian "Red Universe" (365) may be an affliction, a wound, even a kind of blindness. Earlier in the novel, Strickland introspectively characterizes his condition as being "fast to his perception like some flying creature to its paralyzed wings" (83). The simile conveys a sense of brokenness, helplessness, and of the loss of a vital capacity. Clearly, he is neither content nor comfortable with his way of seeing things. At a later point, Strickland privately ponders the veracity of his affectless vision, considering whether his view might not, in fact, represent a form of misperception:

> Perhaps the trouble was that things had some aspect he could not perceive. Sometimes he suspected they must. Sometimes he almost hoped for it . . . It might be that he perceived in relief and reversed all signifiers. Thus

>his impatience and his penetration and readiness to fuck,
>all the consequences of what he failed to see. (326)

In this regard, the minuscule Mayan carving that Strickland wears on a chain around his neck is emblematic: the carving represents a man bound to a stake, assaulted by a vulture which is eating his eye. The helpless position of the prisoner depicted on the carving recalls Strickland's own experiences as a filmmaker in Vietnam when he was punished in a similar fashion by a group of United States Army "tunnel rats" who had taken exception to the antimilitary character of his work. Strickland's own interpretation of the Mayan carving is that the prisoner is being punished for witnessing the truth, a truth unwelcome to the community. Such is Strickland's self-flattering conception of his own social role: a bearer of unwelcome words, a messenger with uncomfortable and even unbearable tidings. But at the same time, the carving clearly resonates with Strickland's earlier description of himself as "fast to his perception," and thus at a deeper level of meaning represents Strickland as the self-tormented victim of his own nightmare and negative vision, as a man being devoured by his own cruel, raw perception of life.

Like Owen Browne, then, Strickland is a self-divided man. His outward identity has brought him social and economic success, but at a deeper level it neither satisfies nor fulfills him; indeed, it is a source of torment to him. And, in a manner similar to Browne's psychic process, a latent identity begins to express itself in Strickland's life, by subtle signs at first and then in more dramatic ways. One early sign of a subversive yearning of Strickland's psyche is the unaccountable presence among the reels of film that he has shot in Central America of a considerable amount of footage devoted to birds.

Strickland is both puzzled and struck by the bird sequences, at a loss to explain their curious presence or their strangely moving effect upon him. Clearly, though, the imagery of birds contrasts with the image of "paralyzed wings" by which Strickland portrays his predicament, and may thus represent an unconscious desire to remedy or transcend his condition.

The most powerful expression of Strickland's latent self is his sudden and profound infatuation with Anne Browne, Owen's wife. Despite Strickland's cynical disbelief in such an emotion as love, and despite the fact that Anne is entirely unlike the type of woman he customarily favors—"the mysterious and perversely turned" (174)—he becomes utterly obsessed with her both erotically and emotionally.

Unlike any of his previous amorous relationships with women, this time Strickland is not in control of either the development or direction of the affair. Contrary to his every conscious belief and wish, he feels keenly jealous of the absent Owen, afraid of losing Anne, and possessed by her: "This bitch has got my brains, my blood" (338).

Yet despite the intensity of Strickland's desire and affection for Anne, he refuses ultimately to permit his nascent other self to gain a dominant influence in his psyche. In a single stroke he stifles it altogether, decisively reasserting his former identity and restoring it to control.

Strickland does so by choosing his film about Owen over his love for Anne. Indifferent to Anne's great pain and in defiance of her expressed wishes, he insists upon making his film and even betrays her outright by stealing from her materials that she has declined to let him use. In the end, it is the cynical "carnie" side of Strickland's makeup that prevails, the showman, the con man whose professed high moral purposes are only a "square up," a specious excuse for the selfish deception and exploitation of others.

The consequences for Strickland of his betrayal of Anne and his corresponding betrayal of his own better instincts are persistent feelings of sadness, of regret and longing, and a keen sense of isolation: "For the first time in his solitary life, Strickland felt himself alone" (399). The more practical consequences of his theft of Owen's logs include incurring the displeasure of Anne's very powerful father, which results in a drubbing for Strickland at the hands of two hired thugs, and in his loss of virtually all of his material for the Owen Browne project.

A seemingly trivial consequence of his actions is Strickland's loss of his parking space on the pier—his "priceless midtown spot, convenient and secure" (47)—revoked summarily by Anne's influential father as a response to Strickland's misdeeds. Beyond the immediate inconveniences of no longer having a place to park or store his automobile, Strickland's lost parking space possesses certain metaphorical resonances, suggesting a loss of personal immunity and security, of casualness and complacency, as well as a loss of artistic confidence: "There would never again be the old nonchalance of the hand" (403). Finally, the image of the lost parking space suggests a banishment or estrangement from his life as it has hitherto been—an unspecified, perhaps undefinable, but vital and definitive loss, like the loss of hope.

In a sense, Ron Strickland and Owen Browne are mirror images of each other: the cynic and the idealist, linked by the reverse parallels of their experiences in Vietnam, by their love for Anne, and by their common condition of self-dividedness. Both men are compelled and for a time overpowered by antithetical energies within their psyches, and both are driven, each in his own way, to the dangerous edge of things. But whereas Browne by means of his dark passage achieves a degree of insight and a kind of redemption, Strickland resists the process, refusing to surrender or to sacrifice, and ends, therefore, in a state of diminishment and loss.

In the novel, Anne achieves the most successful resolution of the problem of self-dividedness and its attendant psychic crisis. Though she remains at home while Owen sails the seas where he is assailed by storms without and within, Anne's life ashore is far from calm and stable. She is compelled upon an arduous and perilous night sea journey, a tempestuous inward passage with many parallels to her husband's voyage.

As in the case of Strickland and Owen, Anne's daily life holds early premonitory signs of the psychic crisis that subsequently overtakes her. These include a certain uncharacteristic recklessness of behavior in playing the stock market (losing heavily), and more seriously, the frequency and amount of her alcohol consumption. Nor is Anne a social drinker; she drinks alone. At the same time, we perceive in her the practical, responsible qualities and realistic outlook that will serve as mental ballast during the uproars and tumults to come.

Anne begins to unravel shortly after Owen sets out to sea. At first, like Owen, she tries to summon the courage, patience, and endurance that sustained her in years past during Owen's long absence in Vietnam. But, as is also the case for Owen at sea, the resources of former times prove to be no longer effective. Anne's drinking continues, steadily increasing to the point where she begins to experience loss of memory, alcoholic blackout. She becomes filled with anxiety, attempts to take up again the practice of her religion, and attempts to stop drinking altogether. Her familiar sense of orientation in the world and her sense of identity begin to dissolve:

> Sleeping and waking, the notion of being lost, of having wandered out of the right life, kept turning up in different guises. She imagined mirrors in which she could not find herself. (280)

At the same time, Anne understands that she has lived her life largely unaware of herself, ignorant and neglectful of other facets of her character, oblivious to her real fears and desires: "for her consciousness had mainly been a synonym for being awake and a tool with which to discharge responsibilities" (280). She also realizes that her outwardly successful and rewarding marriage and family life has, in reality, been far from satisfactory: "The fact was they had been wasting their lives. She had been bored sick without knowing it" (293).

During this confused and unstable time, Anne permits Strickland to kiss her, accepting him as her lover. (It is at this same time that Owen is riding out the howling gale in his disintegrating boat somewhere in the Atlantic—the crucial event of his voyage.) Previously, Anne has shown herself to be very shrewd where Strickland is concerned, wary of him, astutely aware of his deviousness and compensatory behavior. But just as Owen experiences the increasing hegemony of a latent self, so too does Anne. When she awakens on the morning after her initial explosive bout of lovemaking with Strickland, she reflects that "It had been as though she were someone else altogether" (304).

Accordingly, Anne becomes uncertain of who she is and what she wants. In an exchange with Strickland her replies to his innocuous observation suggest the distance that she now feels with regard to her former identity:

> "Nice place," he said.
>> "I always thought I liked it. Now I don't know."
>> "I spoiled it for you? That what you mean?"
>> "No," she said. "That's not what I mean."
>> "Last time," Strickland said, "I thought you went
>> very well with the place."
>> "Last time I did." (305)

Unable to resist the imperatives of her latent self or to arrest her descent into alcoholism, Anne abandons herself to a life of erotic degradation and dissolution with Strickland, feeling at the same time intense shame and guilt for her actions. Gradually, Anne even comes to identify herself with Strickland's casual libertinism and cynicism, as if spiritually infected or morally contaminated by him. On one occasion, talking about Owen to Strickland as they lie together abed, Anne remarks, "He believes in all those things people used to believe in. Before there were people like you. Like us" (338).

Like Owen, Anne becomes—in consequence of her amorous affair—involved in a process of deception, forced for the sake of propriety to hide her relationship with Strickland from her family, her neighbors and associates, from the yacht club, and even from Mr. Baily, the man who services the propane tanks at her summer home on Steadman's Island. In a sense, Steadman's Island, where Anne conducts her affair with Strickland, parallels Owen's uncharted Island of Invisibility: the two islands represent hiding places, isolate tracts where the minds of both partners suffer eclipse.

Anne's darkest moment, the point at which she is nearly obscured by the shadow within her, occurs when she considers suicide, counting out twenty-five Xanax tablets, then placing them again in the tube. Unlike Owen, Anne resists self-destruction, and having done so begins to work toward light and new life.

Anne's inward resources, her true qualities and capacities manifest themselves in the face of the ordeal of Owen's death at sea and the knowledge of his deceptive acts in the boat race. Her new clarity and insight is suggested by the description of her as "clear-eyed" (389) looking out at the gray sky. Her actions are now motivated by the unselfish motives of love and duty. She aims to protect her loved ones, her daughter and her late husband. At this point, Anne decisively disencumbers herself of Strickland, refusing the shallow consolations and the self-serving counsel that he offers, rejecting him in terms that make it clear that she recognizes and despises his inveterate duplicity.

When we last see Anne in the final chapter of the novel, some months after Owen's death, she is clearly a woman who has come through—a renewed, tempered person, one who has attained control and direction in her life. Anne has solved her alcohol problem, has become responsible, judicious, determined, and intensely aware of and responsive to life. She is poised to embark upon a final phase of self-refinement or self-realization, a solo around-the-world voyage in a small boat being built to her specifications.

The concluding image of the novel, Anne leaving her now empty house to move with her daughter to another colonial house in view of the ocean, letting "the teak door swing shut behind her" (409), suggests the crossing of an inner as well as an outer threshold, moving from enclosure to exposure, venturing forth, advancing, and leaving behind the dead past.

The lives of certain minor characters of *Outerbridge Reach* resonate in significant ways with those of the central characters of the novel. Matty Hylan, for example, is at once a kind of precursor to Owen and Owen's absolute antithesis. Hylan, a big time wheeler-dealer, high-rolling business tycoon whose machinations cause the collapse of the stock-market, is (like Owen) a deceiver who disappears. Hylan, who fancied himself a sailor-sportsman, was to have sailed the very boat in which Owen sails in the around-the-world race. But whereas Hylan disappears in order to avoid prosecution and to enjoy the fruits of his deception, Owen ultimately rejects deception, answers for his transgressions, and disappears to restore himself to honor and honesty. In this sense, Hylan embodies the sort of man whom Owen might have allowed himself to become.

In a similar manner, Pamela Koester has a kind of kinship of opposites with Anne Browne. Pamela is "a suburban soubrette turned occasional prostitute" (31), the subject of Strickland's last documentary film. She is childish, irresponsible, disorderly, and unprincipled. She affects a scornful amusement at the straight world as typified by the Browne family and all they stand for, but she is beguiled by Owen and is an enthusiastic supporter of his bid to win the boat race. Pamela is genuinely shocked and outraged to learn that Strickland is having an affair with Anne, remarking that if she had Owen for a husband she would be true to him. Pamela embodies Anne's mirror image or antiself: promiscuous, infantile, dissolute, yet a would-be faithful wife for Owen. As in the relationship between Hylan and Owen, Pamela represents the expression of possibilities latent in Anne, the sort of woman whom she might have permitted herself to become.

The characters of Strickland and Harry Thorne are likewise comparable. Both men have cultivated an outward manner calculated to discomfit and disconcert others (Strickland with his quick cold laugh and his flat, cold gaze; Thorne with his challenging, unfaltering stare), both are outwardly lacking in sentiment, yet both have an element of the romantic latent within them, and both possess a streak of the "showman" (51, 325). Both men share a secret condition of woundedness, bearing some grave covert injury to the heart or spirit. Anne notes once how Thorne's usually guarded eyes reveal themselves on one occasion as "lustrous, like those of a man who carried some humiliating wound" (290). Strickland acknowledges his own inward wound and yearns for the society of someone similarly afflicted:

> Sometimes he had the fantasy there was some wound
> he might inflict that could make her into a creature
> more like himself. For company's sake. So as not to
> be lonely. (356)

Strickland is, of course, the rebel artist while Thorne is a business magnate, but Thorne is not without a certain delicate aestheticism, nor is Strickland without a component of crassness. For all his toughness, Thorne tends to idealize people, longing to be "reduced to reverence, to be worthily impressed, to be edified even, by something human" (388), and for all his creative sensitivity Strickland is contemptuous of "the field of folk and its bellyaching and its feeble strategies" (79). Yet it is Thorne who is disappointed and disillusioned by the conduct of Anne and Owen, while Strickland discovers in the couple unexpected qualities of imagination, integrity and authenticity. And yet, too, Thorne in the end and in spite of everything, keeps his word to Anne, helping to finance her boat, while Strickland, despite Anne's trust and love, betrays her.

In a sense, Strickland and Thorne supplement each other in a negative way, each man lacking just those attributes and insights that the other possesses. Perhaps the clearest exposition of their relationship as opposite, incompatible types—informed by mutually discordant beliefs and perspectives, and embodying irreconcilable truths—can be seen in the following exchange:

> "Some people go out and do things," Thorne said. "They put life and reputation on the line. Others seem to see their role as following after. Checking up. With a flashlight. Looking for cracks."
>
> "Or a shovel," Strickland said, "looking for bullshit." . . .
>
> "What I'm saying," Thorne said, "is that there's a difference between people who actually do things and people who find fault and poke holes and make judgments."
>
> "It isn't true," Strickland said, "that I don't do anything. A film is something."
>
> "Not one of your films, Strickland. A film of yours is just an attitude about something." (354)

Of the remaining secondary and minor characters of *Outerbridge Reach*, Buzz Ward and the Finnish boat designer-builder, Lipitsa, deserve mention because, though their presence in the novel is by no means extensive, they represent poised and whole men in a book otherwise populated by persons who are deceitful or defective.

Buzz represents the moral center of the novel. Alone among the characters of *Outerbridge Reach*, he has found a suitable tempo for his life and a fitting structure for his experiences. As mentioned earlier, he is retiring from the navy after twenty years of service and is embarking upon a new career as a minister. During the Vietnam war, Buzz flew twenty-five combat missions and spent five years in captivity as a prisoner of war, of which fourteen months were spent in solitary confinement without light. He has gone through his ordeal of terror and isolation (as Owen does later), and he has also faithfully and cheerfully discharged the domestic duties of a husband and a father. And now, as befits a person at his stage of life, he is preparing to cultivate the spiritual aspects of his identity and to give to others whatever spiritual comfort or counsel he can offer them. Buzz is anything but sanctimonious: he still drinks whiskey and howls with the wolves, is still full of humor, still sociable and unpretentious. But clearly he possesses a simple, solid strength and a humble, human wisdom.

Lipitsa, too, possesses those qualities of quietness and firmness of temper that bespeak harmony and dignity in an individual. He is described as having "the build of an oak stump and eyes the color of wild grapes" (90), comparisons that suggest an affinity with natural forces. Lipitsa is an accomplished craftsman, a master boat builder whose offices possess a "churchly resonance" (90), an austere grace that likewise informs the creations of his eye and hand. Though somewhat reserved in manner, he is courteous and not without humor, and it is in this and his essential poise that he is different from his American counterpart in the novel, the carpenter George Dolven, who, though he performs "thorough and conscientious work" (124), is cranky, sarcastic, and self-infatuated. Lipitsa, almost alone among those Strickland encounters in his pursuit of footage for his documentary on Matty Hylan, is not in the least interested in being interviewed or filmed. Apparently Lipitsa's life and work are adequate to him and he has no need to become a transient celebrity, "famous for fifteen minutes," in Andy Warhol's apt and oft-cited phrase.

Persons such as Buzz Ward and Lipitsa, living their modest, useful human lives, doing their work in the world, present a wholesome contrast to the hustling and whoring of people such as Hylan and Pamela, and to the meretricious world of discotheques and drugs, board rooms and yacht clubs, and all the vanity and viciousness, the shallowness and desperation of those sad and futile scenes.

The recurring sailor images help bear the metaphoric meaning of *Outerbridge Reach*. Implicit in the image is the notion of human life as a sea voyage, and all men and women as mariners. As we see in the novel, there are true sailors and false sailors, the former being upright, the latter base. Among the second type are Matty Hylan, whose "chosen image [is] that of a sailor" (48) but who is at best no more than a pirate, and Captain Riggs-Bowen, the most ostentatiously nautical character in the novel but certainly no true sailor, rather a snob and a hypocrite, who, though he "prattled endlessly about discretion, was a loose-lipped showoff who could not keep from seeking credit for what he thought he knew" (406). Preston Fowler, one of the competitors in the boat race, is clearly no true sailor either, being a "shady character" with a "soul-withering false smile" (105); and of the same spurious self-regarding species is Pamela who shamelessly asserts, "I know all about boats . . . I used to sail" (76). Whatever the level of their actual skill in sailing, these persons lack spiritual seamanship; they are, as it were, deficient in the essentials of celestial navigation.

Among the true sailors in the novel can be counted Patrick Kerouaille, another competitor in the race, "an amiable Breton schoolmaster" who writes his own books (in contrast to others such as Ian Dennis who has his nautical adventures ghostwritten for him) and whom life at sea inclines to "mystical ruminations" (105). And, of course, Lipitsa is a true sailor who as a young seaman in the late 1930s served aboard one of "the last four-masted sailing ships" (92). Finally, their failings notwithstanding but by virtue of their courage, their ultimate fidelity, and their great heart, Owen and Anne Browne are also true sailors. Both Anne and Owen understand, as do all true sailors, that "The ocean encompassed everything, and everything could be understood in terms of it. Everything true about it was true about life in general" (409).

Another recurring image that serves as a metaphoric representation of the characters' inner nature is that of birds. Riggs-Bowen, for example, is likened to "a raptor" (109), while Lipitsa's shipyard is described as being melodious with "bird calls of a mystical complexity" (90).

Owen seems to have as his totemic bird the stormy petrel. One such bird perches for a time on the mast of his boat, another leads him on to the Island of Invisibility. The stormy petrel seems to Owen an auspicious sign, a bird of good omen, and he associates it (through his remembered reading of Joshua Slocum's account, *Sailing Alone Around the World*) with the miracle on the lake at Gennesaret when Simon Peter walked with Christ on the waters, but faltering in his faith began to sink. On the day Owen commits suicide, he first searches the sky for a petrel but finds none. Owen's last thought as he sinks into the ocean is that it is "deeper than Gennesaret" (385). The stormy petrel thus seems to represent Owen's sustaining faith, his dream and motive aspiration, without the aid of which, like Simon Peter, Owen cannot maintain himself upon the waters of the world but must sink and drown.

Strickland, it will be remembered, was at a loss to account for all the footage of birds—"rising flamingos, swallows in the cactus, doves and vultures in the palm trees" (30)—with which he returned from his Central American sojourn. Later in the novel, walking in a park in New York City, Strickland finds himself "fascinated at a level beyond words" (21) by the flight of pigeons. But, ultimately, his true totem, his chosen tutelary power, is the vulture: on the carved Mayan talisman that he wears it is a vulture devouring the eye of the captive, and at the screening of his Central American documentary only the footage of vultures remains in the film. Strickland has edited away, suppressed all other birds, the emblems of his spirit's aspirations of ascent, and has embraced as his totem the vulture—the predator, the eater of carrion. The vulture corresponds to Strickland's affectless, cynical vision, which in the end he permits to exercise the dominant influence in his life.

Anne, too, has a totem bird: the sparrow. Once during a moment of drunken affection she calls Strickland "my sparrow" (338). In this instance she is mistaken—Strickland is not, as we have seen, a sparrow—but the epithet expresses Anne's positive associations with that bird. At last, during the period of self-rehabilitation following Owen's death, Anne attains contact with her totem bird, and it becomes for her, as was the petrel for Owen, a spiritual emblem, an inspiration and a guide:

> One morning she had lain listening to a white-throated
> sparrow chanting in the single living elm across the
> street. Everything seemed obviated in its plainsong.
> There were many around the house in South Dart-
> mouth and she looked forward to that . . . She thought
> she saw a model for herself in the order and simplic-
> ity of the sparrow's call. (409)

Another important motif in the novel is laughter, not mirthful laughter but malicious, mocking laughter. We encounter it in the "unsound
laughter" (15), the "cold quick laughter" (281) of Strickland, and in
Pamela's "screechy laughter" (182), her "chattery ersatz laughter"
(324). We hear its echoes in Owen's memory of the "loony drunken"
(301) scornful laughter of his father whose "dry . . . heartless" (302)
laugh is recollected with such disquieting effect years afterward by
his son. We hear it in the "malign delight" (130) of Owen's teenage
daughter, Maggie, and her friends, "convulsed with laughter at the
Agnus Dei" (130). And perhaps most dismaying of all, we learn of
it in the laughter of the four-year-old son of Jernigan, one of Owen's
colleagues, whose wife piteously wonders, "What do you do for a
kid with a terrible laugh?" (39) Such laughter is the consequence of
an almost universal lack of reverence for things, of ravenous cov-
etousness and unrestrained self-indulgence, and of the absence of
any sense of what is authentic and essential in life:

> Sold our pottage, overheated the poles, poisoned the
> rain, burned away the horizon with acid. Despised our
> birthright. Forgot everything, destroyed and laughed

away our holy things. What to do for our children's
terrible laughter? (301)

The motif of blindness suggests a defective vision in a figurative sense, a perceptual and moral blindness that impairs our ability
or willingness to discern or to judge. The "thick-lensed glasses" (30)
of Strickland's assistant Hersey, which he wipes with Sight Savers,
the "cold eyes" (33) of Pamela, and the perpetual dark glasses of
Harry Thorne's chauffeur all suggest forms of limited vision. Strickland suspects that his "demystified" (326) mode of vision may be a
kind of blindness, leading him to wonder whether "he had long ago
gone blind" (327). Yet he also perceives Owen Browne as blind,
impercipient, depicting Browne in one film sequence as "The Blind
Orion Searching for the Rising Sun" (160). Later, alone at sea,
Owen himself becomes "preoccupied with blindness" (372), even
wishing that he were blind, conceiving of blindness as a kind of freedom from the burdens of false identity and false perception. And,
indeed, Owen's final medium of contact with the world at large is
through "Mad Max," a blind teenage amateur radio operator who
Browne uses as an intermediary.

The issues of limited vision and moral and perceptual blindness, together with the question of the validity of awareness derived
from sensory experience, lead us to the central theme of *Outerbridge
Reach*: the problem of the nature of the true or the real.

In the novel, both Strickland and Browne are motivated by a
desire to know and to serve truth, each man embodying a conception
of what he believes to be real. "I work in the service of truth" (22),
proclaims Strickland, while Owen declares, "The truth's my bride"

(383). Yet both men, as we have seen, are self-deceived, and both deceive others. Moreover, there is but small area of agreement between the two men; their respective notions of what constitutes truth would surely be quite incompatible with each other. The conflicts within and between these two figures in their efforts to conduct their lives in accordance with truth suggest that truth and reality are more complex, more equivocal, more at issue than Strickland's and Browne's too categorical conceptions would allow.

Yet in the course of the novel, the distance between the beliefs and viewpoints of the two men narrows significantly. The tentative convergence of their separate perspectives—each party gaining greater range of perception, understanding, and knowledge—implies that a knowable, operable order of truth is perhaps after all susceptible of discovery and accessible to us. Indeed, the many errors, misguided acts, and disasters that result from a lack of some feasible, usable concept of what is fundamental and authentic in life make it imperative to attain and maintain such knowledge in our personal lives and the life of our world.

In *Outerbridge Reach* the problem of truth is further treated through the novel's inquiry into two interrelated processes upon which our apprehension of reality depend: perception and communication.

Our powers of perception are depicted in the novel as being seriously impaired by our habits of preconception and by our lack of discernment. We unquestioningly or unconsciously accept ideal or stereotypical images of reality, and as a result see only what we expect to see, or ultimately become disillusioned at the disparity between our false expectations and our actual experience in the world. We are too often misled by deliberately created false impressions, by wiles and artifices.

Take for example Owen's romantic expectations as a young man of the kind of man he would become and of what the experience of combat would be like. The first expectation he derived from his eager, adolescent reading of the fiction of Ernest Hemingway, the second from the television series *Victory at Sea*—neither of which bore resemblance to the truth of his experiences.

Harry Thorne, too, tends to idealize, in his case blindly projecting upon others his own latent desires for nobility and purity. Then, when subsequently becoming disillusioned with them for falling short of his ideals, he fails to note their actual praiseworthy qualities, their real nobility.

In a similar, if opposite, manner, Strickland is mistaken in his conception of Browne, seeing him initially as merely another "pilgrim" (115), a naive booster of bourgeois values—in reality one of Strickland's own perceptual clichés. In like manner, Strickland at the outset views the Browne family in terms of another of his cherished stereotypes, as the all-American, middle class, insouciant, insular, nuclear family; he fails to perceive in them the fires banked within, their passions and their anguish.

Deceptive appearances and duplicity abound in the novel: the ideologically pious facade of the Central American republic that is the subject of Strickland's probing documentary film as opposed to its actual conditions and practices; the rosy, heroic romanticization of Cuban society in the documentary program that Owen views on television; the external beauty and grace of Pamela in contrast to her inner squalor; the guileful Matty Hylan with his elaborate scams and perfidious stratagems; Anne's marital deception; Owen's false log and reported false positions; the erroneous claims made for the Altan Forty boat, which proves to be unseaworthy; the sham integrity of

Riggs-Bowen; and many other such cases. Clearly, according to the terms of *Outerbridge Reach*, deceiving others and being in turn deceived constitute a significant proportion of our experience in the world.

The novel also considers the effectiveness of the ways in which we communicate to each other the truths we think we know. These means are in *Outerbridge Reach* chiefly verbal, written, and visual, and include speech, books and letters, instruments of communication such as the radio, the television, the telephone, and media such as painting, photography, and film.

Repeatedly, the novel shows the distortions and deficiencies of attempts to communicate. As simple an act as interpersonal speech seems to fall far short of imparting the intended meanings of the speaker. We see, for example, how Owen attempts to express his feelings to those closest to him, his wife and daughter, and how again and again he fails to do so: "Somehow he could not succeed in saying what he meant" (185). Likewise, in the interviews he has with Strickland and with the psychologist, Dr. Karen Glass, Browne is unable to convey through verbal formulations his true thoughts and sentiments. After his interview with Strickland, Browne feels ashamed of his replies; and after his session with Dr. Glass, Browne remarks to Anne, "I felt as though I wasn't telling the truth" (149). Similarly, later, Anne reflects upon the peculiar and unsatisfactory nature of attempting to converse via long-distance marine telephone: "It tended to flatten out meaning . . . Its shorthand economies suggested false or pretended comprehension. The tendency was not toward truth" (228).

Strickland is consciously convinced that his chosen medium of perception and expression, the camera, "never lies" (79), and yet it is apparent that at another level of awareness he recognizes that it is the way in which he frames or lights a photographic image or cuts a film that causes the particular image to evoke from the observer the desired response. He admits this to his assistant Hersey and later to Anne, telling her that no latent meaning can be conveyed by his film "unless I want it there . . . They'll see what we want them to see" (306–7). Harry Thorne, himself a victim of newspaper photographers, would certainly concur. Thorne is bitterly aware of how the camera can be employed to manipulate, to mock, to create "unflattering pictures, sinisterly lit from below" (387).

Yet even where there is no intention, unconscious or otherwise, to edit reality, to distort it or to dress it up by means of specific photographic techniques, how effective or valid a means of communication is the camera? Having just beheld his first iceberg in the brightness of the Antarctic sunlight, marveling at the subtlety of its colors and the complexity of its shapes, Browne films it with a camcorder loaned to him for the voyage by Strickland: "But even as he filmed he knew that he had failed to record the ice's mystical, Shackletonian quality. How to photograph a psychological principle?" (283).

Painting, too, can be a problematic medium of communication, as we see in the significantly dissimilar responses of Strickland and Anne to the canvasses of Winslow Homer at the exhibition of his work that they attend together at the Metropolitan Museum.

Nor does writing fare much better than other media in *Outerbridge Reach*. Buzz Ward's conscientiously considered and carefully composed letter to Owen is immediately misconstrued by Owen, who gives it only a cursory reading. Similarly, Browne's own precisely, tersely worded message to Duffy, the public relations man assigned to him by Thorne, is transmogrified by Duffy when recomposed into a press handout, divested of all its original force and resonance, reduced to banality.

Owen discovers that when he attempts to record in his log the scenes and events that he has witnessed on his voyage and the emotional and intellectual responses that they have evoked in him, he cannot express in words the true dimensions or the reality of his experiences. His log entries seem to him contrived, evasive, wholly inadequate. He comes to realize that the accounts written by previous voyagers, the books that he has read and admired, are similarly deficient: "They are writing about what cannot be fully described . . . They reduced things and provided no more than what they knew was expected" (249). The solo-sailor writers, Browne believes, have consciously or unconsciously imitated each other, together creating a veritable genre: the sea adventure story. Their accounts, expressive of no more than conventional emotions and formulaic reflections tailored to suit the expectations and tastes of their reading public, represent a kind of counterfeit, an imposture: "No one had ever brought the truth ashore. It was not to be had" (334).

If, as the novel suggests, our perceptions of the world are largely undependable to begin with, and are then attenuated by our imperfect attempts to communicate them, it would seem that we are living our lives at several removes from reality. Indeed, it would further seem that, rather than sharing a common world or a common conception of truth or even a common delusion, we are instead living in a myriad of isolated, solipsistic, individual little pseudoworlds. Thus the conflicts that occur in the novel at every level from the intrafamilial to the international: fathers and daughters quarreling and mutually estranged, self-righteous pacifists brandishing their ill-informed and militant opinions, contras and revolutionaries killing each other, massacres and atrocities among the "intelligent, humorous and kind" (158) people of Sri Lanka, senseless acts of international terrorism such as the demolition of the satellite receiver, and on and on. And all this transpires because ignorantly, arrogantly, we cherish the notion that we alone or we together with a band of like-minded people are in possession of the truth and privy to the real.

Yet despite all the evidence in *Outerbridge Reach* of the errors and deficiencies that impair our perception of what is real, and that mar or prevent effective communication, the novel also offers counterinstances, testimony to the presence in the world of other and vital orders of truth and other modes of perception and communication.

In one of his last letters, W. B. Yeats wrote, "When I try to put all in a phrase I say: 'Man can embody truth but he cannot know it.'"[3] This concise, penetrating formulation expresses an operative principle in *Outerbridge Reach*. While the novel shows us the extreme difficulties that impede the quest for truth, it does not suggest that there is no truth. In a sense, the lives and actions of certain characters embody truth. Buzz Ward, for example, embodies the truth of humility, compassion, and hope. Ward's wife, Mary, embodies the truth of faithfulness and tenderness, and Lipitsa, the truth of patience, labor, and dedication. And Anne and Owen, by virtue of their courage and their determination, also come to embody truth, including the truth of learning to be a sailor and navigate the sea of human fate.

Certain characters also experience moments when quite suddenly, forcefully, truth is revealed. Such glimpses seem to occur when the ego or the rational mind is temporarily in abeyance, through fear or loneliness or fatigue. Take for example Buzz Ward. After months of solitary confinement in a North Vietnamese prison, he contrived at last to observe through a small hole in the wall of his cell the simple, humble, mundane daily activities of some nearby peasants, and realized with the force of a revelation "How sane they are and how little they expect from life" (320). Strickland experiences another such epiphany when he beholds Pamela in the light of an early morning after she has been up all night long taking drugs and watching images of herself on a video screen. Suddenly, for an instant, all the real desperation and vulnerability of her character is revealed, the essential ingenuousness that she dissembles beneath her pose of cynicism and street-sophistication is nakedly displayed:

> On her face, caught perfectly by the morning's faint
> radiance, was an expression like a child's. Standing
> there . . . she looked for all the world as though the
> morning light could somehow save her. She seemed,
> through the homely offices of shadow and line, hope-
> ful and expectant . . . She looked mournful and lost
> and, indeed, vulnerable. (36–37)

Another such quick, intense grasping of truth occurs when Owen, confronting the abyss during a fierce storm at sea, discovers not only the true nature of the craft in which he has embarked, but suddenly comprehends the true nature of the society of which he has been a part, seeing it as being like the boat it has produced: shoddy, phony, and worthless.

Various incidents in *Outerbridge Reach* also suggest that true communication is attainable, though such communication most often occurs outside of the usual channels and means. Dreams and portents constitute in the novel species of communication whose messages, though truthful and pertinent, go unheeded simply because we are not disposed to receive them. Anne, for example, dreams of her marriage as a form of captivity, and of Strickland as "a kind of louche salesman, who appeared to be encrusted in armored scales, part condittiere, part lizard" (280). She recognizes in her dream her need for "an antivenom kit" (280) as an antidote against the serpent cajoleries of Strickland. Similarly, Owen's recurrent weeping dreams and his dreams of his father point out the deep discontent he feels and identify the unresolved nature of his relationship with his father. The dreams of Anne and Owen are revelatory and cautionary, but they are ignored. In like manner, the numerous omens and portents that precede Owen's ill-fated voyage are all disregarded: the cheap piece of plastic tubing on the Highlander Forty-five boat that causes its failure; Owen's fall overboard during his shakedown cruise; his fall on the dock just prior to his departure; his recurrent and urgent misgivings about his voyage; the photograph that shows the Browne family facing a gathering storm; Anne's repeated failure to break the champagne bottle across the bow of Owen's boat at its launching. Despite their number and their persistence, such methods of communication are not recognized.

Other methods of nonrational communication in the novel include the inexplicable feeling of affinity and rapport that develops between persons, that "intense, elusive emotion" (199) of caring about another human being. Such a form of rapport occurs between Strickland and Browne just before Owen departs. Subsequently, Owen discovers a strange rapport with Mad Max, though they have never met and though they communicate with each other by means of Morse code across great distances. Similarly, Anne and Duffy develop a comradeship in spite of their differences of age and background.

And, finally, there are those mysterious forms of communication with the numinous that occur in the novel: the synchronicities that take place between word and event as Owen listens to the missionary radio station while at sea; and the signs in the form of birds: Strickland's unaccountable footage of birds, Owen's petrel, Anne's sparrow.

Taken together, these numerous instances of intuitive perception and communication suggest that our conventional concept of truth should be enlarged and extended to include the kinds of information that can only be given by this numinous communication.

Stone's use of multiple points of view in *Outerbridge Reach* is also related to the novel's central theme of the nature of truth. By shifting narrative point of view from one character to another within single chapters and alternating among the various characters from chapter to chapter, the novel communicates the elusive, complex, and subtle nature of the world we inhabit and the inherent limitations of each person's experience of that so various world, showing the sheer reductiveness and partiality of each individual's habitual manner of organizing and interpreting reality.

A secondary theme of *Outerbridge Reach* is the character and condition of the American republic. The novel begins with a stock market crisis, the collapse of false promise founded upon greed and fraud. This ominous event prefigures the later revelation of the shoddy state of the Atlan Forty boat in which Owen is sailing, its sleek design belied by its cheap, inferior construction. The boat may be seen as a metaphor for America, the pleasure craft as ship of state, disintegrating due to "Bad workmanship and sharp practice. Phoniness and cunning" (300).

The America of *Outerbridge Reach* is one of beggars and crack smokers, boarded tenements, graffiti, ruined children's parks, and ragged black men gathered on street corners. It is also an America of hermetically sealed high-rise office buildings and soulless condominiums; a country where "Nothing works anymore" (6), and where "the spirit of No Can Do" (70) prevails; a land of "frantic egoism, millions of ravenous wills" (217), where corporate power and wealth such as that enjoyed by Anne's father, Jack Campbell, is founded ultimately upon the muscle of vicious, violent thugs such as Donny Shacks and Forky Enright.

The novel's powerful, comprehensive metaphor for all the forces that have broken and ruined American ideals and dreams throughout the history of the republic is the coastal salvage yard at Outerbridge Reach, the end of the line for old boats. The history of Outerbridge Reach is one of suffering and sorrow: "Thousands of immigrants had died there, in shanties, of cholera, in winter far from home. It had been a place of loneliness, violence and terrible labor" (74). Now, with its prison-like fences and floodlights and its moldering masses of old hulks half-sunken or stacked upon each other five high, Outerbridge Reach is like a graveyard of human hope, a dead-end anchorage, a place of dereliction, decay, and desolation.

Significantly, Outerbridge Reach is owned by hard-boiled realist Jack Campbell. The symbolic collision there of Owen's boat, *Parsifal II*, with a rusty, worn-out old tug—even as Owen is listening to the innocent dreams embodied in the singing of Russ Columbo—foretells Owen's personal fate and tells also the fate of innocence and dreams in a harsh and brutal world.

Another aspect of the theme of America in *Outerbridge Reach* is the preoccupation of the several characters with notions of winning and losing. Their conceptions of what constitutes victory and defeat are shallow and crass, founded upon no more than the desire for self-aggrandizement—riches, ambition, pleasure—and the corresponding fear of remaining unexceptional and unadmired. This unquestioning compulsion to win according to the world's terms can be seen in Owen and Anne and in their daughter, Maggie. It also constitutes the motive power of Pamela, Strickland, Harry Thorne, Matty Hylan, and the contestants of the boat race. Indeed, the winning ethos represents a guiding national belief that effects every aspect of American life and consciousness. The dream of success has replaced all the other and nobler components of the American dream.

It is Duffy who identifies the dimensions of this pernicious obsession with winning in his criticism of the late football coach Vince Lombardi, in whom Duffy discerns the embodiment of the vicious, superficial and single-minded drive to win:

> Vince Lombardi nearly destroyed this country . . . He was a fucking monster . . . He caused the Vietnam war. (180–81)

In opposition to all the waste and futility of this misdirected energy, the novel proposes the sort of awareness and discipline that is achieved by Buzz Ward, and ultimately by Anne, their poise and their direct existential grasp of reality, their connection to the authentic and the essential, their lives of "order and simplicity" (409).

CHAPTER SEVEN

Damascus Gate

In his latest novel, *Damascus Gate*,[1] Robert Stone moves from the New World to the Holy Land, to the city of Jerusalem as it exists in the closing years of the twentieth century. Sacred to Muslims, Jews and Christians, and populated by the pious and fanatics of all faiths, the city of Jerusalem is a magnet for spiritual seekers and religious cultists of every kind, the confluence and the battleground of diverse cultures and ideologies. Divided by the bitter hostility between Israelis and Palestinians, it represents the very locus of the dangerous edge of things.

The overarching, underlying, interweaving theme of *Damascus Gate* is that of vision and division: the universal struggle between the forces of disunity and discord, opposition and conflict, and those promoting attraction and combination, harmony and unity. This struggle takes place at every level: the metaphysical, the historical, the material and the mental, between and within nations and factions, and within each human heart.

Christopher Lucas most fully embodies the divided and conflictive condition of the world and of humankind. Throughout the novel, Lucas oscillates and wavers in his ideas of religious faith and lack of faith. He is, by turns, believing and unbelieving, yearning to believe then denying his need to believe. He rages against faith, against God, dismisses spirituality as an illusion, then yields again to the irresistible attraction of faith.

Lucas, a freelance American journalist, professes to have come to Jerusalem in order to cure himself of "the fond, silly regard for religion" (8) which persists in his heart and spirit despite the keen skepticism of his newspaperman's mind. Yet in this regard Lucas would seem to be unaware of his own deeper motives. Rather, it would appear that he has journeyed to Jerusalem in unconscious pursuit of some decisive epiphanic affirmation of faith, in search of conversion. His favorite location in the city is the Damascus Gate (associated, of course, with the journey and conversion of Saul of Tarsus), a place that possesses for Lucas "the suggestion of a route toward mystery, interior light, sudden transformation" (9).

Lucas's inner division is further complicated by his uncertain religious identity: he cannot decide whether he is a Jew or a Gentile. The offspring of a mixed marriage, Lucas has grounds for allegiance to either faith, and to neither. Raised as a Catholic, during his childhood and adolescence, Lucas was brutally persecuted by his parochial school classmates for being a Jew. During his residence in Jerusalem he is frequently asked—by Jews, Muslims, and Christians—whether he is Jewish or Christian. Lucas replies sometimes in one manner, sometimes in another, though never framing his answer for reasons of convenience. He regards himself as a "half-caste" (5) and a "half-breed" (75), confused and rootless.

A far more serious matter for Lucas in this regard is the way in which others choose to classify him religiously. The anti-Semitic archaeologist Lestrade sneeringly insists upon seeing Lucas as a Jew, despite the fact that the two men share the same religious upbringing and training. At one point, a group of enraged Palestinians unhesitantly classify Lucas as a Jew, whereas certain Jews decline categorically to accept him as belonging to their religion or culture. In the Holy Land, as Lucas learns, the issue of religious identity can be more than merely a minor concomitant of one's existence; it can have very immediate and practical bearing, entailing dire and even fatal consequences.

Though he strives to affect indifference, the question of religion is for Lucas germane to his sense of identity. During his college years he was a religion major; currently he attends the Hebrew University, taking courses in classical Hebrew and in Jewish spiritual traditions, as well as studying on his own abstruse works of Jewish mysticism. One Sabbath evening in Jerusalem, he is drawn to join the worshipers at the Western Wall. On other occasions, Lucas is attracted to church services: on Easter he heads for the Church of the Holy Sepulchre; and later he is drawn desperately to attend Mass at a desert monastery. In conversations with religious figures in the novel such as the Reverend Eriksen and Father Herzog, Lucas is surprised to discover the depth and intensity of his longing for answers and for spiritual guidance.

At the same time, Lucas is repelled by the manner in which religious faiths lend themselves to exclusivity and intolerance, and by their seeming indifference or irrelevance to the struggles and sufferings of humanity. Moreover, Lucas possesses a strain of cynicism, fatalism, and reductive rationalism that effectively precludes for him any enduring acceptance of religious faith.

Lucas has a personal and professional preference for the kinds of news story "that exposed depravity and duplicity on both sides of supposedly uncompromising sacred struggles," because he finds such stories "reassuring, an affirmation of the universal human spirit" (11). When, for example, he learns from a British historian that the official story of Massada and its courageous defenders is largely invention and that the real story of the siege is far less edifying, Lucas again feels relief: "People were people, for what it was worth. The fundamental things remained" (77).

Similarly, Lucas indulges a propensity to ascribe base and banal causes to certain exalted emotions on his part or on the part of others. Thus, on one occasion after having been seized suddenly by an intense, urgent desire to attend Mass, Lucas dismisses the impulse as having arisen from his recent increased level of drinking, his lack of tranquilizers, and his head cold. He assures himself that his state of mind was aberrant and purely physiological in origin, the biological efficiency of the brain having been temporarily impaired by an altered chemical composition of the blood.

Employing a metaphor as an explanation for his religious impulses, Lucas rationalizes his curious and uncharacteristic (but psychologically revealing) desire to go to Mass as a result of "an undigested bit of beef" (338). (It will be remembered that in Charles Dickens's *A Christmas Carol*, the figure of Scrooge attempted in this fashion to explain away the apparition of Morley's ghost.) Lucas also glibly accounts for the mystical predilections of a middle-aged American man named De Kuff by characterizing De Kuff's spiritual strivings and struggles as being merely chemical in nature.

By believing always in the lowest and most ignoble motives for human behavior and by conceiving always the dullest and most reductive explanations for what transpires in the mind and in the world, Lucas bars from serious consideration the potentially disturbing implications that certain phenomena might otherwise possess for him. It is a self-protective strategy to which he has habituated himself. By refusing to acknowledge that there might be selfless actions or ideals worth serving or a spiritual dimension to existence, Lucas evades the painful process of then having to evaluate his own life in the light of such absolutes. The defects of this mode of resisting moral and spiritual attack from without are that, when it functions optimally, it leaves him marooned and deprived of nourishment within the confines of his defensive perimeter, and that, as we have seen, the assaults on his ego fortifications do not always come from without, but come at times from within.

Within his citadel of skepticism, rationalism, pessimism and ironic wit, Lucas feels empty, isolated, and lost: "His weariness with things was frightening; it smacked of obliteration, a wall of anger and fatigue that felt as though it might sweep him into nothingness. Worst of all was loneliness" (59). Lucas's inward condition of psychic deprivation and depletion expresses itself symbolically in his sexual impotence: his incapacity for sexual union makes manifest in a physical medium Lucas's psychological inability to unite with anything beyond the sterile, isolated ego-self.

From this blighted state Lucas reclaims his life, restoring and reorienting himself, after first enduring a siege of darkness, traversing a personal inferno, teetering on the dangerous edge of things.

The darkest phase of Lucas's night journey occurs when he is pursued alone in the darkness across the desert by a group of hate-crazed Palestinians who, believing him to be a Jew and a djinni, wish to torture and kill him. Lucas finds that he has no allies, neither among the more reasonable factions of the Palestinians nor among the Israeli soldiers. He experiences the ultimate solitude of the hunted man, severed from all human sympathy and succor, the object of the unreasoning, implacable malice of other men.

Lucas at last evades the howling, murderous mob by finding sanctuary among a tribe of gypsies. The rescue of Lucas by the Nawar tribe represents a kind of homecoming, a finding of his own true tribe. Like Lucas, the Nawar are independent outsiders and thus oppressed and despised by all sides. Their way of life—centered upon music and dance—is tolerant and optimistic, their religion inclusive: "They celebrated life, using wine and arak when they could be had. They honored Muhammad, Moses and Issa, all prophets of God" (334–35).

Lucas's subsequent abduction by and beating at the hands of an ultra-Zionist sect (whose members, in ironic contrast to the Palestinian mob, do not regard him as being Jewish but merely a meddlesome interloper) confirms his feelings of being an outsider, his ultimate rejection of any identity predicated upon an exclusive religious affiliation, whether as Jew or as Gentile.

Lucas achieves a more affirmative resolution of this same question of religious identification during what could be termed the second phase of his night journey, during a night of rioting and violence in Jerusalem. In the course of this perilous night, despite very immediate dangers and the practical attraction of claiming a religious affiliation, Lucas resolutely declines to declare himself either a Christian or a Jew. Yet he may be said to resolve the issue by transcending the merely apparent dichotomy represented by the two categories. During the night of rioting, caught between armed ultra-Zionist conspirators and violent Palestinians, Lucas—although quite naturally concerned for his personal survival—repeatedly puts his own safety at risk in an attempt to accomplish a moral and humane end: preventing the detonation of a bomb that could be the catalyst to a full-scale war. In pursuit of this end, Lucas rescues the unpleasant and offensive archaeologist Lestrade who is implicated in the bomb plot. Apart from Lestrade's immediate usefulness, however, Lucas saves him just because Lestrade is a fellow human being and thus deserving of mercy. Or as Lucas phrases it, "although Lestrade was a prick, a fascist and an anti-Semite, it would be the Christian thing to save him. Or the Jewish thing. The Judeo-Christian thing" (436).

The conflict between the seemingly incompatible Jewish and Gentile components of Lucas's background and heritage is obviated entirely by his recognition of the essential likeness of the two faiths, their common ground in human mercy and their shared sense of the sacredness of life. In place, then, of uncertainty and of the tension between the two identities or rejection of both, there is in Lucas's psyche a new unity that, characteristically for Lucas, does not conform to the notions and doctrines of the orthodox of either faith. He remains, as it were, a spiritual gypsy.

Apart from the ethical dimension of religious identity, there is the question of belief—belief in a creator, in a cosmic design, a spiritual realm. As previously noted, Lucas is caught between a powerful yearning for belief that exerts its force largely outside his conscious awareness, and a profound religious skepticism born of his rationalism and his experience of human suffering in what seems to him a world without purpose or meaning. At the outset of the novel, it is Lucas's conscious rationalism and skepticism that dominate his desire to believe, a deep-seated impulse which his critical intelligence manages to stifle and suppress, dismiss and deny.

Yet despite his apparent complacency in the matter of religious belief, Lucas finds himself "pursued by unreasonable yearnings" (134) of a spiritual character, longings and cravings that express themselves as wistfulness and as impulse and compulsion. At length he must recognize that he was mistaken to imagine that he had disposed of his desire to believe, outgrown his religious impulses: "he had confidently and wrongly thought himself beyond all that. In fact it was part of him, his inward man" (135).

But the recognition and acceptance of one's desire for belief is still distinct from the possession of belief itself, and Lucas cannot get clear of his dark view of existence as purposeless and full of pain, and of religious belief as a dangerous illusion. This inward conflict materializes in the novel in the figures of a young blond woman and a strange, malign little girl, both of whom Lucas briefly encounters.

Lucas first glimpses the young blond woman in the chapel of a Benedictine monastery near Haifa, which he is visiting both for professional and personal motives. Seeing her piety and prayer, Lucas envies her, desiring devoutly to possess "her faith and her secrets, her life" (261). The woman represents for him an embodiment of all that he has lost and all that he would wish to be. Later, upon an evening in Jerusalem, Lucas thinks he sees her among the Christian pilgrims entering the Church of the Holy Sepulchre and he follows her there.

He is mistaken, however; she is not to be found in the church, and Lucas is inadvertently locked in for the night together with a group of pilgrims keeping vigil there. Falling asleep in a side chapel Lucas dreams or hallucinates a conversation with a little blond girl named Diptheria Steiner, who claims to be the daughter of Rudolph Steiner, a German mystic. As her name and her lineage suggest, and as her choice of conversational topics reveals, Diptheria embodies the harmful, baneful aspects of religious belief: narrow doctrinaire self-righteousness coupled with complacent acceptance (indeed, approval) of a wrathful God who punishes and destroys all those who do not conform to the most orthodox beliefs and the most stringent religious disciplines.

The figure of Diptheria personifies religious belief as a tool of selfishness and a force of division in the world, lending itself to holy wars and pogroms, to persecution and genocide. Lucas's pursuit of the young woman and encounter with the girl constitutes a kind of allegory of the spiritual quest: how seeking after a noble and worthy goal, we may instead unexpectedly and unknowingly be seized by what is ignoble, degraded to self-satisfied baseness. Latent in even the highest endeavors of the mind and spirit, abides that misbegotten and malevolent offspring of belief—the imp of the perverse.

Still in pursuit of an epiphany, driven by the accumulated energies of an impulse long pent up, Lucas at last journeys "off the map" both literally and figuratively, and his quest for vision culminates in hallucinations of a character and import quite opposite to that of Diptheria Steiner.

Again, for reasons both personal and professional, Lucas accompanies the members of a messianic-millennial cult on a pilgrimage into the mountains of the Golan, near the Syrian border. Lucas uses a road map to help him navigate into the remote area, but soon his journey brings him to the edge of his map, and without reference or guidance, he proceeds further into the mountains.

Symbolically, of course, Lucas is entering psychic *terra incognita*—unknown, unexplored inner regions, a wilderness of unconscious drives and desires. Under the influence of the wild landscape, the group-mind, the charismatic leader of the cult, and a dose of the drug Ecstasy, which has been surreptitiously administered to him, Lucas approaches epiphany and draws near to belief. For one brief instant he does believe, then in the next moment belief is withdrawn and he feels that he "no longer knew what he believed or denied" (400).

But if Lucas is ultimately unable to attain belief, he demonstrates admirably his capacity for practical compassion, for reason and decency. Despite the vivid hallucinations induced in his mind by the Ecstasy, and despite the abandoned behavior of the cult members who are moved by the drug and by their exalted mood to extremes of rapture and terror, Lucas succeeds in perceiving the peril in which the group finds itself and preventing their coming to harm as the mountain weather turns cold and a storm approaches, and as the frail, aged leader of the cult, De Kuff, reaches the extremity of his strength. Steadying himself and focusing his attention on the task at hand, Lucas organizes the orderly withdrawal of the bedraggled group of seekers from the wilderness.

Significantly, as soon as he begins to think and to plan, Lucas finds that he can once again use the road map for orientation. Back from the dangerous edge of things, he is back on the map. In a sense, though he may not consciously be aware of it, Lucas has had his epiphany after all; in an undramatic fashion, he has realized his true vocation, the specific mode of devotion for which he is especially suited. Lucas's calling is not to the mystical or contemplative life, but rather his way is that of compassionate action in the world. Lucas's spiritual path and spiritual task is service to others, both through his journalistic dedication to truth and through the exercise of ordinary decency, steadfastness and common human sympathy.

If Lucas's sympathetic powers are affirmed and augmented by his humane actions in the mountains of Golan and later in the hazardous night streets of embattled Jerusalem, those same powers are many times enhanced in his love for Sonia. Sonia, an African American follower of Sufism, who works for the International Children's

Foundation, inspires in Lucas immediate and powerful attraction, reawakening in him his capacity to love.

But Lucas's ardor for Sonia constitutes another of the ordeals of his night journey, for his is a thwarted love, a hopeless and desperate love. Sonia does not at first return Lucas's feelings; later, when at last they establish a mutual affection and become intimate, Lucas's sexual impotence precludes the erotic consummation of their love. Yet despite the pain and shame that he feels at his sexual failure, Lucas persists in wooing her, dedicating himself to shielding her from the potential dangers and disappointments attendant upon her commitment to the De Kuff cult. Ultimately, his devotion to her is rewarded in a passionate and liberating act of sexual union that has for Lucas the effect of a spiritual and emotional resurrection: "He felt as if he had been near to death and come alive" (391).

By means, then, of a series of encounters, trials and ordeals, Lucas is saved from his self-inflicted perdition, from the blind and blank psychic diverticulum in which he had ended before coming to Jerusalem. The Holy Land is for him a place of existential self-encounter, the outcome of which is at least a partial healing of his inner division. Lucas moves beyond fatalism and resignation and learns again to dare and to act and to love. He gains considerable self-knowledge and attains a greater degree of psychic integrity. In nearly every sense—intellectually, emotionally, ethically, spiritually, sexually—Lucas is cured of his impotence.

At the end of the novel, as Lucas departs Jerusalem, his destiny is by no means fully worked out, nor is the resolution of his inner struggle fully or finally achieved. Significantly, he has failed to achieve a lasting union with Sonia, who embodies the highest aspirations of his spirit. Lucas thus occupies a sort of midpoint or halfway station between what he once was and what he may yet become.

Despite his disappointment in love, Lucas has regained the power to love, and despite his continuing lack of real belief, he has realized the profundity of his need for belief. If he cannot be said to have attained wisdom, than he may at least be said to have gained what must be seen as the beginning of wisdom: an acquiescence to his fate, an acceptance of his life.

Lucas leaves the Holy Land bearing two precious souvenirs of his sojourn there. In his mind he bears away a compensatory insight: the perception that, although loss is inevitable, in a deeper or a higher sense nothing of great value is ever lost, but rather its presence in the heart or the mind is made only the more real, the more vivid and distinct through its distance or absence. And in his pocket Lucas bears away a handful of stones he gathered atop Mount Sinai, talismen of that sacred place where, it is said, Divinity intersected human history. The stones are emblems for him of a fond and wistful faith that such a momentous event may truly once have taken place, and may again take place—in some manner mysterious and impossible to comprehend.

Another central figure in the novel who is torn by inner discord and caught between vision and division is Raziel Melker. Raziel (who is also known as Razz and as Ralph) represents a kind of mirror image of or contrary counterpoint to Lucas, in that whereas Lucas's surface disbelief and despair are subverted by his suppressed spiritual impulses, Raziel's conscious spiritual purposes are undermined by negative energies arising from his unconscious. Raziel is thus at once an earnest and dedicated spiritual seeker and the secret spoiler, the hidden destroyer of his own aspirations and ideals.

Restlessly seeking an elusive absolute, Raziel, who is a musical prodigy, pursues through a variety of musical forms the song of songs, the primal and ultimate tone, while pursuing at the same time through a variety of spiritual traditions—orthodox Judaism, Zen Buddhism, Tantra yoga, Christianity, and the Kabbala—final truth and illumination.

Raziel is, in turn, pursued by his own self-destructive inclinations, which manifest themselves especially in his use of narcotic drugs. Raziel's spiritual drive is for a time diverted by this pernicious practice as he becomes addicted to heroin, a condition that transforms his quest for transcendence into a search for oblivion.

Freeing himself from his addiction, Raziel embarks upon a far more exalted spiritual endeavor: an attempt to effect universal redemption. This nobly conceived (if unlikely) enterprise is, however, soon brought to naught, undermined by Raziel's ruinous negative propensities, which impel him to involve himself in a nefarious political conspiracy and to introduce among his companions and fellow believers the use of a hallucinogenic drug in order to induce in them pseudomystical states. Equally fatal to the accomplishment of his elevated purposes, Raziel resumes the use of heroin and relapses into addiction. In this manner, Raziel's magnanimous project for human redemption collapses in disaster, insidiously eroded from within by the same mind that has supplied the creative intelligence for the enterprise.

Raziel's darker, destructive aspect is implied by his outward manner and appearance, which seem incongruous with an attachment to spiritual values. His characteristic black attire, his lizard-skin boots, his perpetual sunglasses (worn indoors, even at night), together with his air of impudence and derision, hardly bespeak the ascetic or the mystic. Rather, his trappings and deportment express the presence within him of the manipulator, the mocker, the malicious trickster. Appropriately, Raziel is described as being left-handed, a detail whose metaphoric implications become clear when at one point, speaking perhaps more truly than he knows, Raziel jeeringly says of himself: "Think of me as Din. The Left Hand. The Spoiler" (403).

Yet despite his dark side, his demonic aspect, and his unknown destructive inner companion, Raziel is a young man of undeniable spiritual gifts, including a kind of second sight or clairvoyance. His religious beliefs, his spiritual ideals and aspirations are unfeigned and heartfelt, and he labors arduously and diligently to realize them. Even Lucas, who from the outset of his acquaintance with Raziel is skeptical and mistrustful of him, must grudgingly admit to himself that Raziel is "a prodigy" and that there is about him the special quality of being "second born" (135).

Caught in the pull of contrary forces, riven by inner contradictions and conflicts, torn between his creative and destructive energies, between the sacred and the profane, between his (literal and figurative) myopia and his clairvoyance, between hope and despair, Raziel both redeems and destroys himself in a final act of love and of selfless devotion. Raziel's attempted rescue of De Kuff from the violence of an enraged mob of Palestinians is perhaps the purest act of his life. Undertaken at great personal risk, it is an act motivated by simple affection and sincere concern for another's safety. In so acting, Raziel, though effectively destroyed, achieves, briefly but decisively, victory over his shadow self, and at last attains the salvation that he has sought for so long.

The central theme of vision versus division is also represented in certain subsidiary figures. Among the followers of the De Kuff cult, for example, there are two sets of close relatives: the twin brothers, Horst and Charlie Walsing, and a father and son with the family name of Marshall.

The Walsing brothers in their duality constitute the very embodiment of the human condition. Indistinguishable from one another in appearance, inseparable companions, Horst is an accomplished musician, while Charlie is mentally retarded. The former brother embodies the aesthetic and spiritual potentials of humankind, while the latter embodies the brute physical aspect and the unenlightened mind, which are a hindrance and an impediment, a burden to the other, and which must somehow be elevated and redeemed.

The Marshalls, father and son, are highly skilled but unscrupulous accountants, formerly affiliated with organized crime in the United States and currently in flight and in hiding from warrants issued against them there. The Marshalls are involved in a continual dispute between themselves over the possession of a set of ledgers that they have brought with them. While the interest of the younger Marshall is in the financial transactions recorded in the ledgers, the older Marshall, who is an accomplished Kabbalist, is concerned only with the mystical properties and import of the numbers. Their struggle for possession of the ledgers is a metaphor for the ongoing struggle between the mind and the spirit, between the secular and the sacred, between the selfish desire for appropriation of things in the created world and the desire to discover the mystical significance of existence.

Those figures in the novel who do not or cannot embrace some version of spiritual vision find in political ideology or national identity a secular counterpart to mystical apprehension of the meaning of existence. As Lucas observes, "Everyone wanted an answer, a guide for the perplexed. Everyone wanted death and suffering to mean something" (210). Take for example the exaggerated reverence of ex-Marxist Basil Thomas for the impersonal transcendent force of "History;" or the dedication of Rashid, the young Palestinian medical doctor to the cause of the "Palestinian Revolution;" or the lives of high-ranking Israeli government officials such as Avram Lind and Naphtali Shaviv consecrated to service to the land of Israel.

Yet such secular visions as those embraced by these and other figures in the novel are also vulnerable to contradiction and internal division, most frequently in the form of a confusion of self-interest with the interests of the cause one serves, or in the form of a narrow self-righteousness that is counterproductive to the establishment or furtherance of one's ideals.

The two secular visionaries with whom the reader becomes most closely acquainted in the novel are Nuala Rice and Janusz Zimmer, both of whom exemplify the discord and conflict inherent in devotion to worldly and temporal ideals.

Nuala is an Irish Marxist, an orthodox and unreconstructed Communist who works for the Children's Foundation. She is a hardened veteran of aid work in Beirut, Somalia, and the Sudan. We learn that her life is divided between "good works and various intrigues, erotic and otherwise" (16). Indeed, it is difficult at times to distinguish between Nuala's erotic appetite and her political passion, and to know to which of them she gives precedence, which of them represents her primary motivation.

Moreover, Nuala's ideological commitment to the cause of the "Palestinian Revolution" (coincident with her romantic involvement with Rashid), leads her into an incongruous alliance with a drug smuggler and an even more inconsistent connection with the Israeli internal security agency. Yet in both of these liaisons Nuala perceives, as she phrases it, "coincidences of interest" (368). Equally incompatible with humanitarian ideals and more reprehensible, perhaps, is Nuala's calculated deception and endangerment of her closest friends in the furtherance of her political goals.

Yet, upon another occasion and under other circumstances, Nuala shows herself capable of transcending all ideological perspectives and their attendant categories and imperatives, in her purely humane attempt to save the life of another—the life, in fact, of one of her avowed political enemies.

Liquidated ultimately by her ideological enemies, Nuala dies at too early a stage of her intense and passionately lived existence to have begun to reflect upon the divisions and contradictions that proceed from her vision of human unity.

Janusz Zimmer shares much of Nuala's secular vision and shares also the kinds of inner contradictions and moral incongruities that arise from the attempt to further in the world one's convictions and ideals. Like Nuala, Janusz believes in history and dedicates himself to serving that force and its processes. Unlike Nuala, though, he is not a Marxist but rather what might be termed a secular Zionist: Zimmer believes in the historical destiny of the state of Israel. Committed unconditionally to serving the state—or at least to serving that political faction which he has determined best represents the interests of the state—Zimmer undertakes in that cause various covert operations, including the organization of an elaborate bomb-plot sting that constitutes the central action of the novel.

Zimmer's covert mission necessitates his manipulation, deception, and betrayal of a number of people who give him their trust, even their love. Moreover, Zimmer feels a certain wistful kinship with those whom he misleads, thwarts, and exploits—the ultra-Zionist factions—both because he believes that they may, after all, represent the "purifying wind" required to make the state of Israel "the singular place it had been meant to be" (480), and because, like himself, they devote their lives to a cause. Thus in his endeavor to bring "purity of purpose" (480) to the state, Zimmer employs impure means; in his effort to further what he perceives as truth, he perpetrates fraud and falsehood. In this way, Zimmer's particular integrity compels him to duplicity, and his faith constrains him to treachery and betrayal. His tragedy, like that of Nuala and the other secular visionaries of the novel, is that of a mind searching for coherence and worthy purpose in the world but generating, instead, only further confusion, corruption, and conflict.

But if there is at work in the world or in the human psyche a divisive force acting to create and perpetuate disunity and discord, to promote disharmony and contradiction, there is also an opposing, unitive force that draws together and gathers in mutual attraction, that causes mingling and merging, and that expresses itself in human feelings of sympathy and solidarity and in visions of mystical unity. This latter force acts upon the lives of several characters in the novel, including certain secondary and peripheral figures as well as Sonia who is, in ethical and spiritual terms, the most substantial of the book's main characters.

The potential for merging spiritual traditions into a more inclusive identity is suggested in the novel by the presence of two minor figures, Abdullah Walter and Father Jonas Herzog. The former, an American Jew from California, became a Sufi sheik in Jerusalem, enjoying there the admiration and affection of the Muslim community, and even the patronage of the grand mufti.

Father Herzog, of French-Jewish origin, is a convert to Catholicism and an ordained priest in the Benedictine order, living and working in a monastery near Haifa. Despite his conversion and ordination, Father Herzog still considers himself to be Jewish; his Jewish heritage representing for him the essential condition of his being, the material that he must work into a more finished form (as every human of whatever condition likewise must do). His Jewishness is for him a given, a foundation, both a burden and a boon, or as he phrases it, "my means of grace" (263). Following the words of Saint Paul, Father Herzog believes that all earthly categories and classifications are merely apparent and temporary and that they are obviated by the unity of the human spirit in God in whom all souls are one: "There is neither Jew nor Greek, there is neither bond nor free, there is neither male nor female" (262).

Adam De Kuff in his spiritual development arrives at a position similar to that of Father Herzog. At the outset, De Kuff is a virtual embodiment of the condition of inner division: a manic-depressive with schizophrenic tendencies, a Jew who is a Catholic convert but who has relapsed into a state of spiritual perplexity and anomie. Under the influence of Raziel, who acts upon his spirit as a catalyst, De Kuff experiences a sudden revelation of the oneness of all beliefs and all faiths, the oneness of humanity and God. He awakens to a sense of divine mission and begins to preach and teach.

De Kuff struggles bravely against the mental illness that torments and undermines him, and exerts himself in an effort to bring into reconciliation and integration the multiplicity of voices or souls within himself. In a sense, he is himself a microcosm of the world with its myriad voices and its multiple faiths and philosophies, and his struggle possesses both an inward and an outward aspect, as if the process of redeeming his own spirit and the redemption of the world were inextricably interwoven.

Ultimately, although De Kuff at last succeeds in manifesting harmoniously the souls within him and thus attains spiritual wholeness and fulfillment, he is in the same instant destroyed by a violent, quarrelsome world unprepared to receive his message that "God is One. And faith in Him is One. And all belief is One. And all believers in Him, regardless of sect, are One. Only the human heart divides" (474).

Clearly, in a strict sense, De Kuff is not the redeemer that his followers take him to be. And yet, in another sense, he is that redeemer, in that he embodies, for however brief a moment, a principle, a potential; and that principle, that potential, that illustrious invitation and supreme opportunity are once again rejected by the world. De Kuff's unitive vision and his violent demise at the hands of a mob suggest that the redeemer comes again and again until we recognize and accept Him.

Perhaps no other figure in *Damascus Gate* is burdened by so much potential for inner division and conflict as Sonia, a biracial, bireligious, young American woman who is the offspring of Marxist parents, members of the American Communist Party. Yet with the exception of Father Herzog, no other character in the novel possesses such poise and integrity. Sonia almost effortlessly transcends the apparent polarities of her background and integrates them in such a manner as to attain a tolerant outlook and a generous spirit.

Sonia combines in her life religious faith (Sufism and Judaism) with practical humanitarian idealism. She has worked for the American Friends Service Committee and served as an aid worker in Somalia, and she is sincere and diligent in the practice of her spiritual disciplines. It is clear that she regards both forms of belief, both modes of action, as being mutually reflective.

Sonia is not, of course, a paragon. She is not untroubled by doubt, nor is she immune to temptation or human weakness. In the course of the novel she is subjected to experiences that test the substance of her spirit.

The first trials and temptations that Sonia must confront present themselves in the form of two men to whom she is emotionally attracted: Raziel and Lucas. Prior to the internal chronology of the novel, Sonia has had an amorous relationship with Raziel. Now her former lover returns to her as a kind of spiritual seducer, asking that she extend her belief to accept the coming of the end of days, the imminent transfiguration of the world. At this same point in time, Lucas enters her life, challenging with his scorn and skepticism her hard-won faith, and, in effect, asking her for his sake to renounce belief.

Appropriately, Sonia's ultimate trial—a struggle within herself —takes place in the darkness and solitude of a labyrinth, a maze of ancient corridors and chambers under the city of Jerusalem, in which, entering upon a brave errand of mercy, she becomes lost. Nearly overcome with fear and loneliness, Sonia yet resists the false reassurances offered her by the conspirators whose plot she has come hence to thwart. Despite her terror, Sonia asserts herself against the dreadful silence and darkness of the labyrinth and against the menace of armed conspirators, persisting by sheer bluff and brashness to frustrate their purposes.

Neither Sonia's disappointment in the failure of the lofty enterprise of Raziel and De Kuff to redeem the world, nor her ordeal in the underground labyrinth of old Jerusalem discourage or diminish her, but rather they confirm her faith and her sense of duty. She has come through her temptations and her trials intact, neither relinquishing her spiritual beliefs nor surrendering to the more grandiose devotion of Raziel. Similarly, while preserving and acting upon her humanitarian ideals, Sonia has not succumbed to the kind of glamorous but futile ideological adventurism of Nuala.

Sonia's inner victory in the labyrinth is decisive for her and prophetic of her chosen life afterward in the world, where she aims to cultivate both her piety and her subversive, practical compassion. Sonia intends, she says, to try "to be the best Jew I can be" (492) and to resume her aid work among the oppressed and impoverished of the world. In this manner, she will assert herself against the darkness and the silence of the labyrinth that is life in the world, striving to further the ultimate spiritual redemption of the world by effecting redemption within her own heart and spirit, and working to restore divine justice and balance to the world by defying and undermining all the external forces and agencies that impede for humankind the process of social justice. As she says of herself, she is "here to learn" (454) and also "here to make trouble" (493).

It is fitting that when she is lost in the labyrinth beneath the ancient streets of Jerusalem, Sonia ultimately finds her way into what is the chamber of Sabazios, for it may be said that unknowingly Sonia worships and serves this deity. Sabazios Sabaoth was an ancient eastern syncretic god worshipped by a small group of devotees, including both Gentiles and Jews, at some time prior to the early Christian era. Sabazios's followers conceived him as both multiple and one in nature, at once divine and human, male and female (compounded of Zeus and Persephone, Hermes Trismegistus and Isis).

The iconographic representation of Sabazios suggests a theological worldview that incorporates and harmonizes primitive
totemistic elements with a complex theology and sophisticated mystical doctrines. The statue of Sabazios is described as being a Hermes-
like figure, its (broken) right hand raised in benediction, its left hand
holding a staff around which curl two serpents. The face has "a
beatific smile, reminiscent of a bodhisattva's," while on its head it
wears a cap, "like the figure of Liberty in the Delacroix painting
of the Revolution of 1830" (456). The cap, as we later learn, is Phrygian, because Sabazios was once a Phrygian god whose cult was
brought to Jerusalem by Jews from Phrygia. Clearly, though, the
association with Liberty fortuitously completes for the modern mind
the inclusive, comprehensive character of the deity—multi-faceted,
many-leveled, encompassing every human aspiration from political
liberty and social justice to mystical transcendence.

Another syncretic deity of the ancient East whose name occurs
at intervals in the novel is Serapis, who, as we are told, was "at
once the subsumation of Apis and Osiris and Aesculapius, a son of
Appolo" (148). Together, these amalgamative deities, Sabazios and
Serapis, personify the principle of inclusiveness, growth by addition,
growth toward wholeness and unity. They are products of the process
of joining together thoughts, impulses and perceptions of different
kinds and fusing them into larger, fuller conceptions.

The various characters in *Damascus Gate* may be viewed as
either serving or opposing this principle of comprehensiveness, as
promoting by their actions either vision or division. Some figures in
the novel, such as Nuala and Zimmer, and the Temple bomb-plot
conspirators, confident in their ignorance and impercipience, assert

categorical and exclusive positions and strive vehemently to further
their causes. Other figures in *Damascus Gate*, most notably Sonia,
endeavor—sincerely, if sometimes uncertainly—to attain greater
breadth and depth of vision and are content humbly and hopefully to
serve their convictions.

The ever-present latent potential for unity in the world is
expressed in the novel by the recurrence of the ringing of church
bells and by the muezzin's call to prayer. Despite the bitter division
of the world, its many contending tribes and factions, its conflicts
and violence, its mutually destructive wars, these sounds summon us
to recollect and to reconcile with ourselves, with each other, and
with God. And in spite of our inertia, our hypocrisy, our elaborate
evasions, the bells and the muezzin's cry continue to bid us to think
of our loss, to remember and recover truth, holiness and oneness in
the mystery of love.

Likewise, in *Damascus Gate*, music serves as a redemptive,
reintegrating force. We encounter in the novel many forms of musical expression, including reggae, jazz, Ladino, traditional eastern
music, opera, classical and rock music—each musical mode representing a fragmentary phrase of the primal and ultimate music of the
universe, or so at least certain of the novel's musicians believe.

Sonia, for example, employs her musical gifts as a mode of
spiritual discipline, an exercise by which to accomplish inner transformation. Similarly, Raziel and De Kuff, both accomplished musicians, agree that "at the base of music lay principles of metaphysics
that were hidden by the distractions of everyday life" (61). Accordingly, Sonia, Raziel, and De Kuff make use of music in their effort
to effect the transfiguration of the world, their aim being to recover

and to restore the divine ground tone of the cosmos, "making every-thing be music again . . . the way it was in the beginning" (389).

Mysteriously, music corresponds to and partakes of the process of mystical union. Even music's most secular servants become at moments "almost sacerdotal" (276) in their devotion and passion. Even the most rational of minds must at moments come under the influence of music's strange, subversive power, as when during one of the De Kuff cult's concerts, Lucas's psychiatrist friend, Purchas Obermann, gives himself over to the music; or when at times listen-ing to music Lucas momentarily forgets his disbelief and feels in the tones and notes "The promise of human transcendence, of great things to come" (190).

In mystical terms, music constitutes one of the emanations—radiations of the godhead—that persist in the created world, intan-gible waves of original divine energy that permeate the physical realm, like invisible signatures or reflections of the Almighty. Other such emanations include the human spirit itself, conscience, love, mercy, and beauty, especially the beauty of the natural world.

At intervals throughout the novel, we are presented with imagery that reminds us that despite all the squalor and defilement of the Fallen World, there still persists a residual freshness and purity and innocence as of the first day of creation. The mornings especially are a time when such vestigial primary beauty can be perceived.

The novel begins on such a morning: "The day was innocently glorious; spring sunlight scented the pines and sparkled on the stone walls . . ." (4). And there are in the novel other such glimpses of the lingering paradisiacal potential of the world: "There was dew on the olive trees and riotous bougainvillea. Doves lowed on the whitewashed walls, and below the sea sparkled. The world in the morning . . . Despair was foolishness" (257). And, again, later in the novel: "the air was fresh and dewy, the chill mountain air of Jerusalem as yet unsullied by exhaust fumes" (295).

At other hours of the day as well, despite human pollution—both moral and material—of the world, a simple, elevating natural beauty endures. Thus, we are told that "the evening smelled of car exhaust and jasmine" (265), that "By dusk the smog sometimes drifted off and the evenings were again herb-scented" (268), and that "There were still nightingales in the Jerusalem Forest nearby. Their flutings and repeated, intricate riffs could soothe and stir the heart" (417).

Parallel to the residual purity and innocence in the natural world is the remnant of human idealism that endures among certain persons, both old and young, who are glimpsed in the course of the book. In contrast to the narrow fanatics and the cynical opportunists that abound in *Damascus Gate* are those who are guided by hope and humanitarian ideals and who are dedicated to promoting human welfare.

Among those characters guided by hope are the idealistic physician Dr. Kleinholz; old Berlin Sparticists who operate a pension near the beach in Tel Aviv; the "old timers," including the venerable veterans of terrible wars and fearful ordeals, the aged Communists, Zionists, and Kibbutzim who still sing the old songs and keep the old faith, and who possess a vitality, a strength and a *joie-de-vivre* that belies their years; and the youthful modern counterparts of these unreconstructed old idealists—the aid workers and human rights activists, the United Nations peacekeepers, including Inge Rikker,

Helen Henderson, Ernest Gross and Sonia, and the unflappable Captain Angstrom with his quiet, resolute courage.

Yet another figure in the novel who exemplifies human hope and innocence is Lucas's nameless neighbor in Jerusalem, the old man who patiently, diligently tends his crop of kale, cultivating healthy plants from stony ground. The humble devotion of the old man suggests an ideal image of what each individual human spirit ought to do in this barren, inhospitable world. In contrast to the grandiose plans and vainglorious lives pursued by so many other figures in *Damascus Gate*, the old man represents a model of simplicity and sanity, a living embodiment of the teaching of Saint Francis of Assisi: everyday each man must hoe his own small garden.

In opposition to the scattered manifestations of primal purity and latent redemptive energies in the world is the nightmare of history, the endless cycle of human violence, persecution and retribution. Throughout the novel we are reminded of the terrible burden of the past, its calamitous consequences in the present, and the probable disastrous impact of past and present upon the future. Outrages, ancient and modern—Mosada, the destruction of the Temple, the Crusades, the Inquisition, the Holocaust, Stalinism and the Cold War, the Six Day War—serve still to hold humankind confined in "circular darkness" (222).

The blind and futile, self-perpetuating round of violence and vengeance between enemies is exemplified in the novel by the appalling retributory actions committed by "Abu Baraka;" the barbarous torture-murder of a young American sailor at the hands of the Lebanese Shiites; the cruel end of Hal Morris who is beaten to death by a Palestinian mob; and the no less cruel execution-style murders of Nuala Rice and Rashid in retaliation for Morris's death. In these and other instances of vengeance in the novel, innocents are punished for offenses they did not commit; these are cases of mistaken identity, punishment by proxy, or random victims selected solely for their representative value. Each act of revenge reacts ultimately upon the avengers and serves only to maintain the momentum of mutual destruction, to ensure the continuance of the nightmare cycle.

Appropriately, imagery of confinement and of having lost one's way in darkness recurs in the text: locked chapel doors, the menace of dark narrow streets, passages leading nowhere or ending in walls with sealed doorways, an ancient stone privy haunted by demons, a cellar where conspirators meet, a tiled interrogation room, underground tunnels and chambers buried deep beneath the streets of the city. The world and human existence are imaged in the novel as a labyrinth, a wilderness of rooms.

At one point, in a moment of sudden and utter confusion, Sonia asks herself wildly, "Who are we? What place is this?" (93). Her questions resonate through the narrative, fundamental to her own life and to the lives of other figures in the novel. These questions take on a desperate urgency for Sonia when she loses her way in the darkness of a labyrinth of ancient corridors and chambers. For Lucas, too, the questions have pertinence, but his view of the nature of the labyrinth in which he feels that he is lost is more passive and more pessimistic. "It was all a series of rooms one never found one's way out of," he reflects. "You had to be content with that, or die, or go completely crazy" (249). Later, following his beating in an interrogation room, Lucas employs the same trope, representing his life as "a series of such rooms, expanding endlessly" (354). In a like but more extreme manner, Razz, who feels caught between worlds, trapped in the interstice between the material world and the world of the spirit, between time and eternity, becomes so disoriented both physically and metaphysically that he is "not always completely certain what room he was in" (471). Razz's final, comatose state may be compared to close confinement in a sealed room: "walled off within his own darkened brain" (483).

Yet, the conspirators, celebrating the success of their endeavor, gather together in a "dusty, joyless room" (474), a metaphor for their narrow moral and metaphysical enclosure. Indeed, the surname of one of the chief conspirators, Zimmer (whose name in German means room), may suggest his unaltering state of confinement, as if despite his outward physical freedom of movement, he remains essentially enclosed within the narrow scope of his limited views. In the end, Zimmer and his fellow conspirators have superimposed upon the labyrinth of human existence in the world another labyrinth of intrigue and trickery, double-dealing and deception, thus adding maze to maze, darkness to darkness.

Less prominent in the text, but of no less thematic import, is imagery of egress. The title of the novel and the characterization of the Damascus Gate as "a route toward mystery, interior light, sudden transformation" (9) together constitute powerful counterimages to those in the novel of endless rooms and blind passages, and those pertaining to the condition of being lost or disoriented.

Lucas first encounters Sonia—his soul image—by impulsively entering an open door on a secluded side street of the city, "as dizzying and inviting a doorway as Lucas had seen in the city" (17). There, too, within a courtyard he discovers an ancient dome decorated with designs suggesting metaphysical principles and processes, and he reflects that it is fitting "that it should be tucked away so obscurely, on an unvisited street behind a moldering door" (18). In a similar manner, Raziel discovers in the unprepossessing figure of De Kuff, the presence of the redeemer—the doorway out of history into eternity. Raziel later recounts to Sonia this transfigurative experience: "I couldn't believe it . . . In the old man's eyes—the way out" (416).

Certain Kabbalistic terms and symbols in the novel resonate with the recurrent imagery of enclosure and egress. "Shells and light" is a phrase frequently employed by Raziel and De Kuff to designate the relationship between the temporal, material world and the eternal realm of the spirit. The shells are all the false, limiting constructions —whether personal, social, conceptual, cultural, or national—that impede us in our perception of eternity and our union with divinity; they are the enveloping, imprisoning husks of custom and constricted mental vision from which we must emerge. Another image drawn from the Kabbalah and signifying the ultimate egress of human redemption and transcendence is that of the snake which, molting, leaves behind its empty skin, and is symbolically born anew.

The spiritual theme of *Damascus Gate* is enhanced by numerous biblical allusions that suggest the continuity and the manifold manifestations of the human spiritual quest. Sonia, for example, is compared variously to the Old Testament figures of Leah and Rachel, the Shulamite of Song of Songs, and the Witch of Endor. De Kuff sees himself as a modern Jonah, swallowed by his psychosis, while he is seen by others as a descendent of the prophets. Lucas is compared to Uzzah, the soldier who at the risk of his life rescued the world from disaster by preventing the Ark of the Covenant from falling. And all the figures in the novel, all the lives in the world, are likened to the sparrows of Psalms 84 and 102, who have either found a home in the love of the Lord, or who remain forlorn and alone, full of unhappiness and dread.

Another biblical reference relevant to the theme of spirituality is to Samson's riddle, which at intervals throughout the novel Lucas ponders. The formulation "out of the eater came forth meat, and out of the strong came forth sweetness," takes on in the novel a metaphoric meaning beyond its original contextual significance in the Samson story. Samson's riddle represents for Lucas a potent paraphrase of the mystery that so perplexes him—the enigma of evil and suffering in a world created and ruled by a benevolent deity.

Considered in this perspective, the lion—"the eater," "the strong,"—of Samson's riddle may be seen as a metaphor for the ravening, devouring maw that is the created world—the blind, brute forces of appetite and survival. Yet ultimately, the riddle prophesies that these forces will be overthrown. When at last with the coming of the Redeemer the created world is transfigured—slain by the hero in the terms of the riddle—its role will be inverted and it will instead become for us a source of nourishment and sweetness.

Lucas's references to the poem "To the Infant Martyrs," by Richard Crashaw (1612–1649) provide a parallel to this view of a final triumphant reversal of the terms of pain and salvation, of devouring and nourishment . The poem constitutes a nexus of the novel's motifs of music, of enclosure and egress, and the motif of nourishment from the Samson riddle. Viewing human suffering and death from a spiritual perspective, Crashaw's poem presents physical death as a liberation from the cage of the body, as an occasion of elevation from mere human speech to celestial song, and as the beginning of a supreme and infinite nourishment of the spirit.

And so throughout the pages of *Damascus Gate*, the old immortal questions resound; the perennial mysteries of existence are revolved and revalued, reformulated and reinterpreted. Of course, the novel does not propose new resolutions or final answers to the issues of reality, identity, faith, and salvation. Rather, the book explores certain more unaccustomed connections among and configurations of these issues, and offers to us as readers imaginative insights into the confusions and conflicts arising out of the confrontation of contemporary lives with eternal questions.

Damascus Gate implies that through deficiencies of imagination and defects of perception we continually fail our ideals and betray our visions. Confounding righteousness with our own beliefs, confusing the tangible and material with the ideal and the ineffable, finally we come to accept as true and real a world of phantoms and mirages generated by our self-deception. Thus, in the novel we see fundamentalist Christians mistaking metaphor for fact, and acting upon their narrow, literalist interpretations of scripture by engaging in a conspiracy to destroy what they regard as the heathen shrines of the Moslems and in their place to rebuild the Temple of the Almighty in Jerusalem. Of a like cast of mind are the Israeli politicians, Avram Lind and Naphtali Shaviv, who self-importantly and self-servingly identify the fate of the nation of Israel with the status of their own political careers; the ultra-Zionist settlers in the Gaza with their notions of divine sanction for their aggressive, acquisitive endeavors; and all the various fanatical factions of the Palestinians in their vengeful self-righteousness, mindlessly prosecuting their *jihad*, or holy war.

In a similar manner, drugs become for many characters a surrogate for or a counterfeit of desirable mental states or genuine spiritual experiences. Numerous kinds of drugs are consumed by the various figures in the novel, each type of drug reflecting the particular need of the user. Nuala has her energizing, aphrodisiac khat; Lucas his alcohol and hashish and later his Prozac. Sonia has—until she renounces them—her pain pills "to promote inner harmony and self-fulfillment" (20), while De Kuff has—until he forsakes its use—his antidepressive, mind-stabilizing lithium. Razz reserves for himself his soul-cushioning, care-soothing heroin, while to his fellow cultists he surreptitiously dispenses a vision-inducing hallucinogenic. In every instance the fundamental error inherent in the use of drugs is that of mistaking the spurious for the genuine. And in nearly every instance the particular user's original purpose and direction becomes deflected through the habitual use of a drug. The shortcut becomes a sidetrack. Like religious or political obsession, drugs in the novel constitute a forgery and falsification of human experience, a failure of perception and imagination.

Challenging the diversity of error in the world are those few figures in *Damascus Gate* who discover and exercise the faculty of spiritual perception—the recognition of a reality, intangible and invisible, which transcends the sphere of our ordinary, practical life. Take, for example, Father Herzog, a man of poise and integrity, uncompromising in his faith, unobstructed by fear or self-protection. Or De Kuff, who in his moments of clarity upholds the unity of truth and affirms the primacy of spiritual reality, and, accordingly, the primacy of things symbolized over their symbols.

De Kuff affirms vision and imagination against the errors of the material-minded and the literal-minded, who have in his view mis-identified the Holy Land of Israel with an actual geographical locality, who have confused the struggle for righteousness and against evil with actual armed conflict, and who have conceived of redemption as an immanent historical event. "No land is holy," De Kuff asserts, "All earth is exile. The redemption is in the mind . . . The redemption is unarmed. The battle is with the self. The land is in the heart" (400).

Sonia arrives at similar insights. For her, as for De Kuff, the realm of the spirit is an immutable truth of which material reality partakes in only a much adulterated fashion. Spirit to her is primary, the physical world inferior and subordinate, a dim reflection of the spiritual world. Sonia, too, understands that words and images are symbols, vehicles of understanding, and are not to be apprehended merely in terms of their explicit references to objects or phenomena in the material world. Thus, for her the true *jihad* is not that which Hamas or the dispossessed Palestinians call *jihad* but is, instead, the struggle between light and darkness, between self and Self, that must take place in each human mind and spirit, or, as she calls it, "the struggle without weapons" (372). And, like De Kuff, Sonia perceives that attempts to rebuild the Temple in Jerusalem are hopelessly misguided and utterly futile, for the true Temple can only be built within: "The Temple has to be in the heart. When everybody builds it there, maybe then they can think about Beautiful Gates and the Holy of Holies" (493).

I have stated that *Damascus Gate* is not concerned with proposing new resolutions or final answers to the metaphysical issues that occupy many of the figures in the novel, and that constitute so impelling a motive for their actions. But with regard to these same spiritual questions, does the text itself express a position? No metaphysical views are set forth directly in the text by the narrator, nor can any single figure in the work be regarded as being the author's spokesman; nonetheless, such views are implied in the novel. Implicitly, the novel suggests that amid all the chaos and violence, the fission and division, the errancy and ignorance of human life in the world, a process of evolutionary development may be discerned, a principle of teleological dynamism may be operative.

Take, for example, the interior movement of the figures depicted in *Damascus Gate*. A common denominator of the main characters in the novel is their development—in terms of self-realization and spiritual apprehension—from potentiality to actuality. Each of the central figures undergoes a process of inner growth and refinement, each moving closer to personal insight and spiritual perception and comprehension, each moving toward the realization of his or her inherent inner form, each striving to manifest that form.

In the case of Raziel and De Kuff, the fullest accomplishment of their latent spiritual identities takes place only moments before their deaths. In contrast, Sonia's spiritual growth is of a more even and equable pace, and of a stronger and more stable constitution; while Lucas, in the end, by recognizing and accepting the deep-rooted, ineradicable character of his hunger for a redemptive, unitary vision may at least be said to have made a beginning, to have taken a first but crucial step toward the fulfillment of his spiritual aspiration.

An implicit spiritual perspective may be found also in the novel's depiction of the world of persons, places, and things as possessing a double aspect, a dual nature—one element or mode of which is hidden and latent, the other of which is manifest and apparent; one aspect of which is of higher value and quality, the other inferior.

Thus, in the novel, we are made aware of the dual nature of numbers, their merely practical application in mundane human affairs, and their value as a mode of mystical knowledge. A similar duality of nature can be seen in the letters of the alphabet, which may be employed for purposes pragmatic or occult. Symbols themselves may be dual in character; snakes and sparrows in the novel suggest both the condition of spiritual darkness and the state of ultimate spiritual fulfillment.

Human institutions likewise partake of the essential duality of created things. Religion is at once a divisive force and a vehicle of mystical transcendence. The city of Jerusalem is both a venal, banal, polluted, and overcrowded Middle Eastern metropolis, a mecca for fanatics and extremists of every stripe, and "the center of the world, where earth touches heaven . . . where the destiny of man was written . . . Where what was above met what was below, where that which was before met that which was to come" (484).

Individuals in the novel are no less divided in character. Dr. Purchas Obermann is both a dedicated healer of the human psyche and an inveterate womanizer. Linda Eriksen is a biblical scholar and a Christian missionary, irremediably promiscuous and a treacherous spy. Ian Fotheringill is both a ruthless, amoral mercenary and a sensitive and temperamental *haute cuisine* chef. Raziel Melker is at once a manipulator and a mystic; De Kuff both manic-depressive and messianic. In every instance, flawed wills and minds, trivial and ignoble motives coexist with higher impulses and worthier purposes.

The duality of the world is given concise, symbolic representation in a minor event that occurs near the end of the novel when Lucas goes diving in the Red Sea. Above the surface of the water is a field of ragged coral bleached by the harsh light of the desert sun, while below the water is a visionary landscape of intense colors and animated architectures, so ravishingly lovely that Lucas perceives it as representing a "counterpart of the Kotel, the wall of a temple to the Lord of Creation" (496). Yet, even in this realm of bright beauty, there may be seen in the depths of the water, "far, far below," the dun colors of prowling hammerhead sharks. Even at its most idyllic and Edenic, then, the created world retains its essential duality. But the exquisite and transporting loveliness of the natural world can call to mind the ultimate source of the Beautiful of which natural beauty is but a reflection. Metaphoric proof of this is furnished when during his dive, Lucas reflects that the delicate, comely creatures of the coral wall conduce "to remind you that out across the blue infinity lay the Indian Ocean, the Indies" (496).

Damascus Gate depicts the world as a place of contending forces whose ultimate symbols are light and darkness. These forces express themselves in the dual nature of the created world, and the conflict of these forces constitutes the necessary condition for the process of spiritual evolution, the slow growth of the "seeds of light scattered in darkness" (13). This process ends in liberation from the realm of multiplicity, restriction and darkness (the temporal, material world), and the restoration of the primal, pristine state of Light Eternal.

The novel, arguing that this process of becoming takes place in the world, gives evidence of certain indwelling urges and irrepressible impulses in the human mind and spirit, together with such glimpses and intimations of the eternal or the divine as may be gleaned by each individual. There is, for example, in our sullied, blighted world of selfishness and depravity, the mystery of the persistence of qualities of nobility, strength, sympathy, compassion, mercy and love, and of the human capacity for repentance and regeneration. Also mysteriously present in the human heart is an appetite for beauty and the creative expression of this inherent craving in arts such as music and poetry—arts that provoke our hope and yearning and that elevate our spirits with their evocations of transcendent realms of being.

The driving craving for freedom also suggests these impulses for growth, unfolding, and fulfillment. At a temporal, material level, this urge expresses itself in the desire to transcend the human condition, to establish political freedom and social justice. At a spiritual level, this same urge is expressed in the desire to transcend the human condition, to escape from time and matter, to achieve redemption, salvation. In this sense, the political activists Nuala and Rashid, and the mystics Raziel and De Kuff, alike are motivated by the same essential impulse. In their lives the same teleological energy is given expression in different ways, brought to bear upon different aspects of the same fundamental condition: human unfreedom, all that impedes true being, both external coercion and constraint, and the prison of self-conscious selfhood.

Thus, our inherent form, our latent identity—both as individuals and as a race—is of freedom of being; that is the motive, the potential that imparts to our lives their motion and their course; that is the force that urges us forward and onward. And thus human history is the record of our individual and collective striving to manifest that form, to realize that identity in a world ruled by the constricting forces of necessity; it is the chronicle of the dead ends and false starts, the failures and betrayals, the sudden advances and slow progress of our journey toward that goal. This metaphysic, drawn from the pre-Socratic philosophers, from Neoplatonism, and from modern Existentialism, constitutes the ultimate frame of reference according to which the persons and the events presented in *Damascus Gate* may be interpreted, the perspective from which the interactions of the personal, the historical and the spiritual are seen as mutually reacting aspects of a sole, purposive process, conducing toward a single, ultimate end.

This underlying system of principles informing and sustaining the external configuration of characters and events in *Damascus Gate* forms the final elaboration of the spiritual, psychological and socio-political themes of the author's earlier work. In *Damascus Gate* the recurrent relationships and issues of Stone's previous novels culminate in a coherent, comprehensive pattern, a design which could even be said to illuminate the works that precede it. In a similar manner, the numerous resonances and parallels of *Damascus Gate* with specific figures and motifs characteristic of the author's earlier work create in the mind of the reader who is familiar with Stone's writing, not a sense of self-referentiality of the author or the oeuvre, but rather a sense of convergence and concentration of theme, a sense of the unity and growth of Stone's vision as an author.

Scattered throughout *Damascus Gate* are moments of incongruous and almost outrageous humor that mitigate the feeling of menace generated by the plot action and the sense of solemnity that derives from the spiritual theme of the novel. But apart from their dramatic function, such instances also express an apprehension of comedy that is inherent not only in the human condition but also in the very nature and character of the world. The comic aspect of the novel points out the essential ambiguity of the world, which together with its rather obvious attributes of pathos and tragedy, and its destructive and entropic dimensions, seems also to possess, disconcertingly and intriguingly, a certain sportive propensity for the improbable and the ludicrous, a quality of playfulness.

CHAPTER EIGHT

Short Fiction: *Bear and His Daughter*

Robert Stone, it would seem, generally prefers to work on a larger scale than that afforded by the short story (even his novels tend to be large), and so over a period of more than thirty years, he has published no more than seven works of short fiction. These stories were recently collected in a volume titled *Bear and His Daughter*.[1] Within the limitations inherent in the short story, Stone creates what seem almost to be compressed novels, compact, complex, and potent in their control, their language precise and resonant, worked to a cutting edge. Imbued with Stone's unsparing, unwavering eye, imbued with his struggling spirituality, these distinguished stories make up an important part of the author's body of work.

"Porque No Tiene, Porque Le Falta" is the earliest of Stone's published short stories, dating from 1969. The title and the epigraph of the story (both taken from the Mexican song "La Cucaracha") suggest the absence of a necessary quality without which, as in the song, one cannot "travel on." In the context of the story, this vital and essential quality is the capacity for creative courage, those attributes of venturesomeness, imagination, humor, and verve that enable one not only to remain undaunted and undamaged by the annoyances, disappointments, cares, and terrors of everyday life, but to prevail over them, transforming them into romantic, heroic adventure.

The story, which takes place in Mexico, opens with images of danger and evil: scorpions on the beach, a manta in the bay, and the ominous presence of the "Sinister Pancho Pillow" in a villa on the headland. The low, dark clouds of an approaching thunderstorm add an element of foreboding to the already tense atmosphere of the story.

The protagonist of the story, an American poet named Fletch, suffers from a nameless malaise which expresses itself in sensations of physical coldness and in "an odd passion for constancy" (50). Fletch wants conditions, including even those of light and weather, to remain just as they are at the present moment; any kind of change causes him to feel uneasy. At the same time, he seems curiously aloof, detached, "dispassionate" (51). He is unable to relieve his indefinite sense of ill-being and his incipient fear either by means of alcohol or marijuana.

The antithesis of Fletch's dispirited desire for constancy and security, and his lassitude and general dismay, are Fletch's acquaintances and fellow Americans, Fencer and Willie Wings. As their names suggest, Fencer and Wings playfully resist or transcend life's adversities. In contrast to Fletch, they are energetic and high-spirited, possessing genial confidence, good humor, and a sort of jaunty and audacious grace. From the very moment of the arrival of Fencer and Wings at Fletch's house, there is an immediate lack of rapport and a clash of sensibilities between them and Fletch. This is especially true of Willie Wings, who lets it be known that he regards with disfavor "literary" types, among whom he is inclined to number Fletch. To be "literary," according to Wings's implied definition of the term, is to possess false consciousness, to be in a negative state wherein one mistakenly values abstraction over experience and imagination; it is to lack awareness and responsiveness.

As the three men set out together on a journey by car to the summit of a nearby volcano, the tension mounts mile by mile. Within Fletch there is an ever-growing fear, reaching a state of paranoid panic, that his companions mean to do him harm. He determines to escape from them but in the meantime can only huddle and crouch in dread in the back seat, stare dully at the landscape, and respond with bored hostility to Wings's conversation.

Addressing himself specifically to Fletch, Wings recounts an incident—a recollection from the days of his youth or perhaps a complete fabrication—that serves as a parable of the kind of inventiveness and spiritedness necessary to counteract the ever-menacing, dominion-seeking forces of negativity. Wings relates the story of how once he witnessed through a hole in the wall a man who was masturbating in a hotel room—ordinarily, if such a sight were ordinary, a most depressing, unedifying spectacle. Yet by the sheer energy and panache with which the man applied himself to his set purpose, it achieved a sort of splendidness, a kind of poetry, or as Wings expresses it: "all by himself in that there hotel room *he wailed*. He set his consciousness on fire!" (62). Clearly, Wings's purpose in telling the story is to inspire Fletch, to hearten him and incite him to bring his own capacities as a poet to bear upon his present wretched condition.

Fletch, however, is quite unmoved by Wings's parable, and he remains preoccupied with schemes of escaping from the car and from the company of Fencer and Wings. At both a physical-geographical and a metaphysical level, both externally and internally, we may say, Fletch resists ascent: he does not wish to ascend the mountain with Fencer and Wings, and he resolutely refuses either to be impressed by or to participate in the mystical perspectives and reflections of his two companions.

The sudden appearance of the Sinister Pancho Pillow foils Fletch's first attempt to escape, and contributes an additional element of tension to the story. Pancho, according to Fencer and Wings, is a figure of mythic proportion, a fearful and baleful presence. Not only is he the devisor of various, nefarious plots and the perpetrator of unspeakable acts, but he is also the very embodiment of predatory, parasitic, negative energy.

Fletch's successful flight from Fencer and Wings, commencing at dusk as they approach the summit of the volcano, precipitates in him a dramatic reversal of mood and outlook. From his earlier state of depression and fear, Fletch now experiences joy, and—despite the discomforts and perils that he faces in his new situation, including the cold of the desert night, the danger of falling in the darkness, the presence of snakes, Gila monsters and other poisonous or hostile creatures—he now feels "completely unafraid" (71). In contrast, too, to his earlier huddling and crouching in the car, he now moves with "animal grace" (72) down slopes and steep trails illuminated only by flashes of lightning and the light of the moon. And, in place of the dullness, passivity, and indifference toward scenery and surroundings that he exhibited during the journey from the coast to the volcano, Fletch now feels a powerful sense of sharpened and strengthened perception.

Arriving at the mountain town of Corbera at around the hour of midnight, Fletch feels quite sufficiently self-possessed and "at peace with the world" (74), enough so to venture an encounter with Pancho Pillow and his associates, and then, finding their company disagreeable, he deftly, artfully effects an act of escape and evasion.

A final trial of his newfound powers and poise awaits Fletch upon his return at dawn to his house, where he discovers his wife, Marge, and Fencer in the act of making love. Here, too, Fletch displays exemplary equanimity, quietly observing and then discreetly departing without allowing his presence to become known: "It took him nearly five minutes to crawl out; a masterpiece of silence" (79).

His night journey at an end, Fletch is now able to engage with Willie Wings in the kind of banter that betokens a man of spirit. Wings, for his part, acknowledges approvingly the qualities of mettle and wit that Fletch now manifests: "Fletch, babe, I had you wrong, brother. You really are a poet" (80).

The story affirms that grace is available to us, we can call forth and sometimes sustain a mode of imaginative awareness, which can lift us—momentarily at least—above the confusions and contingencies, the perturbations and misfortunes, the banalities and insipidity of quotidian existence, and which can perhaps also impart to us intimations of a larger, more profound experience of reality.

The suggestion that there exist other supernatural systems of correlation and causality, other occult dimensions and levels of reality, is conveyed in the story through certain mysterious resonances and synchronicities, through confluent events rich in elusive significance and enigmatic implication. Such events include, for example, the sudden appearance of Sinister Pancho Pillow at the very moment that Fletch is attempting to alight from Fencer's car (an occurrence viewed by Fencer and Wings as being a prime example of pure psychic causation, as if dread and fear somehow attract their ultimate fulfillment); Fletch's sense of intimate connectedness with the incidence of lightning and the power failures in Corbera, and the subsequent presence in La Florida bar of the electric shock machine with its painted emblem of "a clenched fist emitting bolts of lightning" (73); the Mexican truck driver's drunken song about the seduction of a man's wife by his friend, which prefigures or coincides with Marge's infidelity with Fencer; and Willie Wings's anecdote concerning voyeurism that anticipates Fletch's subsequent assumption of a similar role. These correspondences, affinities, links, and parallels imply purposes and designs conceived at other levels of the psyche, principles operative at other strata of reality.

"Porque No Tiene, Porque Le Falta" is an original and effective mixture of stylistic elements. It is tense and tight, precisely observed, yet hallucinated, and shot through with quirky humor. Thematically, the story stakes out the author's claim on those frontier territories of experience, those corners and margins of consciousness where terror contends with revelation, destruction with renewal.

Stone's next short story, "Aquarius Obscured," published in 1975, complements the foregoing story. Both take place during the same era and in the same milieu, that of the counterculture of the late 1960s and early 1970s, and both focus their narratives around persons whose minds are afflicted with delusion. If the former story suggests a degree of sympathy for certain personal styles and animating ideas of the counterculture, the latter represents a witty commentary on the follies and excesses of the movement.

The main character of the story is a young woman named Alison who lives in a house in San Francisco with her little daughter, Io, and a man named Big Gene. Big Gene is a junkie, and Alison, who is by education an astronomer, is a former topless dancer and an occasional user of amphetamines.

The opening paragraphs describing Big Gene's actions strike the key note of the story. Gene has been unmanned and dehumanized by dope, reduced by opiates to a state of infantilism, solipsism, and utter indifference to everything that does not serve his need for junk. He is completely feckless, selfish, and self-deluded, boasting to Alison of having "control" (154) when clearly that is the very attribute he most acutely lacks. Like some form of psychic parasite, drugs have drained from him all will and vigor and left only immutable lethargy and inertia.

Alison seems at first to be the opposite of Big Gene. She is exasperated by his apathy and irresponsibility, and frightened by the dangerous deterioration of their lives:

> The scene was crumbling. Strong men had folded like
> stage flats, legality and common sense had fled. Cere-
> bration flickered. (154)

It is Alison whose work has supported them, and she who must look after both Io and Big Gene's dog. And now she feels herself nearing the end of her tether. The question she poses to her little daughter— "What'll we do?" (155)—is asked in genuine perplexity. In order to sustain her genial spirits in the execution of her responsibilities, in order that her tasks and burdens might be "more gracefully endured" (156), Alison consumes at times prodigious quantities of ampheta- mine.

A handful of such illicitly manufactured pills ingested just prior to taking her daughter Io on a visit to the aquarium precipitates the events of the story. Increasingly under the influence of the pills, Ali- son, guiding her daughter among the luminous tanks of fishes, at last stands before the tank of a lone dolphin and enters into telepathic communication with him.

Alison's conversation with the dolphin exposes all the trendy clichés of thought and feeling with which she has allowed herself to become imbued, all of the crude and credulous, fatuous and half-baked, simplistic and categorical opinions that so often passed for penetrating insights in certain milieus during the sixties. In a sense, the exchange between the dolphin and Alison recapitulates in miniature the evolution of the ideological and metaphysical attitudes of the counterculture.

Significantly, it all begins as a vague dream. On the night before her trip to the aquarium with Io, Alison has had a deeply affecting, though only dimly recollected dream in which she was somehow miraculously delivered from the confusion and anxiety of life in the world and "carried into a presence before which things had been resolved" (159). At the aquarium the following day in her state of amphetamine-induced psychosis, Alison partly recalls the dream and believes that the lone dolphin in the tank, in fact, embodies that resolving presence, and that she has been summoned by him.

In the beginning of their dialogue, the dolphin engages Alison's guilty, self-apologetic sympathy for his being, as it were, a member of an oppressed minority. She expresses moral indignation on his behalf and on behalf of his species, self-righteously denies any complicity in the oppression of dolphins, and ends by declaring to him her love and her willingness to serve in his cause.

The scene parallels and parodies the sort of self-abasing worship on the part of many New Leftists for self-styled revolutionary African Americans or for Third World peoples. At the same time, it parallels and parodies the kind of unreflective devotion, the surrender of ego and intellect, in which many hippies indulged in the veneration of their particular self-proclaimed cult messiah or guru. The same con-man patter fits the solicitation of either ideological or metaphysical commitment:

> "As your perception changes," the porpoise told her,
> "many things will seem strange and unfamiliar. You
> must unlearn old structures of thought that have been
> forced on you. Much faith, much resolution will be
> required." (163)

Alison is moved to ardor by the dolphin's rhetorical flights, seduced
by his subtle flattery of her as being a carefully chosen and vital
instrument of a noble cause, a comrade-in-arms in a just and histori-
cally momentous struggle. She immediately attempts to instill in
herself discipline and a martial spirit, and begins to practice rigorous
self-criticism.

The dolphin's impassioned oratory reaches a frenzy of aggressive animosity worthy of Joseph Goebbels, calling for the domina-
tion of the world by the "superior species," the dolphins, and the
eradication of the "weak and decadent" humanity by means of a
"final solution" (165), and glorifying the purifying effect of merciless, vengeful violence. Only then does Alison begin to draw back
and to question the character of the cause to which she has so hastily
and so whole-heartedly pledged herself.

Alison's dawning disillusionment with the porpoise's program
is immediately countered from his side with an abrupt change of
rhetorical strategy as he shifts into a Charles Manson-like style of
speaking: slangy, pseudo-mystical, and sleazy-sophistical, a hippie
con. But by this point Alison's critical faculties are engaged and she
emphatically rejects the whole rigmarole. As in Lewis Carroll's
Alice's Adventures in Wonderland, to which Stone's story bears a
glancing likeness, the heroine's recognition of the insubstantiality
of her interlocutor causes his sudden collapse into impotence and

insignificance. And, as in Lewis Carroll's tale, the whole conversation between Alison and the dolphin has, of course, taken place only within the imagination of the female protagonist.

Her prolonged reverie or auditory hallucination now ended, Alison returns to conventional reality, bearing with her a certain residual paranoia. Approached by a friendly young man who is obviously attracted to her, she conceives the suspicion that he somehow— perhaps by some species of ventriloquism—was involved in deceiving her into believing that she was actually conversing with the dolphin. Either as an act of reprisal or perhaps quite gratuitously, Alison contrives to steal from the young man two very expensive camera lenses, then drives him away from her with a stream of insults and abuse. The incident confirms the chronic agitation and tumult of her mind.

Outside of the museum, the sunlit day has disappeared; dusk is approaching and it is becoming cold and foggy. The mood seems somber now, even ominous. Alison's admission to her child of her deluded condition, echoing the earlier occasion on which she sought advice from her daughter, seems more a statement of resignation than of contrition or resolution.

As suggested above, the progress of Alison's day—from her early morning dream of deliverance, to her drug-deluded encounter with the dolphin and all of the ensuing zealous dedication to extremes of perceptual and ideological change, to her subsequent disillusionment, and her return to a cold and foggy world—seem to repeat in brief the unfolding of the counterculture from its early heady idealism in the mid-1960s, through its later excesses and imbecility, to its dissipation during the early years of the 1970s. The character of Alison embodies certain psychological, moral, and intellectual flaws inherent in the movement that caused its relatively rapid deterioration.

At the same time, though, it is worth noting that Alison does ultimately prove to possess sufficient good sense and strength of character to resist the temptations of authoritarianism. Considered in this
manner, the story represents a trenchant satire on the counterculture
and a comic epitaph commemorating its demise.

If a defect of the era of the mid-1960s to the early 1970s was
its excessive and facile sense of optimism and millennial anticipa-
tion, its disposition to embrace uncritically various extreme causes
and obscure creeds, its specious and often misdirected idealism, then
surely during the decades that have followed we have had cause to
regret an inclination of precisely the opposite character: a paucity of
hope, a dearth of readiness to believe and to strive. This darker,
starker mood of the closing decades of the twentieth century is
vividly evoked in two stories by Stone, "Under the Pitons" and
"Helping."

"Under the Pitons," a harsh and hard-boiled tale of drug smuggling in the Caribbean, is a contemporary counterpart to "Aquarius
Obscured." In contradistinction to the earnest, gullible dopers of the
sixties, people of the nineties, as depicted by Stone, are devoid of
metaphysical or ideological inclinations, their bent being inherently
hedonistic, their aims mercenary. But if their orientation is more
practical and their motivation more materialistic than those of their
counterculture predecessors, their behavior is no less dangerously
deluded.

"Under the Pitons" concerns the fate of four young amateur
smugglers in a rented boat, running a load of marijuana and cocaine
from Saint Vincent to Martinique. For each of the four—two cooks,
a waitress, and an ex-model—the venture is their first such under-
taking, and accordingly they have underestimated the many perils of

such an enterprise. Even the buy itself is not without alarming incident, and now before completing the deal and collecting their profits, the smugglers must hazard the winds and tides, the currents and coral reefs, the pirates and informers, the police, the customs, the coast guard, and the resources of the Drug Enforcement Agency.

Yet more perilous still than all of the tangible external risks they face are the potentials for suspicion and violence among themselves: drug-induced paranoia, murderous anger born of mutual mistrust, self-defensive slaughter undertaken to forestall anticipated hostile action by others. And, finally, no less a danger than any of the foregoing, there is the constant possibility of making an irreversible, irremediable error, performing a wrong action—proceeding from faulty judgment, from ignorance or inattention—that can have the most desperate consequences. As one of the smugglers reflects: "there were a thousand dark possibilities on that awful ocean" (141).

The disastrous end of the four young smugglers' enterprise is foreshadowed in the story's opening incident when in the darkness of night on the ocean their boat very nearly collides with a barge being towed by a tug. The barge is unlit, silent, its towline submerged. Regarded in a metaphoric sense, the barge, "a big, black homicidal juggernaut" (122), is the very prototype of catastrophe: unforeseen, unapparent, undetected, and swift and devastating in its impact. Moreover, in this instance, the boat's pilot, an Irishman named Liam Blessington, is "stoned at the wheel" (122). In an environment and under circumstances where there is so little margin for error, the use of drugs can only be disadvantageous. Through sheer good luck, disaster is on this occasion averted, but the incident is ominous.

Similarly ominous is the later incident when Blessington and another of the smugglers, an American woman named Gillian,

spontaneously, perhaps even unconsciously, conspire to kill one of
their partners, Freycinet, a tough, domineering, drug-crazed French-
man who is the prime mover of their enterprise. The true nature of
their actions and intentions is unclear even to Blessington and
Gillian. After the event, Gillian asks, "Hey, what were you gonna do
back there, Liam? Deep-six him?" To which Blessington can only
reply, "I honestly don't know" (137). Like the submerged towline of
the unlit barge, there are submerged in the darkness of the mind dangerous impulses, swift and obscure, and utterly devastating in their
consequences. Clearly, there are more ways than one in which to be
"stoned at the wheel."

In a sense, the smugglers' ketch is a contemporary version of
the medieval image of the *Narrenschiff*, or ship of fools, an allegorical representation of the voyage of human life and of the vices, frailties, and vanities that can lead to grounding, foundering, ruin, and
death. Viewed in this perspective, the small world of the smugglers'
boat—a fragile realm of tentative, tenuous order upon vast, deep,
and dangerous seas—corresponds to the world we all inhabit. Similarly, the condition in which they live, under the constant threat of
chaos from without and within, is no more than an intensification of
the situation in which we all are caught, and their dreams and their
weaknesses are but reflections of our own. The tale is thus a cautionary one, implicitly urging us to remain vigilant and to exercise
restraining and directing influence upon our thoughts and actions,
and to be mindful of our true course.

Ultimately, a series of errors of judgment and lapses of attention by the smugglers leads to their undoing. Both the degree of their
complicity in the fateful loss of their boat and their separate fates
immediately after the event reflect the nature of their individual

characters. Freycinet precipitates the disaster by his reckless and aggressive behavior. His girlfriend, Marie, is the victim of her naive imperceptiveness. Significantly, both Freycinet and Marie attempt repeatedly and in vain to regain control of the drifting boat, striving desperately to repossess the stable, secure realm from which their heedlessness has forever barred them, clinging single-mindedly and futilely to their illusions. More realistic in her reaction to the catastrophic loss of the boat, Gillian succumbs to the overdrafts drug use has made upon her physical strength and surrenders to her nihilistic indifference. Blessington survives because he is at last able to exercise sound judgment, to summon self-control, and perhaps also because, alone among the smugglers, he possesses both the capacity to hope and the humility to believe.

The protagonist of "Helping," Elliot, struggles between the attitudes embodied by Gillian and Blessington, between nihilism and belief. Elliot is a combat veteran of the Vietnam War for whom the experience of wartime violence and terror was deeply disturbing and profoundly unsettling to his mind and emotions. In the nearly twenty years that have passed since the war, Elliot has earned a master's degree in social work, has married, and has pursued a career as a counselor for veterans at the state hospital, but at the same time, he has also been an ungovernable alcoholic and has spent time in jail.

As the story opens, Elliot has been attending meetings of Alcoholics Anonymous faithfully for fifteen months and has in that time successfully resisted the impulse to drink. But his will to resist is undermined by two events: a trip to Boston on a dreary and desolate November afternoon, and a few months later a session at the state hospital with a client who reawakens Elliot's dormant trauma.

Elliot's compulsive drinking is but one manifestation of the powerful destructive urges that exist in opposition to his conscious purposes. These negative energies express themselves as frustration and despair, as terror and anger, in the urge to do violence, and in the attraction of oblivion, the desire to be relieved finally and forever of the burden of consciousness. Struggling against such dark, ruinous impulses are Elliot's desire for beauty and order, his half-thwarted tenderness and compassion, and his profound but unavowed wish for redemption.

During the approximately eighteen hours during which the story takes place, Elliot battles against erosion of will and loss of purpose, and his precipitous decline into drunken, angry, violent behavior, but at a crucial moment, he succeeds in summoning sufficient moral strength to resist being overwhelmed by his destructive impulses, after which point he begins to turn once again toward feelings of sympathy and contrition.

The immediate cause of Elliot's malaise and the subsequent collapse of his self-control is an image of dream and memory, the image of a baleful black sky. First described to Elliot by one of his clients who dreams it recurrently, the image resonates in Elliot's mind, representing to him a potent compression of his war experience:

> He was looking up at a sky that was black, filled with smoke-swollen clouds, lit with fires, damped with blood and rain. (87)

Elliot is deeply disturbed by the image and is unable to drive it from his mind; it remains with him through the day, causing him to become increasingly nervous and edgy. That evening, to dispel its persistent influence, he begins to drink. The image of the black sky reanimates Elliot's suppressed war trauma, evoking within him the sensation of eerie terror associated with imminent violence and the proximity of death. In a deeper sense, the black sky is a metaphor for a universe without design or purpose, without meaning or mercy, a world of viciousness, of cruelty, and of savagery only.

Ironically, in his urgency to escape the dreaded presence of the black sky, Elliot only summons it forth all the more palpably. His drinking causes him to create about himself a world of disorder and violence—mocking and taunting his gentle wife, provoking a dangerous confrontation with a loathsome young man named Vopotik and his biker friends, then arming himself and sitting in the darkness in a state of rage waiting for the enemy to appear. By his actions, Elliot makes of the image of the black sky a prophecy to be brought to fulfillment, rather than a nightmare to be resisted. In this regard, the quotation from Euripedes' *Medea* recalled by Elliot in his drunkenness is particularly appropriate: "The gods and I went mad together and made things as they are" (98).

The external weather of the story parallels Elliot's inward weather, serving as a metaphoric externalization of his psychic condition. The "cold and lonely" (83) November streets of Boston with their gutters filled with dead leaves correlate to Elliot's interior desolation. The gathering snow storm and the frozen cold that "closes over him" (92) correspond to and are emblematic of his gathering anger and his cold ruinous fury. The motif of cold is closely associated in the story with imagery of darkness—the darkening day, the night—suggesting the negative, destructive forces latent in Elliot.

Elliot's despair and anger are provoked not merely by his memories of the war but by his perception that the condition of warfare is universal—that life is a grim and vicious contest of each against all, and nature and humanity are wantonly and ruthlessly cruel. The image early in the story of Elliot lying sleepless in his bed on frozen winter nights, listening to the baying of packs of dogs running down starveling deer in the snow, suggests a Hobbesian universe of "nature red in tooth and claw." The incident of the deer prefigures and resonates with the terrible revelation later in the story that the three-year-old child of the low-life, white-trash couple with the surname Vopotik is being slowly beaten to death by his malicious, demented parents. The boy's father is a biker, and like the dogs that run down deer, we are told that "They travel in packs" (108). Elliot does not view the Vopotik's depraved behavior as being by any means exceptional or uncommon in the world. Helpless innocence is ever destroyed by the brutal and the vicious. As Elliot remarks to his wife apropos of the vileness of the Vopotiks, "You go messing into anybody's life, that's what you'll find" (104).

Candace Music and Elliot's wife, Grace, hold perceptions and perspectives opposite in character to the bleak, fatalistic views held by Elliot. Candace is a librarian and "a Quaker of socialist principles" (92), a gentle and generous-spirited woman whose library is an oasis of human dignity and harmony, providing refuge to young and old, rich and poor alike. Formerly, she and Elliot worked together at rendering some fragments of Sophocles into English verse, a task undertaken for simple love of beauty. Candace Music embodies qualities of tolerance and compassion, together with a quiet but confirmed optimism. Unlike Elliot, she possesses values and ideals which she cherishes, and beliefs and convictions which she strives to realize in the world.

Grace, too, possesses a stubborn resolve of purpose in the furtherance of her duties as a lawyer for the state department of welfare and as a wife. On the evening the story takes place, Grace is depressed about having lost her court case to have the Vopotik child removed from his parents, and shocked and saddened by Elliot's unexpected defection to alcoholic anarchy. She indulges herself in questioning the ultimate utility of caring about and attempting to help others. She even permits herself a little anodyne in the form of a couple of shots of Elliot's whiskey. But such is her strength of character and the firmness of her ideals that it is clear that she will not abandon her patient efforts to bring a little order and justice to the world, to uphold mercy, and to offer succor to those in misery and distress. Unlike Elliot, Grace is animated by a sort of dogged and sober meliorism, deriving ultimately perhaps from her strong religious convictions; and unlike Elliot, Grace is reduced to a despondency—momentary only—not by her own pain but by the pain of others.

Aside from being persons in their own right, and constituting an alternative in the story to Elliot's beliefs and behavior, Candace Music and Grace (surely their names are significant) also represent latent tendencies within Elliot and potentials he has not realized. Accordingly, Elliot may be attracted to Candace Music and Grace precisely because they personify the very qualities that he so acutely lacks and desperately longs to possess: belief, poise, compassion, and a disposition to act according to principles, in spite of adversities and reversals.

Throughout the story, Elliot reveals his self-dividedness and makes repeated efforts to deny, suppress, or evade acknowledgment both of his own pain and of his capacity for feeling compassion for the pain of others. In order to dissemble from others the true nature and extent of the emotional and mental wounds of the war, Elliot has contrived to control his anguish by a pretense of ease in talking about Vietnam, and by the careful preparation of "little discourses and picaresque anecdotes to recite on demand" (93). When such ruses fail on occasion, as in the case of Candace Music who sees through Eliot's defensive pretenses, then Elliot feels "great secret distress" (93), and retreats and withdraws, rather than confronting or being confronted with his condition.

Another of Elliot's strategies to deflect the pain—both within and without him—is his ironic manner and his bitter wit, which is especially apparent in his conversations with Grace. When her questions are too direct, too pointed, or when the incidents that she recounts are too distressing, too disturbing to him (as, for example, that concerning the broken fingers of the three-year-old Vopotik child), then he deftly parries them by means of some sardonic remark.

To avoid conceding even to himself his afflicted psychic state and his susceptibility to feelings of shame and self-pity, Elliot also rigorously maintains inward composure and strictly censors his most tender impulses. At one point of the story, while waiting for Vopotik, sitting armed and angry in the darkness, Elliot begins suddenly to weep, but regarding his tears as a weakness, as "childish and excremental," he immediately "stifle[s] whatever it was that had started them" (110). Similarly, just after he has resisted the impulse to kill his neighbor, Loyall Anderson, and has also experienced relief at having missed the pheasant at which he shot, Elliot acknowledges to himself that in truth he wishes "no harm to any creature," and he begins to feel "fond and sorry for himself" (115). But "As soon as

he grew aware of the emotion he was indulging, he suppressed it"
(115).

Yet in spite of Elliot's clever evasions and willful denials of his
own inward pain and vulnerability, and despite his attempts to anes-
thetize himself with alcohol, irony, and anger against such knowledge and against real recognition of the suffering of others, he is at
last compelled in dramatic fashion to acknowledge his pity and his
need. The decisive moment for Eliot occurs during his early morning encounter with Loyall Anderson. Dehumanized by his ski mask
and insufferable in his sanctimonious self-assurance, Anderson comes
within a hair's breadth of being killed by Elliot. Elliot has gone so
far as to remove the safety from his shotgun in preparation for firing
it at Anderson, when suddenly he experiences a change of heart.

Elliot's rambling, incoherent, threatening talk inspires fear in
Anderson, and it is this fear manifest in Anderson's voice and manner that saves his life, for this fear arouses pity in Eliot since he is
himself so very thoroughly acquainted with fear. Quite abruptly,
Anderson is transformed in Elliot's perception from arrogant, complacent, sententious enemy into pitiful, fearful fellow human.

After his encounter with Anderson, and the release of tension
caused by shooting at and missing the pheasant, Elliot experiences a
moment of clarity and insight as he sees his wife standing at the bedroom window of their home looking out, having been startled from
sleep by the report of the shotgun. Elliot sees that his ungovernable,
all-consuming anger has at last placed even Grace on the other side
of his psychic defenses, has made of her an enemy. He realizes that
his loathing and his rage ultimately encompass everything, including himself. He recognizes that his most deadly, most dangerous

adversary is, in fact, within the wire, behind the gun; it is anger itself that is his mortal enemy.

The ending of the story is deliberately ambiguous, the formal resolution suspended, as Elliot, hoping for forgiveness, stands in the cold but also in the light, waiting for Grace, and waiting for grace.

The story's central theme of the struggle between destructive forces and redemptive energies has significance, of course, for all humans and all cultures and countries, but the author also links this conflict to the historical destiny of the United States.

At the very beginning of the story, Elliot makes a journey to Boston on an autumn afternoon, and despite the city's "elegance and verve," he senses there "a broken promise" (83). The broken promise alluded to here is a prefigurement of Elliot's own subsequent broken promise to his wife and to himself not to drink alcohol, but there is a larger dimension of meaning in the allusion. The reference goes to the very roots of the identity of the American nation, to Boston as a seat of what may be called the American promise, or the American dream.

The sense of the broken promise of America, the nation's failure to live up to its ideals, is further conveyed by characters like Blankenship, the pathetic outcast, by the anonymous vagabond in the Conway Library, by vicious riffraff such as the Vopotiks and their associates, and by sanctimonious, smug, privileged prigs such as Loyall Anderson and his wife. The broken promise manifests itself in the bureaucratic absurdities of Elliot's work as a social counselor, and in the futility of his wife's legal efforts on behalf of the helpless and the innocent. The betrayal of the dream, the breaking of the promise, is also associated in the story with the Vietnam War, whose long-term impact upon the collective American psyche is depicted as profoundly, insidiously destructive, like a contagious nightmare or a psychic parasite.

Like Elliot, the American nation, it is implied, is in peril of succumbing to its negative, destructive impulses, to anger and violence, to self-indulgence and cynicism, to bitterness and despair. To redeem its promise and reclaim its dream, the nation must rediscover and must realize "the lost America of love" (as Allen Ginsberg named it in his poem, "A Supermarket in California").[2] This lost America, the heroic America envisioned by its prophets and poets, is seen in the compassion and dedication of Grace, and may be glimpsed in the Conway Library where Candace Music presides over an enclave of utopian potential, a place of dignity, wisdom, fellowship, and hospitality.

In two subsequent short stories, "Absence of Mercy" and "Miserere," Stone examines more closely the contrary apprehensions of the world which provide motive force for such persons as Elliot, and as Grace and Candace.

A fuller expression of Elliot's bleak view of a purposeless, pitiless universe is set forth in the explicitly titled "Absence of Mercy." The story presents incidents in the life of a man named Mackay, occurrences and situations indicating that, despite all of our wishes and intentions and all of the pretenses of our cultural and social institutions that suggest otherwise, life is inherently, irremediably disorderly and violent.

Mackay first learns the terrible disparity between the world's false appearance and its fierce reality during his childhood years as a pupil at a Catholic boarding school for orphans and unwanted children. Run by Pauline Brothers, the school should, of course, embody and advance the Christian virtues of mercy, compassion, and forgiveness.

Instead, the school not only inhibits among its "scholars" (as the boys are euphemistically called) the growth of these qualities, but also fosters in their stead a spirit of ruthless competition and violence.

After years of witnessing and receiving corporal punishment cruelly administered by the teachers, and living through the persecution and abuse perpetrated by the students, Mackay emerges from the school with a view of the world as a "physical and moral chaos of all against all" (28). This Hobbesian perspective is confirmed by his subsequent experiences in a teenage gang, and by an incident in which during a drunken argument with his friend Chris Kiernan, Mackay is knocked unconscious by him. And Mackay's grim estimate of the nature of things is not contradicted by his later experiences with institutions such as hospitals, the military, and the police.

Yet in time, as a man in his late twenties, married and the father of an infant son, with a gratifying job and a pleasant apartment, a cultured, creative wife and a circle of friends consisting of "people of spirit and artistic interest" (36), Mackay begins to view life in terms far less harsh than formerly, feeling that the world in which he now lives is a different and better one from that in which he grew up.

An unsettling sign that Mackay's nascent optimism is illusory comes to him via a news story concerning the death of his old friend, Chris Kiernan. Kiernan, with whom Mackay shared the terrors of boarding school and the later perils of gang membership, has been slain in the subway while attempting to rescue a lone middle-aged woman from the menacing and abusive behavior of an aggressive drunk. Like Mackay, Kiernan had made enormous efforts to leave behind him his sordid and violent past. He had gone to college, married, fathered a child, found secure employment. Yet despite all his exertions to create for himself a safe, civilized life, Kiernan has died a violent, senseless death.

Kiernan's violent and untimely death leads Mackay to construct of his life an elaborate denial of the implications of that terrible event. To this end, Mackay disavows violence in every form, swearing never to strike his children, and embracing a pacifistic position with regard to international politics. He espouses a "progressive right-mindedness" (39), and lends his support to the promotion of the causes of peace and human brotherhood. Unconsciously, superstitiously, Mackay hopes by these means to ward off the fate that overtook his friend.

But, as in the case of Mackay's earlier optimism concerning the changing conditions of life, his careful, conscientious efforts to avert the violence and disorder of the world are ultimately no more than a kind of mental Maginot Line built of wish and illusion—futile defenses easily outflanked by reality. At last, upon a deceptively benign spring day, Mackay finds himself in circumstances precisely parallel to those in which one year earlier his friend Kiernan was killed.

In an attempt to protect an elderly woman from the menacing of a young male on a subway platform, Mackay intervenes in the situation, only to become abruptly drawn into fierce, mortal combat with a homicidal madman. The lunatic against whom Mackay struggles for his life is the very incarnation of the world's random violence and absence of mercy. His eyes are "without order or justice or reason" (42); his body gives off "an evil smell" (43). Driven by terror, pain, desperation, and blind fury, Mackay finally succeeds in saving himself from his relentless, murderous assailant, only to be chased by the angry crowd of subway commuters who mistakenly believe he is the aggressive party in the hostile encounter with the madman.

Through his traumatic clash with the madman, Mackay learns a new mode of perception, a vision of the state of things that confirms the apprehensions of his childhood. Behind its external aspect of coherence, the world is lacking in cohesion or order: "The disconnectedness of things [is] fundamental" (44), as fundamental as the absence of mercy. The story ends with Mackay running through the streets in headlong flight, desperately wondering if he can evade his pursuers, and wondering whether anywhere there is refuge or sanctuary to be found. In Mackay's battered, bewildered flight is an image of the human condition in a pitiless world, a world of treacherously deceptive appearances, a world ruled by chance, a world of animal aggression, of conflict and violence, where in the end higher human intentions, desires, and ideals count for nothing.

"Miserere" proposes quite another response to the incomprehensible tragedy of human life in the world, a response similar to that made by the figures of Grace and Candace Music in the story "Helping." Like Grace and Candace, the characters Mary Urquhart and Camille Innaurato in "Miserere" are committed to active compassion and to the service of supernatural principles.

Mary Urquhart is a woman well acquainted with pain. Thirteen years before the winter evening on which the story opens, Mary's husband and three small children perished in a grotesque skating accident. She then spent years in alcoholic oblivion. But at length, despite her conscious will and her every defense, she developed an acceptance of things, a new perspective on existence, after which she took instruction in the Catholic faith and was received into the church. Although as a consequence of her loss, she continues to endure great psychic pain, Mary no longer drinks. By means of an inner order, by faith and a firmness of mind and will, Mary seeks to counter the disorder of the world.

Mary's commitment to her new faith is serious and deeply felt. Her piety expresses itself both in prayer and in action and sacrifice. She is active in antiwar, antiapartheid, and antiabortion work, and in her daily life she performs numerous small acts of kindness. These range from buying, out of her meager librarian's salary, books as gifts for inner-city children; engaging in ongoing personal dialogues with homeless, hopeless alcoholics in an attempt to help them to reform; and praying for the wretched and lost souls whom she encounters. As another far more demanding duty of love, Mary ensures that aborted fetuses are not merely disposed of as if they were mere refuse, but instead receive the sacrament of baptism and are interred with dignity in hallowed ground.

Mary's accomplice in this latter undertaking is Camille Innaurato, a middle-aged, unmarried, unsophisticated, asthmatic, working-class Catholic woman, whose life apart from laboring at a local factory has been one of sacrifice for and service to others. Despite differences in social background and level of education, Mary and Camille share an uncompromising dedication to the spiritual welfare of the aborted fetuses, most of which have been taken from the wombs of African American mothers.

The two women persevere in what they regard as a sacred duty despite the risk of legal accountability for removing the aborted fetuses from the premises of the medical waste disposal company, in spite of the considerable personal effort and expenses involved in their task, and in the face of the indifference or embarrassment of the official church with regard to their endeavor. Their persistence derives from a deep sense of concern and obligation, from pity and reverence, and finally from a compelling impulse to guard and honor the human image because it is the image of God.

The physical location and seasonal setting of the story generate a stark, somber atmosphere with suggestive resonances. The nameless New Jersey city in which the action of the story occurs is divided into opposing neighborhoods of misery and selfish indifference. One part of the city consists of dilapidated wooden tenements and candlelit crack houses, a bleak strip mall sheltering homeless alcoholics, sad gas stations attended by Indian immigrants who labor long hours and are frequently shot in holdups, and ill-lit thoroughfares of broken street lights whose fixtures have been stripped by junkies scavenging for scrap metal. Elsewhere in the city, the ethnic working class and lower middle class defend their enclaves of hard-won respectability against the larcenous incursions of the poor; while in the comfortable, clean, and spacious outer suburbs of the city the mood is one of calm, assured self-satisfaction. The mutually hostile quarters of the city, together with the bitter winter evening and the dark, deep-frozen winter night, suggest that the human spirit itself is in winter; all sense of human unity or community withered; the flower and fruit and foliage of conscience stripped away exposing the bare branches of selfishness; all the sources of charity and mercy frozen. And obliquely and with potently understated irony, we are reminded that New Jersey styles itself "the Garden State."

In "Miserere" the church becomes no more than a reflection of the corrupt will and selfish indifference of the society in which it occupies its privileged and irrelevant place. The representatives of the church in the story are Father Frank Hooke and Monsignor Danilo,—the former weak and vain, the latter venal and hypocritical, and both of them quite unconcerned with the spiritual welfare of the aborted fetuses.

The true church, the Christian spirit of sacrifice and charity, is exemplified in the story in the figures of Mary Urquhart and Camille Innaurato, neither of them prosperous or successful, or outwardly imposing or even altogether respectable; indeed, both are doubtless a little pitiful in the eyes of the world. In contrast, though, to the two complacent clergymen for whom religion seems to represent only a pretty sentiment, the church a venerable, comfortable institution, and the priesthood a career rather than a calling, the two women embody a disciplined, stoical, humble, vital faith, a faith that is a personal, existential commitment making difficult demands of its adherents and placing upon them duties and responsibilities that may be onerous and burdensome.

Mary and Camille share a "dry-eyed" (9, 21) vision of life in the world; they have a knowledge of God's fierce mercy, which can seem like cruelty for it may involve the pain of loss of all the worldly things we cherish, including our sense of selfhood, in order that we may recognize and realize in ourselves the reality of God. That has happened to Mary: she lost her husband, her three children, her familiar, comfortable life, and her self as then she knew it. Moreover, she lost the false God she worshipped and trusted, the God of Worldly Protection. Only by means of these devastating losses did she come at last to accept God on his own terms and to assent to his will.

In the context of the story's thematic design, the character of the accident that overtook Mary's husband and children is significant beyond itself, representing a sort of allegory of human fate. Mary's family perished while skating at night on a pond in the woods. The ice was supposed to be thick enough and strong enough to bear them.

The pond was supposed to be well lit. But there was a spot where the light failed and where the ice was thin, and they all drowned together. At a metaphoric level, we all make much the same assumptions in our lives as did Mary's family. We suppose ourselves safe. We do not foresee that our reality may, as it were, suddenly give way beneath us. We do not expect that for us the protective light will fail. We rely upon the seeming permanence and reassuring normality of the familiar world and upon our implicit assumption that somehow surely *we* are protected.

Mary was present when her drowned family was raised from the frozen pond the next morning by the police, or rather when "the thing they had been" (19) was lifted from the icy water. To compound the terrible sorrow of her irremediable loss, Mary noted with deep dismay the resemblance of her dear loved ones tangled together in rigor mortis to clusters of drowned rats that as a child she had seen floating in the river. Similar animal imagery recurs in the story, reflecting through a technique of indirect discourse Mary's perception of aspects of human life. Mary likens the aborted fetuses to manatees and cattle, bats and lobsters. She compares the scavenging junkies of the city to locusts; she sees the Monsignor as having a "lupine smile" (22). The import of such imagery in the context of the story suggests that mere human flesh devoid of the life of the spirit is of the same substance and nature as that of animals, fish, and insects. Mary derives from her Job-like agony of loss the fundamental, radical, redeeming insight that our true and essential human identity is as spirit, and that the ultimate nature of the world is not material but spiritual, and the ultimate reality God.

With this insight, Mary strives to refine her heart and mind, to liberate herself from pride and desire, and to make of herself an instrument of God's inscrutable, implacable will. In such submission however imperfect still, is her only surcease from pain, her only peace, as when in the closing paragraph of the story, her task in securing the sacraments and burial for the aborted fetuses accomplished, she prays and finds herself "alone with the ancient Thing before whose will she still stood amazed, whose shadow and line and light [we] all [are] . . ." (23).

The story "Bear and His Daughter" develops to its furthest extreme this theme of a dimension of spiritual reality which underlies material appearances and which constitutes the deepest principle and ultimate foundation of the world, and the theme of a divine will—wholly other, ungraspable and incomprehensible to us—that impels our lives and shapes our fates. At one level, the story is a sordid and gruesome tale of incest, murder, and suicide, of unsound obsessions and fatal compulsions, fueled by an inordinate consumption of alcohol and drugs and brought to a terrible consummation. At another level, though, "Bear and His Daughter" possesses a mythic dimension, as if the events in the lives of the central figures of the story were merely the outward occasions for the enactment of an ancient and sacred ritual, the fulfillment of a supernatural design.

The central figure of the story is Will Smart, an American poet of national and international reputation, who in the course of a reading tour of the colleges of the mountain states, makes a visit to his thirty-one-year-old illegitimate daughter, Rowan, with whom over the years he has had sporadic contact. In late middle age, Smart is a sundered man, divided yet between what might be termed the lower and higher affiliations of his soul, between his wayward and chaotic outer life and his inward capacity for acute and lucid poetic perception.

Only recently recovered from a nervous breakdown, and more lately relapsed into excessive drinking, Smart finds himself grown older and his physical powers diminished, his potentials and possibilities increasingly curtailed. He has become preoccupied with attempting to recover from his memory a poem that he composed thirty years ago and which somehow soon thereafter he misplaced and then forgot. After the passage of so many years, Smart can still recall snatches of the poem, but apart from such fragments the poem seems to be lost to him.

The subject of the poem is the salmon migration up the Tanana River in Alaska, the dramatic spectacle of the fish struggling upstream to die in the place where they were spawned. The poem was inspired by Smart's having seen in the clear sunlight of an early summer morning the strenuous efforts of the salmon to move upstream, their determined laboring against the river's current, even as they were assaulted from above by flocks of predatory birds. The experience was for Smart magical and epiphanic: "It seemed to him that he had never witnessed a sight so moving and noble as the last progress of these salmon" (174–75).

Smart feels for the salmon both admiration and envy, for they must, he believes, know a sense of triumph, of completion and fulfillment that will be forever lacking in his own life and in the lives of his fellow humans. Yet at the heart of his experience of the salmon migration is a feeling more profound and more expansive, a sense of awe and reverence excited by his perception that in the life cycle of the salmon there is a design, a symmetry that suggests ultimate meaning and purpose in the vast, complex pattern of life. In the tragic and beautiful destiny of the salmon, Smart glimpses a mysterious intention in things, a "mighty merciless will" (194) that permeates and unites the universe. This emotion or insight informs Smart's lost poem. Thus, in his attempt to recall the poem that he wrote upon that occasion, Smart hopes to revive in his mind that elusive, illuminative instant and to repossess or to be repossessed by it.

Smart is haunted, distracted, disturbed, and frustrated by the fragmentary recollection he has of his lost poem. It preoccupies him while he is conversing with others, while he is driving, or while he is engaged in other activities. At night he wakes, straining in the darkness to remember the poem. At lakes and rivers that he passes in his travels, he pauses to look for salmon, hoping that the sight might recall the poem to his mind. At times he weeps with the sense of loss with which the forgotten poem afflicts him. Only in the final minutes of his life, while he is sleeping, dreaming of salmon, does he recover his lost poem. His daughter, Rowan, to whom long ago he gave the poem and who has cherished and preserved the gift, reads it aloud into Smart's ear while he is asleep, immediately before she shoots him through the head.

Rowan, who was a neglected, deprived child, has grown into a confused and desperate woman. As Smart's illegitimate daughter, living at the other end of the country from her father and his acknowledged "legitimate" family, Rowan saw him only briefly and infrequently during her childhood, and the inadequate, incomplete character of her relationship to him has left her with a profound, persistent sense of privation. Their uncertain relationship took a disastrous turn about a year before the time at which the story takes place, when during the tempest of his mental breakdown and in a condition of drunken folly, her father visited her and they had sexual intercourse. The event seems to have awakened in Rowan an obsession with her father, an overpowering desire not only for his attention and affection, his acceptance and approval, but for further sexual intimacy with him. As her father seeks to recover the illuminative moment on the Tanana River in the Alaskan dawn, so Rowan seeks to recover the moment of ecstatic union with her father.

Like her father, Rowan is a self-divided figure, at once sensitive and sincere, imaginative and creative, and compulsive and impulsive, given to excessive consumption of alcohol and of amphetamines, and inclined to unrestrained behavior. Between Rowan and her father exists an almost telepathic rapport, yet their relationship is such, we are told, that there is a "terrible energy between the two of them" (202). In a sense, Rowan represents the mirror image of her father, for whereas in Will Smart's character the creative energies exceed and act to curb the negative, destructive energies, in Rowan's character it is the latter energies that predominate and prevail over the former.

The deeper nature of the relationship of Will Smart to his daughter is mysterious, suggesting primordial myths and archaic rituals of sacrifice, as well as the Jungian archetypes of the shadow and the anima. In this regard, Rowan is identified in some enigmatic fashion with Smart's lost poem, almost as if she were an embodiment or counterpart to that poem. Rowan is approximately the same age as the poem about the salmon migration, and it is she, the neglected daughter, who has through the years guarded and preserved the neglected poem and who reads the lost and longed-for poem to her father at the moment of his death.

Profound, inexplicable metaphysical principles are implied by this ambiguous, occult aspect of the father-daughter relationship in the story. Rowan would seem in some manner to have been—unknowingly, unconsciously but with hidden intention—engendered by her father to be the secret guardian of his poem and the agent of its ultimate restoration to him. The poem develops its theme around the ideas of return, completion, fulfillment, and death. These are, of course, the very states that are attained, the very ends that are realized, when the poem is at last returned to the poet. Also, the insight experienced by Smart upon that morning in Alaska on the Tanana River, the insight that occasioned the poem, was that of a "mighty merciless will" that impels all living things, making of their solitary passions and struggles in the world elements in a grand design, a vast, intricate pattern. On a far smaller scale, such an underlying design may be discerned in the life and death of Will Smart, whose given name suggests that he represents (as do we all) a microcosmic reflection of the divine Will, and that his life and death form a small pattern, making up a single constituent in the infinite pattern configured in the Universal Mind.

The story implies another dimension of supernatural design through the parallel suggested between the lives of Will and Rowan Smart and figures in an American Indian myth concerning the relationship of Sun to the Bear Clan. As recounted in the story by Rowan (derived from her extensive readings in mythology and anthropology), the myth affirms that in order to move across the sky, Sun requires the blood of sacrificed children of the Bear Clan. Only their blood enables him to see and thus to rise and set. If their blood is withheld from him, he becomes blind and his daily journey from east to west becomes impossible, with the result that the earth and all life upon it become static and sterile. The human members of the Bear Clan, we are told, were grandchildren of Sun through his sons and daughters, the Bears. Bear Clan children were sacrificed to the sun in a ceremony that took place under the morning star, executed quickly and painlessly with an arrow through the heart.

In the course of the text, Will Smart is likened repeatedly to a bear; his daughter even calls him "Bear." As a poet, he is metaphorically the eyes of the sun, the seer and singer of the natural world. Rowan, then, both by heritage and through her own role as poet, is also a member of the Bear Clan. There are recurrent references in the story to the acute resemblance of Rowan's eyes to those of her father, in terms both of their physical likeness and their shared way of seeing the world. Indeed, what Rowan seems to regret most in her act of murdering her father is having destroyed his eyes. In her own suicide at an ancient ceremonial chamber under the morning star, Rowan takes care to shoot herself through the heart, doing so not in conscious imitation of the sacrificed members of the Bear Clan, but rather so as not to destroy for a second time her father's eyes.

With its suggestive resonances and mythic parallels, its portrayals of primal, violent passions, and its intimations of hidden spiritual significance and purpose in the world, "Bear and His Daughter" expresses a reality that exists in different degrees or consists of different levels, a structure that is reflected in the story both in the relationship of humankind to the natural world and in the layers of human consciousness at an individual level.

Already in the opening paragraphs of "Bear and His Daughter," through opposing clusters of images, we are presented with the contrast between the realm of nature and the realm of man. The natural beauty of lake water at dusk, mountains, and the light of the setting sun are juxtaposed to the interior of a gambling casino where, in order most effectively to exploit its patrons, the management has contrived to isolate them from natural scenery, from daylight and the diurnal rhythms of the earth. The casino, with its counterfeit Western decor and fake Navajo rugs, is staffed by silent men with "serpent gazes" and "dead eyes" (177), men filled with anger and the capacity for violence, yet as emotionless and expressionless as automatons.

These opposing groups of images establish the essential shape and temper of the story, and in the pages that follow, they are enlarged upon as the novel reveals the breadth and height of the land, its staggering spaciousness, its inhuman scale and age, and the smallness and shallowness of the human presence upon it. Casinos, shopping malls, and tourist resorts, ranches and interstate highways, towns and schools and churches have ultimately only the most tenuous foothold on the desert. The sage and greasewood will far outlast such temporary excrescence as humans in their ignorant conceit may choose to construct and inhabit. The mountains and the lava beds, the enormous sky with its clouds and storms will endure for eons after man's presumptuous structures have vanished. In the face of this landscape with its timeless life and immutable laws, the fugitive fates of the humans who live there seem futile and insignificant.

The ultimate image in the text of the unknowable, primordial forces operative through the natural world is that of "The Temple," a small natural cavern containing within it a platform of black lava which resembles "a table of sacrifice" (183). Antedating both the Indians and the white settlers, the spot inspires in visitors a sacred dread, suggesting a universe of purposes adversarial to the petty acquisitive interests of humankind.

The layers of human habitation upon the landscape range from those of the earliest indigenous peoples through later tribal migrations, and then through the stages of settlement of the white Europeans, pioneers followed by Mormons, followed in turn by other immigrants and internal migrants, culminating in the commercial-consumerist, scientific-technological society currently in occupancy.

In a similar fashion, under the surface of each human's social identity and individual personality, there are other psychic strata—levels
of being that extend from the personal unconscious to a kind of biological consciousness comprising the instincts and drives that connect human consciousness with the natural world, and finally to a
primordial, undifferentiated consciousness, which like the geological
substratum of the earth's landforms, represents the ultimate ground
of being, the supernatural essence that supports and surrounds, permeates and penetrates all that exists.

In the story, Will and Rowan Smart are mediators between
the supernatural, the realm of nature and the human realm. Through
myth, song, and poetry they work to bring human consciousness into
relation with the natural world and the Supreme Imagination—Will
doing so by means of his poetry and public readings, Rowan by
means of her poems and songs, and the lectures on geology and
myth that she delivers as a park ranger.

Allied to, yet deeper than, this semishamanistic vocation, is the
personal spiritual search of father and daughter, their common quest
for "home," their urge to effect a return to their source or origin.
This profound, powerful drive is what Will Smart celebrates in his
lost poem, and what Rowan unwittingly seeks in her incestuous
union with her father: "pursuing the salt of her own generation. Trying to get home" (217).

Like the migrating salmon he so admires, Will Smart's last
struggle is from pool to pool of dreams, "rising against his will" into
the suffocating air of ordinary consciousness, "breathless" (216) with
the strenuous efforts of this final stage of his inward journey, until at
last—in the instant of the recovery of his lost poem and the simultaneous loss of his life—he achieves his goal, attains his homecoming.

In a like manner, and according to her own deepest urges, Rowan—like the sacrificial figures of the Bear Clan whom she celebrates in her park lectures—achieves her end under the morning star, shot through the heart. In this fashion, she, too, effects a homecoming.

The violent destinies of Will and Rowan Smart possess a secret, sacred meaning and purpose, just as the emblematic salmon in the poem, "fulfilling a purpose that was never their own" (194), confirm a supernatural design. Similarly, the reflections in the story's concluding paragraphs of Rowan's Shoshone companion and lover, John Hears the Sun Come Up, place the events of the story in a metaphysical perspective.

John Hears the Sun Come Up is the first to discover the bodies of Will and Rowan. In fact, he had foreseen their deaths and thus to him the discovery is not a surprise but rather a sad confirmation of his foreknowledge of the event. It is John, then, who conducts Max Peterson, the county sheriff (and a former lover of Rowan's) to the sites of the murder-suicide. Their interpretations of the event diverge widely: the sheriff representing the more conventional perceptions of pragmatic European-American culture, John representing the perspectives of a culture based upon myth and ritual, traditions of nature worship and respect for the mysteries of the spirit world.

Blinded by passion, prejudice, and preconception, Max Peterson insists vehemently upon his own impercipient misinterpretations and categorical condemnations of the events of the night. Rowan's extensive collection of books on anthropology, mythology, and religion, he summarily disparages as representing "every kind of queer satanic book" (220). Poetry he dismisses as "shit" (220). The sheriff is utterly at a loss to comprehend the characters of either Will or Rowan except as he can force them into his own reductive classifications;

nor is he other than contemptuously dismissive of the explanations and information offered by John Hears the Sun Come Up.

The fundamental, definitive difference between the sheriff and John Hears the Sun Come Up is the belief of the latter in the primacy of the spirit world. Accordingly, like Mary Urquhart in "Miserere," he does not judge events only in relation to the values and standards of society nor on a human scale alone. John recognizes that factors other than those which are apparent may be determinant in lives and occurrences. In consequence of this view, again like Mary Urquhart, he places a high value upon poetry and song as partaking of a greater reality than that of the material world, and he honors (and shares) Rowan's interest in sacred subjects as represented by her books. And, although he is saddened by the death of his friends Will and Rowan Smart, he is not condemnatory or judgmental of their lives, for while he does not personally approve of incest, he accepts that it may sometimes be "what the spirit world wants" (205).

Having done all that he could do to save the lives of his friends, cautioning them and warning them, John Hears the Sun Come Up accepts their deaths as having been their inexorable fate and he honors their memories. He believes that despite their flaws of character, Will and Rowan Smart possessed strong, good souls, and that their essences, their ghosts, survive in a state of union with the natural world and the spirit world. Will Smart, he believes, has returned to where he saw the salmon—his ghost and his songs forever to inhabit that place. Rowan, too, he believes, by virtue of her songs, her poems and stories, will be "well set up out there in the ghost world" (222), claiming a place in the wild landscape she loved—her eyes, like those of her father, surviving in "lost blue places" (222). And in the human realm, Will Smart's salmon poem, particularly admired among his works by John Hears the Sun Come Up, will be translated by him into the Shoshone-Paiute language and sung by him; the poet's central, sacred vision thus surviving among the human community, uplifting and guiding others.

Apprehended from this spiritual perspective, the lives of Will and Rowan Smart were ultimately neither as deficient nor debased as they must appear in the light of conventional community standards. Whatever was unsound or ignoble in their lives will in their posthumous states of being be refined away; that which was turbid and troubled in their souls will become clear and quiet; and only what was pure and true in their lives will endure.

In this regard, the shared surname of Smart—a word susceptible of two interpretations—suggests that the price of awareness or insight is pain, and, by extension, that the cost at which clarity is attained may be anguish and calamity.

Reading the stories "Miserere" and "Bear and His Daughter," with their potent spiritual implications, I am reminded of similar concepts of tragedy and self-transcendence expressed in the work of the American poet Robinson Jeffers (1887–1962). Like Stone's writings, Jeffers' is frequently concerned with the self-shattering circumstance of receiving—even against one's will and despite one's resistance— a dizzying vision of the supernatural order of being that is at the core of all life, a terrifying glimpse of the fierce will of God. In his poem "Apology for Bad Dreams," for example, Jeffers writes of how "[p]ain and terror, the insanities of desire," are "not accidents but essential," requirements for the transformation of human consciousness according to the teleological evolutionary design of the universe.[3]

Elsewhere in his work, as in his narrative poem "Roan Stallion," Jeffers writes of the extremes and excesses, the convulsive psychic violence necessary to precipitate self-transcendence and vision:

> Tragedy that breaks man's face and a white fire flies out
> of it; vision that fools him
> Out of his limits, desire that fools him out of his
> limits, unnatural crime . . . wild loves that leap over the
> walls of nature.[4]

Stone's stories set forth no theological arguments. They are concerned neither with formal nor abstract religion, neither theory nor doctrine, but rather there are in his tales powerful religious overtones, poetic suggestiveness, and the portrayal of spiritual paradoxes and possibilities. The author's concern in stories such as "Miserere" and "Bear and His Daughter" is with what is ultimate in man and his life, with the mystery of the forces that operate within and through human consciousness, expressing themselves both in those "urges involving death and sacrifice" (200), and in the imperatives of a relentless, redemptive love.

The double vision that quickens Stone's short fiction (as well as his novels) derives from the author's situation as a strict, unflinching realist who does not accept the ultimate reality of the world. Suspended thus between opposites, he first undermines our lazy complacency about the nature of life in the world with painful images of the terrible and the pathetic, the hideous and the absurd. Then, when we have been compelled by him to acknowledge the full horror of the world and the boundless folly of humankind, Stone proceeds to trouble our comfortably reductive pessimism with a disquieting sense of the mystery of the universe and the riddles of human identity and destiny. He means to keep us at the dangerous edge of things, off-balance and alert, inquiring and searching.

CHAPTER NINE

Conclusion

The phrase "a hall of mirrors," which provides the title for Robert Stone's first novel, could serve equally as a collective title for the whole of his fiction. The sense of bewilderment and disorientation in confronting endless reflections, as suggested by the image of a hall of mirrors, together with the hint of a passageway providing access or egress, as also implied in the phrase, represent in metaphorical compression the essential terms of the author's vision.

The wilderness of illusion in the fiction of Robert Stone is comprised of the multiple reflections and projections of the mind itself. We are lost amid our own appetites and desires, our lies and fears, our enmities and vanities, and the myriad names and forms that we have given to them. In Stone's work the levels and layers of illusion, all mutually reflective, extend from the personal to the social, the national, and the international, unto the metaphysical.

At the level of individual illusion, we encounter in Stone's work a number of persons who have formerly had ideals or aspirations, who may possess a talent for music or for literature, who have the capacity to feel compassion, to empathize, and to love, but who have denied their highest potentials, forsaken their ideals, squandered or neglected their talents, and have capitulated to what is weakest in themselves. They have succumbed to one or another of the agencies or modalities of illusion—to anger, to fear, to self-aggrandizement, to despair, or to the desire for oblivion. In consequence of having done so, such figures—including Rheinhardt, Converse, Holliwell, Walker, and others—exist as fragmented, tormented men, as self-haunted embodiments of illusion.

CONCLUSION

At more collective levels, the illusions are disseminated by radio, by television, by films; they are perpetrated for political or commercial purposes; they become the cause of wars and revolutions. People die for them or because of them.

And at the highest or deepest level of being, we are also victims of illusion, for the material world, the senses and the condition of self-conscious selfhood are all seen to be fundamentally insubstantial and ultimately illusory. True reality, true identity, Stone's work suggests, is spiritual in character, transcendent in nature.

While the majority of the characters in the author's novels and short fiction avidly pursue phantoms of power or pleasure, there are also a smaller number who succeed in achieving some degree of spiritual awareness and who act upon their moral insights and their compassion. In contrast to those who have yielded to what was weakest in themselves, these figures cultivate what is most worthy in themselves: fidelity, responsibility, discipline, compassion, truth. Often such figures are martyred by the world, killed or driven to suicide. Some are redeemed only by their deaths, which are undertaken or undergone as acts of spiritual or moral affirmation; others endure and endeavor to live their affirmation in the world. Among these are Morgan Rainey, Geraldine, Ken Grimes, Ian and Jill Percy, Dieter, Hicks, Justin, Father Egan, Lu Anne, Buzz Ward, Owen and Anne Browne, Sonia, Father Jonas Herzog, Camille Innaurato, Mary Urquhart, and others. These are persons who have traversed the hall of mirrors, seeing the reflections only for what they are, seeking a true image, a ground of being beyond illusion.

The quest for primal, essential reality, together with the quest for integrity in a destructive, disorderly world are central themes in the fiction of Robert Stone. The terms of these quests are self-realization versus self-betrayal, communion versus isolation, faith versus negation.

A crucial element of the quest in Stone's fiction is the journey to the dangerous edge of things, to the place of ultimate definitions, ultimate decision. Often the quester is impelled there by some irresistible inner compulsion, borne there by excess of drink or dope or by madness, or else arrives there abruptly through sudden and terrible confrontation with death. By whatever means or for whatever motives the pilgrimage to the edge is accomplished, once there the alternatives are absolute: renewal or destruction, redemption or perdition. Stone's fiction chronicles the fates both of those who balk and fail, as do Converse and Holliwell among others, and those such as Hicks and Justin who fulfill the ordeal and who attain to clarity.

Despite, then, the corruption of ideals—personal, national, and civilized—so abundant in Stone's novels and short fiction, his work also affirms the human capacity for freedom and vision, for love and heroic action.

Stone's fiction is informed by a coherent, evolving vision. There is in his work a distinct progression from the dark naturalism that dominates his earliest novel, through the growth of a tentative sort of spiritual perspective that begins to be evident already in *Dog Soldiers*, to the more emphatic if still sober and restrained affirmations of the human heart and spirit expressed in *Outerbridge Reach* and *Damascus Gate*. This movement may be perceived in the continuity and development of certain motifs in the novels and short fiction, and the corresponding diminution of others. Animal imagery and imagery of predation, for example, become increasingly less prominent in Stone's writing, while music remains throughout his work a salient and potent element, suggesting our potential for attaining to a state of being beyond the agitations and confusions of quotidian existence.

Dreams, too, retain an important position throughout Stone's oeuvre, suggesting the persistence of a latent moral and spiritual awareness that coexists adversarially with the appetites and vanities of ordinary consciousness. A final motif, the ocean, which is a recurrent image in the author's works, reflects the movement of Stone's fiction toward a metaphysical perspective. In the early novels the ocean epitomizes the inexorable biological process of mutual devouring, the Hobbesian universe of each against all, and it is employed as a metaphor for the treacherous and ravening character of all life, whether animal or human. In *Outerbridge Reach*, though, and also in the Red Sea diving scene in *Damascus Gate*, the ocean serves as a source of renewal and spiritual rebirth, and is employed as a metaphor for the mystery of existence and the mystical unity of life; the ocean becomes the ultimate clear mirror in which we may behold our true countenance, learn at last our true name. Undersea coral is likened to a temple to the Lord of Creation, while the blue infinity of the ocean suggests a counterpart to the Infinite Mind.

Another element of Stone's fiction that has altered from his earliest to his most recent writing is the incidence in his work of violence and terror. A distinctive feature of his early novels, such scenes and situations are both less frequent and more subdued in character in his later writing, suggesting a more balanced and inclusive vision of life—one that does not evade recognition of the destructive and negative forces, but that accords them no more than their due proportion in the processes of life.

The effect of Stone's writing upon us as readers is often one of disturbance and disquiet: we are shaken by scenes of violence, offended by sordidness and ugliness, and unsettled by implacable irony. Stone's fiction is frequently a harrowing experience, yet it is harrowing in both senses of the word, in that we are at once vexed and distressed by it, and we are also, as it were, prepared for cultivation: broken, turned, worked, and made ready for sowing, for new growth and new life.

The impact upon us of the element of violence and terror in Robert Stone's fiction is to jolt us out of our habits of perception and conception, and to jar us into recognition of ourselves and our world. Stone's work disabuses us of our comfortable illusions—all the conventions, the pieties and platitudes, the fabrications and fictions, the compromises and hypocrisies by which we evade the truth of life—and compels us to confront in full measure the danger and disorder of the world, and to acknowledge the demonic potential each of us harbors within, our capacity for cruelty, deceit, obsession, and delusion.

Yet, by assaulting and calling into question our familiar modes of seeing and feeling, by showing us how spurious, partial, and insufficient they are, Stone's work restores to us the possibility of reconceiving our identity and our notion of reality, for the author challenges us not only by presenting us with images of fear and fury, but also by directing our attention to the authentic and the essential, the simple and the good, and by affirming our human potential for awareness and courage, for love and renewal.

Stone's work both subverts our repose and undermines our doubt, permitting us neither the complacency of firm assumptions nor the specious poise of skepticism, neither easy certainties nor facile acceptance of uncertainty, but enjoining us instead to relentless interrogation of our condition in the light of what we truly know and what we truly feel, in the light of our aspirations and our anguish, our terror and our tenderness.

CONCLUSION

Perhaps the closest that Stone has come to articulating his artistic credo as a writer of fiction is an essay that he wrote (based on a talk he had given earlier at the New York Public Library) entitled "The Reason for Stories."[1] In his essay Stone argues for the essential, indeed almost inevitable, moral nature of the art of fiction, and expresses his view of the vital part played by the imagination in the relationship of human individuals to their private selves and to the society and the world in which they live. The essay also contains an observation by the author, a succinct statement of the central themes that are embodied in his work:

> I have never been able to escape my sense of humanity trying, with difficulty, to raise itself in order not to fall . . . The most important thing about people is the difficulty they have in identifying and acting upon what's right. The world is full of illusion. We carry nemesis inside us, but we are not excused. (76)

In six very accomplished novels together with a handful of potent short stories, Robert Stone has created an original and distinguished body of writing, penetrating in its scrutiny of our society, acute in its psychological perceptions and moral insights, and compelling in its metaphysical perspectives. Stone's work engages with energy and determination the essential, existential issues, ranging the wilderness of illusion, the vast wreckage that is our world, and salvaging for us some value and truth, some strength and purpose, some simple human hope.

Chapter 1—Understanding Robert Stone

1. Cited in "The Art of Fiction XC: Robert Stone," by William Crawford Woods, *Paris Review* 27, no. 2 (winter 1985): 34.

2. Ibid., 33.

3. Cited in "Robert Stone," by Charles Ruas, in *Conversations with American Writers* (New York: Alfred A. Knopf, 1985), 265–94.

4. Eric James Schroeder, "Two Interviews: Talks with Tim O'Brien and Robert Stone," *Modern Fiction Studies* 30, no. 1 (spring 1984): 151.

5. Ruas, "Robert Stone," 278.

6. For the ideological criticism, see Jonathan Yardley, "Robert Stone: Gun-Running and Jungle Fighting," *Washington Post Book World,* 1 November 1981, 3; Carolyn See, *Los Angeles Times Book Review*, 8 November 1981, 4.

7. For the negative criticism, see A. Alvarez, "Among the Freaks," *New York Review of Books*, 33, no. 6 (10 April 1986): 23–26; Frank Rich, "The Screenwriter's Revenge," *New Republic* 194, no. 17 (28 April 1986): 32–34; Robert Jones, "The Other Side of Soullessness," *Commonweal* 123, no. 10 (23 May 1986): 305–6, 308.

8. Gordon Burn, "Where Mine Is At," *London Review of Books*, 28 May 1992, 20–21; Letters to the Editor by Ron Hall and Tristan Jones, *Times Literary Supplement*, 12 June 1992, 15; Letter to the Editor, *Times Literary Supplement*, 19 June 1992, 15. Tomalin and Hall's book is *The Strange Voyage of Donald Crowhurst* (London: Hodder & Stroughton, 1970).

9. Stone, "The Genesis of *Outerbridge Reach,*" *Times Literary Supplement*, 5 June 1992, 14.

10. Ibid.

11. Stone, Letter to the Editor, *Times Literary Supplement*, 26 June 1992, 15.

Chapter 2—*A Hall of Mirrors*

1. Stone, *A Hall of Mirrors* (Boston: Houghton Mifflin, 1967). Further parenthetical references are to this edition.

2. This poem is to be found in *The Complete Poems of Oscar Wilde* (London: Galley Press, 1987), 693.

3. The phrase is from "Bishop Bloughram's Apology" (line 395), in *Robert Browning: Poetical Works* (London: Oxford University Press, 1970), 656.

Chapter 3—*Dog Soldiers*

1. Stone, *Dog Soldiers* (Boston: Houghton Mifflin, 1974). Further parenthetical references are to this edition.

2. The phrase occurs in the poem "I Think Continually of Those Who Were Truly Great," in *Collected Poems* by Stephen Spender (London: Faber, 1955), 47.

Chapter 4—*A Flag for Sunrise*

1. Stone, *A Flag for Sunrise* (New York: Alfred A. Knopf, 1981). Further parenthetical references are to this edition.

2. Shakespeare, *The Tempest* (Cambridge: Cambridge University Press, 1969).

Chapter 5—*Children of Light*

1. Stone, *Children of Light* (New York: Alfred A. Knopf, 1986). Further parenthetical references are to this edition.

Chapter 6—*Outerbridge Reach*

1. Stone, *Outerbridge Reach* (New York: Ticknor and Fields, 1992). Further parenthetical references are to this edition.

2. *The Short Stories of Ernest Hemingway* (New York: Modern Library, 1938), 241–51.

3. *The Letters of W. B. Yeats,* edited by Allan Wade (New York: Octagon Books, 1980), 922.

Chapter 7—*Damascus Gate*

1. Stone, *Damascus Gate* (Boston: Houghton Mifflin, 1998). Further parenthetical references are to this edition.

Chapter 8—Short Fiction: *Bear and His Daughter*

1. Stone, *Bear and His Daughter* (Boston: Houghton Mifflin, 1997). Further parenthetical references are to this edition.

2. The phrase occurs in *Howl and Other Poems* (San Francisco: City Lights Books, 1956), 24.

3. This poem is to be found in *Selected Poetry of Robinson Jeffers* (New York: Random House, 1938), 174–77.

4. This passage from "Roan Stallion" is to be found in *Roan Stallion, Tamar, and Other Poems* (New York: Boni & Liveright, 1925), 20.

Chapter 9—Conclusion

1. Stone, "The Reason for Stories, toward a Moral Fiction," *Harper's*, June 1988, 75.

SELECTED BIBLIOGRAPHY

Primary

Novels

A Hall of Mirrors. Boston: Houghton Mifflin, 1967.
Dog Soldiers. Boston: Houghton Mifflin, 1974.
A Flag for Sunrise. New York: Alfred A. Knopf, 1981.
Children of Light. New York: Alfred A. Knopf, 1986.
Outerbridge Reach. New York: Ticknor and Fields, 1992.
Damascus Gate. Boston: Houghton Mifflin, 1998.

Short Fiction

Bear and His Daughter. Boston: Houghton Mifflin, 1997.

Other

"The Genesis of *Outerbridge Reach*." *Times Literary Supplement*, 5 June 1992, 15.
"The Reason for Stories, toward a Moral Fiction." *Harper's*, June 1988, 71–76.

Secondary

Interviews

Bonnetti, Kay. "An Interview with Robert Stone." *Missouri Review* 6, no. 1 (fall 1982) 91–114.
Chapple, Steve. "Robert Stone Faces the Devil." *Mother Jones*, May 1984, 35–41.
Karagueuzian, Maureen. "Interview with Robert Stone." *Tri-quarterly* 53 (winter 1983): 249–58.

BIBLIOGRAPHY

Ross, Jean W. "CA Interview." In *Contemporary Authors, New Revision Series*, vol. 23. Detroit: Gale Research, 1976.

Ruas, Charles. "Robert Stone." In *Conversations with American Writers*. New York: Alfred A. Knopf, 1985.

Schroeder, Eric James. "Two Interviews: Talks with Tim O'Brien and Robert Stone." *Modern Fiction Studies* 30, no. 1 (spring 1984): 135–64.

Steinberg, Sybil. "Robert Stone." *Publishers Weekly*, 21 March 1986, 72–74.

Woods, William Crawford. "The Art of Fiction XC: Robert Stone." *Paris Review* 27, no. 2 (winter 1985): 26–57.

Critical and Biographical

Beidler, Philip D. *American Literature and the Experience of Vietnam*. Athens: University of Georgia Press, 1982. *Dog Soldiers* is viewed as an exploration of the effects of the Vietnam War on American life, while at the same time suggesting that the folly of the war proceeds from a vacuum of values at the heart of American life.

———. *Re-writing America: Vietnam Authors in Their Generation*. Athens: University of Georgia Press, 1991. Stone's fiction is considered in the context of the ongoing work of Vietnam writers, whose collective enterprise is seen as a critique and a renewal of American ideals. Stone is regarded by Beidler as "a political novelist in the most traditional sense." Accordingly, Stone's first four novels are examined with particular reference to the Vietnam War. *A Hall of Mirrors* and *Children of Light* are seen as an exploration of the roots of the war in the American psyche, while *Dog Soldiers* and *A Flag for Sunrise* are seen as a treatment of the consequences of the war for contemporary American life.

Burn, Gordan. "Where Mine Is At." *London Review of Books*, 28 May 1992, 20–21. Highlights parallels between *Outerbridge Reach* and

BIBLIOGRAPHY

The Strange Voyage of Donald Crowhurst, by Nicholas Tomalin and Ron Hall, accusing Stone of "unfair appropriation" of the works of the latter authors.

Hellman, John. *American Myth and the Legacy of Vietnam.* New York: Columbia University Press, 1986. *Dog Soldiers* is considered in the context of the literature of the Vietnam War and in relation to what Hellman believes is the American aspiration to be "a redeemer nation."

Karagueuzian, Maureen. "Irony in Robert Stone's *Dog Soldiers*." *Critique* 24, no. 2 (1983) 65–73. The plot of *Dog Soldiers* is perceived as a parallel to American involvement in Vietnam, while the irony of Stone's novel is compounded by parallels to Ernest Hemingway's *The Sun Also Rises*.

Melling, Philip H. *Vietnam in American Literature.* Boston: Twayne, 1990. A reductive reading of Stone's novels *Dog Soldiers* and *A Flag for Sunrise* as supporting Melling's own thesis that post-World War II American foreign policy in Vietnam and Central America was determined by purely commercial considerations, predominantly by the need to establish new markets for an overproducing domestic economy.

Moore, Hugh L. "The Undersea World of Robert Stone." *Critique* 11, no. 3 (1969) 43–56. Views Stone's *A Hall of Mirrors* as a profoundly pessimistic vision of society and the modern world. The undersea imagery of the novel is seen as a suggestion of the cruelty and violence of human affairs.

Myers, Thomas. *Walking Point: American Narratives of Vietnam.* New York and Oxford: Oxford University Press, 1988. Concise discussion of *Dog Soldiers* as a revelation of the darker aspects of the American soul. Moral dissolution, paranoia, and alienation in U.S. society are seen as both a cause and a consequence of the war in Vietnam.

Shelton, Frank W. "Robert Stone's *Dog Soldiers*: Vietnam Comes Home to America." *Critique* 24, no. 2 (1983) 74–81. *Dog Soldiers* is seen to illuminate the moral effect of the Vietnam War on the United

States, revealing the violence and corruption that pervade American society.

Smith, Joan. "Stone Alone." *San Francisco Examiner Magazine*, 24 May 1998, 7–17. Overview of Stone's literary career, with particular focus on *Damascus Gate*. Numerous quotations from the author concerning his life and writing.

Solotaroff, Robert. *Robert Stone*. New York: Twayne, 1994. Acute and comprehensive critical study of Stone's writing up to the publication of *Outerbridge Reach*. Although pertinent and perceptive textual analyses of each of Stone's works are offered, the focus of Solotaroff's study tends toward psychobiography, highlighting correspondences between Stone's own experiences and the lives of his fictional characters. Solotaroff is also very interested in—and very well informed about—links between Stone's fiction and specific historical events and political and social contexts that have served as sources of inspiration or points of departure for his novels and stories.

Weber, Bruce. "An Eye for Danger." *New York Times Magazine*, 19 January 1992, 18–24. Combines elements of a profile, a biographical sketch, an interview, an overview of Stone's oeuvre, and a review of *Outerbridge Reach*.

Wolfe, Tom. *The Electric Kool-Aid Acid Test*. New York: Farrar, Straus & Giroux, 1968. Contains scattered anecdotes concerning Stone's casual affiliation with Ken Kesey and the Merry Pranksters in California and Mexico during the early to mid-1960s. Pertinent biographical background to Stone's short story "Porque No Tiene, Porque Le Falta."

INDEX

INDEX

INDEX